Social Justice and Activism in

Social Justice and Activism in Libraries

Essays on Diversity and Change

Edited by SU EPSTEIN, CAROL SMALLWOOD *and* VERA GUBNITSKAIA

Foreword by Wanda Kay Brown

McFarland & Company, Inc., Publishers
Jefferson, North Carolina

RECENT MCFARLAND WORKS OF INTEREST (MAIN TITLES)

Genealogy and the Librarian, edited by Carol Smallwood and Vera Gubnitskaia (2018); *Gender Issues and the Library,* edited by Carol Smallwood and Lura Sanborn (2017); *Library Partnerships with Writers and Poets,* edited by Carol Smallwood and Vera Gubnitskaia (2017); *Teaching Technology in Libraries,* edited by Carol Smallwood and Lura Sanborn (2017); *Library Volunteers Welcome!* edited by Carol Smallwood and Lura Sanborn (2016); *Continuing Education for Librarians,* edited by Carol Smallwood, Kerrol Harrod and Vera Gubnitskaia (2013); *Job Stress and the Librarian,* edited by Carol Smallwood and Linda Burkey Wade (2013); *Marketing Your Library,* edited by Carol Smallwood, Vera Gubnitskaia and Kerrol Harrod (2012); *Mentoring in Librarianship,* edited by Carol Smallwood and Rebecca Tolley-Stokes (2012); *Women on Poetry,* edited by Carol Smallwood, Colleen S. Harris and Cynthia Brackett-Vincent (2012)

LIBRARY OF CONGRESS CATALOGUING-IN-PUBLICATION DATA

Names: Epstein, Su, editor. | Smallwood, Carol, 1939– editor. | Gubnitskaia, Vera, 1960– editor.
Title: Social justice and activism in libraries : essays on diversity and change / edited by Su Epstein, Carol Smallwood and Vera Gubnitskaia ; foreword by Wanda Kay Brown.
Description: Jefferson, North Carolina : McFarland & Company, Inc., Publishers, 2019 | Includes bibliographical references and index.
Identifiers: LCCN 2019010927 | ISBN 9781476672038 (paperback. : acid free paper) ∞
Subjects: LCSH: Libraries and society. | Libraries and community. | Libraries—Social aspects. | Libraries and minorities. | Social justice. | Libraries—United States—Case studies.
Classification: LCC Z716.4 .S57 2019 | DDC 021.2—dc23
LC record available at https://lccn.loc.gov/2019010927

BRITISH LIBRARY CATALOGUING DATA ARE AVAILABLE

ISBN (print) 978-1-4766-7203-8
ISBN (ebook) 978-1-4766-3510-1

Front cover photograph © 2019 Rawpixel/Shutterstock

Manufactured in the United States of America

McFarland & Company, Inc., Publishers
Box 611, Jefferson, North Carolina 28640
www.mcfarlandpub.com

Table of Contents

Part VII—Expanding Teaching

Foreword

WANDA KAY BROWN

Recently I was invited to address an "Inclusion Committee" at a local retirement facility in North Carolina. While the host was introducing me, a question arose from a non-committee member asking about the mission of the committee. The host shared her story on the importance of inclusion and how it relates to understanding other cultures. From the conversations that followed, it was obvious that there remains a vital need to continue community dialogues on race and inclusion. These authors have done an impressive job in compiling a spectacular showcase of library initiatives designed to address issues of social justice and activism. They are truly to be applauded for their efforts. Those librarians electing to share their stories are also true champions. From each essay, a new set of champions is revealed. These authors are representative of those who have seriously attempted to implement programs and services designed to move us from thought to action. They are librarians and library workers who have graciously agreed to share their efforts with the rest of us. It is from these stories that we gain a deeper insight around advocacy efforts as it relates to social justice, diversity and inclusion. The stories shared within this book provide the reader with an insiders' take on setting goals, exploring options, strategizing, and following a plan through to fruition. The authors also offer practical advice around program planning and sensitivity tips for introducing complex and often times controversial conversational topics. Every library type is represented within the stories shared, and support for outreach efforts is clearly perceivable.

Libraries are valued and respected for their ability to inform, engage, and connect their community of users around topics and issues that are required to be successful. We accomplish our mission through a variety of ways. Most notably our efforts have been concentrated within collection building and through a myriad of program offerings. It is so refreshing to see these authors challenge the standard. Through the stories shared within *Social Justice and Activism in Libraries: Essays on Diversity and Change*, we see libraries implementing new approaches. We see an increase in collaborations with community partners. The authors meticulously outline their thought and strategy process, and detail how their institutions aligned their efforts with others who shared similar commitments and interest. They leverage those partnerships to foster one on one engagement. They provide the platform to lead the community through difficult and challenging conversations. They lead staff through training on how implicit bias is ubiquitous.

Partnering remains key to our profession's continued success. These stories demonstrate how effective partnerships strengthen our voice, expand our ability to reach, and most importantly, demonstrate our profession's value. Their stories are representative of libraries with leaderships that encourage and support open and sincere engagement, actively seek a greater understanding of cultures, and specifically recognize and accept their role in advancing social justice for all. Each story provides a roadmap to a strategy that leads the community on the path from thinking about diversity to an action that reveals a deeper connection with diversity.

Wanda Kay Brown is the president-elect of the American Library Association, 2019–2020, and the director of library services for the C. G. O'Kelly Library, and was the associate dean of Wake Forest University's Z. Smith Reynolds Library. She has served as president of the North Carolina Library Association and president of the Black Caucus of the American Library Association.

Preface

SU EPSTEIN, VERA GUBNITSKAIA
and CAROL SMALLWOOD

In a changing world, with multiple and often conflicting voices, the library's important role as a location of safety and inclusion as well as a crusader for knowledge cannot be overstated. It can be easy to reflect on differing perspectives in our collections and displays, but if we do not practice our values, we are lacking. As leaders in our communities, we, librarians, have an obligation to educate and inform; we must be ready to lead and model the principles we support. The question that arises for many is: how?

It is our hope that the essays in this book offer the foundation and inspiration to move our actions beyond a diverse collection development and social issues displays. We hope as you read this collection that it will motivate you to consider the assumptions you may take for granted, work to support change in our organizations, and seek out creative new programs.

For years we have heard the stories of how libraries and librarians have changed people's lives. We need to ensure that we continue this important role.

Social Justice and Activism in Libraries: Essays on Diversity and Change came about after the lead editor, Su Epstein, recognized the need for a collection written by experienced, practicing librarians in the field. Essays were sought from U.S. academic, public, school, special librarians, and LIS faculty, on the role they can play in social justice and social change, activities supporting tolerance.

The essays are arranged by: Part I—Bringing Underrepresentation to the Forefront; Part II—Establishing Partnerships; Part III—Building Communities; Part IV—Administering with Diversity; Part V—Supporting Activism; Part VI—Generating Programming; and Part VII—Expanding Teaching.

Bringing Underrepresentation to the Forefront

Literacy Support
for the Intellectually Disabled
A New Frontier for Library Outreach

MATTHEW CONNER *and* LEAH PLOCHARCZYK

Introduction

In the course of securing and developing its identity in a changing environment, the library profession has explored new kinds of literacies. Information literacy, computer literacy, digital literacy, and media literacy are just a few terms that have appeared as outgrowths of the library's traditional role in the development of reading skills. Yet despite all the technological advances driving these new fields, literacy in the original sense remains a pressing issue. Perhaps this is due partly to technological advances which have raised the bar for advanced reading skills. The data on illiteracy becomes even more significant in light of the concept of "functional literacy" in which individuals who can technically read and write cannot cope with the demands of independent living (Cree, Kay, and Steward 2012, 3, 9). Addressing this problem would be as significant a social contribution as libraries can make.

Even within the library's traditional domain of literacy, there is a new frontier in the form of a population that has never been acknowledged or supported by the profession. These are the intellectually disabled (ID) who have been increasingly mainstreamed in the educational system. The ID represent a profound test of the profession in both its commitment to diversity and its service ethic. On the one hand, the ID deserve the same support as any population that wishes to use the library, perhaps even more insofar as support is related to need. On the other hand, they represent significant practical challenges. Whereas the library provides services for reading, the ID not only lack necessary reading skills but face special challenges to acquiring those skills. Nevertheless, there is a good deal of creativity emerging to address these issues, and among them the traditional vehicle of the library book club shows great potential.

Background

The American Library Association (ALA) has recognized the interrelation of the above issues by establishing an Office for Diversity, Literacy and Outreach which has published this statement: "The American Library Association recognizes that persons with disabilities are a large and often neglected part of society. In addition to many personal challenges, some persons with disabilities face economic inequity, illiteracy, cultural isolation, and discrimination in education, employment, and the broad range of societal activities. The library plays a catalytic role in their lives by facilitating their full participation in society." It continues, "These materials must not be restricted by any presuppositions about information needs, interests, or capacity for understanding." Passive acceptance is not enough: "Libraries should provide training opportunities for all staff and volunteers in order to sensitize them to issues affecting persons with disabilities and to teach effective techniques for providing services for users with disabilities and for working with colleagues with disabilities" (American Library Association 2017a, b, c).

The natural question that follows is what, in fact, libraries have done to support these goals. Literacy support, as one of the traditional roles of the library, has seen interest across the globe, and public libraries everywhere have displayed ingenuity in their programs. A number of programs for adult learners seek to provide incentives for them to read. Others use the family structure to reach both children and parents. The hallmark of the public library programs is to collaborate with other organizations to encourage literacy (Behrman 2002, Cooper 2004, McNicol and Dalton 2002).

For the academic domain, the authors first examined the support of the intellectually disabled (ID) on college campuses. The authors reviewed the ThinkCollege.net website, a pre-eminent database on postsecondary education for the ID (Think, n.d.). Searches of the database identified 138 institutions with programming for the ID. These programs serve individuals between 18 and 28 years of age. They are permitted to audit regular college classes and have classes of their own focusing on skills that will allow them to function more independently. As part of general self-development and to offer a college experience, the students have extracurricular activities with an emphasis on sports and clubs. Some programs also offer vocational training and job internships. While different in some details, these activities reflect the same philosophy of public library literacy programs in collaborating with various organizations. However, none of the programs listed on ThinkCollege.net made any reference to their campus library involvement; as far as authors know, there is no academic library that provides formal support for the ID, though some studies have raised the issue of library support (Mulliken and Atkins 2009). Neither are the authors aware of any systematic effort to work with the ID among public libraries (with one noteworthy exception below). Yet clearly there is a good deal being done in support of literacy in both the academic and public realms. It is natural to extend these efforts to the ID, and rather than thinking of them as an isolated population, to think of contributing to a growing movement.

While support for the ID raises deep issues of both special education and librarianship, librarians can start making contributions through the traditional vehicle of the book club. Book clubs have proven to be effective for the ID in a number of independent grassroots movements. One organization developed out of the work of a mother whose son had Down Syndrome. In 2003, Jamie Comer had aged out of the educational system and, without any resources to educate or socialize him, was languishing at home. His mother, Nancy Comer, with the help of the local Port Washington Library on Long Island, NY, organized a book club for her son and other individuals with ID in the library. It was so successful that it has since developed into a program called Books for Dessert with its own teaching staff and its own guidebook for those who wish to start their own programs (Books 2017). A similar organization began in 2002 under the guidance of Dr. Thomas Fish, Director of Social Work at the Ohio State University's Nisonger Center for Excellence in Disabilities. It has evolved into a national organization, the Next Chapter Book Club (NCBC), that offers training on an international scale. The premise is that by inserting reading activities into an informal context, the club will contribute to both the socialization and literacy training of the ID. The social mission of the organization has led to a startling range of locations. The book clubs now meet in bookstores, coffee shops, and other public spaces including busy New York City high rise building lobbies. Libraries, so far, have been largely avoided, due to their traditional policy of strict silence. But where this is relaxed, libraries will be free to participate.

Among the 138 colleges and universities that provide programming for the ID, actual literacy instruction is sparse; most of the curriculum supports student learning in the form of auditing college classes or participating in vocationally oriented programs. Yet, four programs have ventured into literacy activities that parallel the work of the NCBC and warrant closer attention.

Literacy Programs

The Panther LIFE program at Florida International University provides a "comprehensive postsecondary program and a system of support through partnerships to eligible students with ID through well-planned, structured and individualized curriculum and related program and community experiences focusing on academics and instruction, social activities, employment and independent living." For a period of time the program ran a book club as part of its activities (School of Education and Human Development n.d.).

The Elmhurst Learning and Success Academy (ELSA) in Elmhurst, IL, offers a program to "provide a full time post-secondary educational experience to young adults with developmental disabilities. The program focuses on academic, work experience, and social and recreational experience." Courses cover "reading and writing strategies and individual literacy needs" (Elmhurst Learning and Success Academy (ELSA) n.d.).

RISE (Road to Independent Living, Spiritual Formation, and Employment) is offered by Judson University in Elgin, IL. It aims to "give students with ID the college life experience in a Christian community and prepare them to live independently and to be competitively employed" (RISE n.d.). The program will begin in fall 2017 but some ideas include:

1. A current events class to engage the ID in familiar topics and to develop problem-solving skills.
2. A class for reflecting on events through readings of the Bible and Christian values.
3. Independent study time with mentors located in the library. Students will either be able to get individualized assistance on their coursework or learn basic library skills.

The John D. MacArthur Campus Library at Florida Atlantic University (FAU), Jupiter, FL, in association with the Academy for Community Inclusion (ACI) program for the ID, organizes a book club for the ID to practice reading skills. Having completed three iterations of the club at this writing, this program enables a more granular study of book clubs as a vehicle for literacy training for the ID.

FAU Book Club

The idea for the book club occurred to librarian, Leah Plocharczyk, who learned about the Academy for Community Inclusion (ACI) program for high school graduates with intellectual and developmental disabilities and wanted to offer library support to its curriculum. Out of her experience in organizing reading circles for other library outreach programs, she proposed one for the ACI cohort, and the idea was enthusiastically accepted by the Director. The librarian presented the idea to a gathering of the cohort, and eight students in attendance volunteered. Since a book club revolves around a book, its selection was crucial to the project. The librarian surveyed the students for their interests in the opening presentation and received requests for comedy and action. After consulting with the ACI program coordinators and surveying a number of books, she settled on Carl Hiaasen's, novel, *Hoot*. This young adult novel follows a boy moving to a new middle school in the Florida area and forging new relationships in the course of solving a mystery. The disorientation of a new school experience, the Florida setting, and even the owls, which are the mascot of FAU, all made the book an ideal match for its audience.

The librarian also consulted theories of literacy. Recent studies, consistent with a more flexible and student-centered pedagogy familiar to instructional librarians, recommend an informal class structure and alternative methods of engaging texts besides drilling vocabulary and grammar (Katims 2000, 4). Accordingly, the librarian sought to present reading as an experience. For the introductory meeting, the room was festooned with images of owls and even owl bookmarks, and there were icebreaking activities for the students to get to know each other. The initial reading sessions were structured carefully with discussion questions, however this did not prove successful. The students offered monosyllabic answers that were often inaccurate, and they had difficulty sustaining attention. In response, the librarian experimented with more interactive approaches that included reading aloud, by herself and by the students. By encouraging discussion and response from the students, she was able to generate a conversation which allowed her to interject questions about the book more naturally. Student engagement improved.

The book club got an unexpected boost from one of the participants who proposed having a party for her service dog who was due to be retired. The mere proposal was already a success for the program's goal of socialization. The librarian and her helper made the most of the opportunity with cake and party hats and the dog presiding over all and appearing to enjoy himself. For the festivities, the librarian also prepared a version of the game, Pictionary, with material that had been selected for its relevance to dogs. This was successful beyond expectations with the students eagerly puzzling over language in the context of the game. It occurred to the librarian that games could become a teaching methodology for literacy. There turned out to be a wide variety of games that could be adapted to literacy instruction, which proved effective for the remainder of the book club. This correlates the experience of Books for Dessert which has also used games in the context of social events for learning (Books 2017 11, 12).

Once the librarian started looking, language games appeared everywhere. Other games included Hangman, and the board games, Likewise and Last Word, some of which were used in modified form. The last two games involved guessing words based on clues. The librarian and her colleague extracted subject cards related to the book so that the game reinforced retention and understanding. Participation was full and enthusiastic and the room filled with laughter as the students jumped at the opportunity to describe a clue.

Another successful game was Sentence Starters which the librarian found online as an icebreaking activity used at parties and events. She made a list of phrases such as, "If I could live anywhere in the world, it would be…." Or "If I won the lottery, the first thing that I would buy is…." She cut them out and put them in a pile for the students to choose, and each student attempted to complete the sentence. This game was particularly effective at putting meaning in context and also advanced the socialization of the group by helping the members learn about each other in a playful and non-threatening way. For example, in response to the question, "If I could live anywhere in the world, it would be…," one member said that she would like to live in the Disney Castle so that she could be waited on hand and foot and go on rides all day long without having to stand in line and pay. This incident supports the observation that the sharing of personal stories promotes interaction that can improve literacy skills. "When encouraged to share their stories as part of a community, students begin to lose their hesitation and more readily assert themselves" (Greene 2015, 29).

Another game, One Word, was invented by one of the coordinators and based on an old game show called Password. A player chooses a secret topic for which she provides one word clues to help the others guess the answer. The game was challenging for the group, forcing the players to bend the rules by using more than one word or resorting to pantomime. But surprisingly, they named this their favorite game by the end of book club. The students appeared to enjoy sharing their opinions and providing information about themselves. One student said, "This is fun, and I like this game. Let's keep playing." The students benefited from the participatory framework of the game and the use of language and pantomime together. While the focus of the game was on a single word reminiscent of traditional instruction of the ID, the formulation of clues tested the understanding of context which is a hallmark of new methodologies. Possibly, the very difficulty of the game was the key to its success in motivating the students to draw on multiple modalities of communicating. If so, this game would counter older thinking about the limitations of the ID to show that the level of difficulty is not the only criteria for an activity. Rather it is the degree of engagement which, if managed properly, can raise the ID to new heights of performance. While the games could not sustain a discussion of the novel by themselves, they proved invaluable as an alternative when the students tired of reading aloud.

The book club culminated in a viewing of a movie version of the book (another reason for the book's selection). As with any population of students, the movie was planned as a way to synthesize and experience the reading material, and it was supplemented with food to make it a social event. The students remained attentive by all indications.

The second iteration of the book club took place in Fall 2016 and saw all eight members of the first group sign up as well as five new students for a total of 13. With the many returnees, the librarian decided to change the book while retaining the successful features of the previous class. The new book was *Strider* by well-known children's author Beverly Cleary. The story follows a young boy whose friendship with a stray dog helps him cope with the stresses of his parents' divorce and relationships with his peers. Yet, surprisingly this work did not engage the students, and the librarian was forced to discard it midway through the quarter and rely on games and other activities. The third edition of the book club returned to the book and movie format with *Teen Beach Movie* which was selected by a third-time attendee who owned both. The curriculum supplemented the book and movie with activities like before as well as a dance demonstration by the movie's owner who had memorized several of its routines.

Assessment

The Books for Dessert program manual addresses the issue of assessment. While it acknowledges the value of formal testing, it rejects this approach because it "contradicts the social sprit of the program." Instead, "progress is measured in a more qualitative manner through the group leaders noting the difficulty of the material covered and the pace at which each group can progress" (Books 2017, 19). Among the case studies at this writing, only the FAU case has enough information to discuss. Similar to Books for Dessert, formal assessment has not been attempted so far because it would be antithetical and disruptive to the informal character of the program. Nevertheless, some outcomes are clear. All participants completed the first iteration of the program and all signed up for the second, and their enthusiasm persuaded new students to join. In terms of the basic indicators of attendance, completion, and continuation, the book club was extremely successful. That is also true of the general pedagogy of language-based games. These activities confirm a student-centered informal approach that combines socializing with diverse learning modes. While the NCBC emphasizes that it is "reading to learn" rather than "learning to read," these methods dovetail with the newest research on teaching literacy to the ID.

The book, however, is the center of a book club, and here the results were more difficult to interpret. Two apparently similar books had quite different outcomes with one proving highly successful and the other not. Yet, this very divergence can prove instructive. The problems lay with *Strider*. While it resembled *Hoot* in following a young protagonist in a state of adjustment, its issues were of a more mature nature. The protagonist comes to grips with his parents' divorce and his father's development of a new romantic relationship. The boy himself also deals with what appears to be a burgeoning romantic attraction of his own. Moreover, these issues were presented indirectly as they would emerge in the mind of a young person arriving at maturity. Another point of difficulty was the protagonist's extensive musings on his writing assignments for English class which were outside the experience of the ID. The more successful book, *Hoot*, had none of these elements. The character's own viewpoint is anchored in a stable and supportive family. While there are reversals of gender roles, these are characteristic of pre-adolescence with a girl physically dominating boys, and conflicts are resolved with overt physical action, often slapstick comedy. The two books together make it possible to gauge the abilities of the students, and over time, book selection could provide a valuable profile of the ID as learners. For the time being, it seems fair to say that those who are embarking on reading, which is a process of abstraction, are best approached with the simplest forms of abstraction in which ideas are expressed physically. Difficult moral issues and complex subjectivities that make for some of the most challenging problems of young adulthood are, if not inappropriate, at least a riskier proposition.

In sum, the experience so far suggests that a book club for the ID, even within an academic library working at the highest end of the education system can be a rewarding enterprise, and this implies that it should work for earlier levels of the education system. Informal discussion with activities and games can engage the ID. A novel length book can also be read provided that it is properly selected and supported.

Conclusion

It remains to integrate the experience of these case studies into the needs of the profession as a whole. For the question of how libraries might provide support for the ID, there is no single answer. But it should be understood that such support is not an all or nothing proposition. A good deal of innovative work is being done by the partners who work with libraries. Public libraries have developed a number of outreach programs to encourage literacy among all age groups. Innovative programs have joined parents and their children in working together to acquire literacy skills. College campuses have opened their doors to the ID through auditing of regular classes and specialized programs including courses, extracurricular programs and training opportunities designed to give the ID a college experience and the means to become independent. Librarians need to be aware of these possibilities. There is no formula for involvement among all the varied situations, but librarians can judge where they might intervene. Actual instruction of reading skills is a complex and evolving subject. But a review of the literature, as well as the case studies here, shows that what succeeds with the ID is not unfamiliar, and does not require special training by librarians. On the contrary, student-centered, participatory, flexible pedagogies open to different learning modes are exactly what librarians have been developing in their own pedagogies for the information illiterate. There is every reason to think that instruction of the ID is more of an extension of current methods than something new and unfamiliar.

Moreover, the traditional library tool of the book club represents a way to cut through a experimentation and theorizing and make an immediate impact on the ID based on the case studies here. The book club format has succeeded brilliantly in the public library format with Books for Dessert, and both it and the NCBC offer support for expanding the idea to academic libraries and into a variety of creative partnerships. Those librarians who accept this challenge stand to make a powerful contribution to their library's role in their community. They are likely to find that rather than serving a long and arduous apprenticeship, they can make rapid contributions to an important new field.

WORKS CITED

American Library Association. 2017a. "A.1.15 Key Action Areas (Old Number 1.4)." American Library Association, accessed May 17, 2017. http://www.ala.org/aboutala/governance/policymanual/updatedpolicymanual/section1/1mission#A.1.5%20Key%20Action%20Areas%20(Old%20Number%201.4).
American Library Association. 2017b. "Office for Diversity, Literacy, and Outreach Services." American Library Association, accessed May 17, 2017. http://www.ala.org/offices/diversity.
American Library Association. 2017c. "Services to Persons with Disabilities: An Interpretation of the Library Bill of Rights." American Library Association, accessed May 17, 2017. http://www.ala.org/advocacy/intfreedom/librarybill/interpretations/servicespeopledisabilities.
Behrman, Edward H. 2002. "Community-Based Literacy Learning." *Reading* 36 (1):26.
"Books for Dessert." Port Washington Public Library, accessed September 14, 2017. http://www.pwpl.org/books/books-for-dessert/.

Cooper, Debra. 2004. "Beyond Four Walls: Adult Literacy Services in Queensland and Public Libraries." *Aplis* 17 (3):156–164.

Cree, Anthony, Andrew Kay and June Steward. 2012. *The Economic & Social Cost of Illiteracy: A Snapshot of Illiteracy in a Global Context*. World Literacy Foundation.

Elmhurst Learning and Success Academy (ELSA). "ELSA." Elmhurst College, accessed August 21, 2017. http://public.elmhurst.edu/elsa.

Greene, David. 2015. "The Field of Adult or Worker Education." In *Unfit to Be a Slave: A Guide to Adult Education for Liberation*. Rotterdam, The Netherlands: SensePublishers.

Hernandez, Christina. 2008. "Books for Dessert: Club for Intellectually Disabled." *McClatchy-Tribune Business News*.

Katims, David S. 2000. "Literacy Instruction for People with Mental Retardation: Historical Highlights and Contemporary Analysis." *Education and Training in Mental Retardation and Developmental Disabilities* 335 (1):3–15.

McNicol, Sarah J., and Pete Dalton. 2002. "The Best Way Is Always Through the Children." *Journal of Adolescent & Adult Literacy* 46 (3):248–253.

Mulliken, Adina, and Ann Atkins. 2009. "Academic Library Services for Users with Developmental Disabilities: Partnership of Access and Syracuse University Library." SSRN Electronic Journal. Doi: 10.2139/ssrn.1398085.

"RISE Program at Judson." Judson University, accessed August 21, 2017. http://www.judsonu.edu/RISE.

School of Education and Human Development. "Project Panther LIFE." Florida International University, Arts, Sciences & Education, accessed August 21, 2017. http://education.fiu.edu/pantherlife/.

"Think College." Institute of Academic Inclusion. University of Massachusetts, Boston, accessed October 12, XXXX. https://www.library.ucdavis.edu/guidde/endnote-directions-export-databasess-web/.

Prison Libraries and Social Justice

Helping Inmates Succeed

ANDREW HART

The Mission of Prison Libraries

Prisons exist for one reason: to correct and rehabilitate persons who have been convicted of committing crimes. Most prisons in the United States have a library of some sort, whether it is a full-time, staffed room of books and media, or library pods located in inmate housing units. Fortunate prison libraries have a degreed librarian present to manage library services for a prison's typical 500 to 2,500 inmates. A prison library is an important, necessary, and treasured piece of the rehabilitation puzzle. Not only does it provide inmates with reading material to pass the time; prison libraries provide community spaces for engaging with others, information to prepare inmates for release, self-help reference material, inspiration to start a business, the ability to discover a new hobby, access to legal resources, and much more.

Prison libraries play an important role in social justice. Libraries on the outside, located in the public and academic sectors, are the great equalizers of society. They provide information and technology resources no matter what one's background and socioeconomic status. They actively work against the digital divide. All people who enter a library are on equal footing. In the United States, citizens have a right to information and learning. Libraries are the gatekeepers and vectors of these rights. Prison libraries are no different, and, one could argue, are tasked with a heavier burden to promote equality and access to opportunities than libraries on the outside.

The mission of a prison library is twofold:

1. to provide opportunities and resources to inmates to permanently and positively change them
2. to prepare inmates for their return to mainstream society with the knowledge to succeed.

Those released from prison are returning at a rapid rate. There are many reasons for this; the biggest reason by far is social inequality. Former inmates are at a disadvantage in a society that is becoming more and more credentialized, technologically advanced, education based, and literate. A large portion of inmates who enter prison already lack these forms of social capital, and arrive in a society in which they are socially bankrupt.

As a result, some decide that the only way to survive is by committing more crime. This starts a nasty cycle of recidivism that prison officials want to break.

Prison libraries can help build up an inmate's social capital (and confidence) before leaving the institution. It is typical to find a dedicated space in a prison library devoted to reentry resources. This can include the following:

- computers to assist inmates with finding available jobs before they are released
- books and software on resume writing
- handouts/brochures on education and applying for student loans
- a list of employers that hire ex-felons
- books on planning a small business, including specific information on starting a business in a prisoner's state
- educational opportunities available to inmates while they are still in prison.

Inmates not only need to build up their social capital, they also need a helping hand to guide and show them what is available, and to be there and provide a reassurance that what lays before them can be accomplished. That person is the prison librarian.

The Role of the Prison Librarian

The job of a prison librarian is multifaceted. Prison librarians wear many hats. They are usually in charge of opening and closing the library, issuing library passes, collection development, readers' advisory, interlibrary loan processing, cataloging, performing general and legal research, notarizing documents, and answering inmate mail. This is all in addition to responding to fights in inmate housing units, enforcing rules, and keeping order in the library. It is a stressful, yet rewarding position in the library world. Prison librarians see inmates come and go, and in some cases, return.

A prison librarian's goal is both to supply inmates with recreational material in the form of books, movies, and magazines, and to provide programs, information, and guidance on preparing to succeed outside the institution once released. It is not uncommon to find illiterate inmates visiting the library to look at pictures in magazines, or to watch movies. Some visit with their friends and pretend to be able to read to avoid embarrassment. The librarian can find educational resources to improve their reading level, and even to assign inmate library workers as reading tutors. If you cannot read in society, your job opportunities, not to mention social and transactional interactions, will be negatively impacted. An illiterate person entering prison and still illiterate when exiting will be in a worse position than before. Prison libraries have the capability to fill in the gap. Opportunities are limited for someone who cannot read; having a prison record drastically decreases the remaining opportunities.

A prison librarian is a valuable source of information in the library, in addition to books and periodicals. Inmates visit the library to ask the librarian for resources not readily available in the collection, such as sample business plans and specific books through interlibrary loan. Inmates can also write questions to the librarian through things called kites. Kites are small slips of paper that inmates write on and then send to staff members through the prison's mail system. This guarantees access to the library if an inmate is not able to make it during a dorm's times of visitation. Quick reference questions can be answered this way. The librarian also makes visits to those in segregation units who cannot visit the library and provides reading material to make it easier to pass the time.

On one hand, prison librarians are educators and rehabilitators, and on the other, they are corrections professionals tasked with keeping order in the prison. Enforcing rules is an important component of the librarian's mission: inmates need to see the librarian as an authority figure. Being fair, firm, and consistent is the prison librarian's motto. Building a rapport with the inmate population begins here. Respect is social capital in prison, among both inmates and staff. Prison librarians gain respect with the inmates by enforcing the rules fairly. If it is perceived that the librarian is being biased or unfair, it will diminish the librarian's authority, and thereby, respect, making him or her less effective in the rehabilitation process. Respect equals trust. Generating a good rapport with the inmate population is therefore paramount for a prison librarian to be an effective agent of social change.

Prison librarians as much as possible strive to replicate the public library. Replicating the public library in the prison setting introduces the inmate population, many of whom have never set foot in a library before, to the services they can expect to find on the outside when released. Forging this connection to public libraries is necessary so that released inmates know where they can go for their informational needs. Knowing where to go, and feeling empowered to do so, helps replenish missing social capital, and gives soon-to-be released inmates the confidence they need to get help. Treating inmates like regular public library patrons also helps restore missing dignity and prepares them for interacting with people on the outside.

The Inmate Population

A prison's inmate population can be quite diverse. People from all backgrounds, ethnicities, and age groups, and those who have committed crimes ranging from murder to theft, are housed under a single roof. Each inmate has their own needs, and some have special needs, such as illiteracy as mentioned above. There are inmates who were wealthy before entering prison, and there are those who lived in poverty. Socioeconomic status (SES) can be used as a predictor for the chances someone has for committing crime, but it cannot be used definitively. Everyone makes decisions based on a complex calculus of life experiences and biological factors. Rich people commit crime just like poor people. Are their experiences different as they move through the criminal justice system? Yes. But once a convicted person enters prison, their experience is mostly equalized (there will be slight deviation in access to material goods for those with the resources to purchase them). Prison is an equalizing force: it levels everyone out to the same status: inmate. Control over one's life and liberty has been lost and given into the hands of the state or federal government.

A shocking number of those who enter prison have a mental illness. This is a tragic consequence of closing mental health facilities, a separate and complicated social justice issue. The resulting lack of mental health services places those with mental illness at a disadvantage and at a greater risk for committing crime. Without proper medication and psychiatric services, those with a mental illness may act out and commit crime unknowingly and uncontrollably. Prisons act as pseudo mental hospitals. In prison, an individual is given medication on a set schedule and has access to psychiatric and nursing staff around the clock. This is a well-known issue in penology, and one for which there is no easy answer.

What can a prison library offer those with a mental illness? The answer is an inviting, welcoming, and calm atmosphere. A prison library is one of the few places in a prison where inmates can find a place away from others and a bit of quiet. Dorms are chaotic at times. A prison library offers a dedicated area away from the perceived chaos and allows inmates to unwind and relax. A prison library can also offer those with a mental illness access to books on their illness. The better one understands oneself, the more one can cope and know the best way to overcome. A core resource that every prison library should have is a copy of the Diagnostic and Statistical Manual of Mental Disorders (DSM). This resource is used by psychiatrists to recognize and treat mental disorders. A resource like this may not be readily available on the outside. A prison library strives to meet the needs of its patrons, and proactively seeks to include resources and material on a variety of topics. Methodical collection development is key.

The Collection

Access to information is a staple in American society. Free access to information is a bedrock belief shared by the forefathers to have a democratic and educated society. In prison, access to information is provided by the library. Without a library, inmates would be left with an informational dearth and move backwards as citizens. Most prisoners will return to society one day. An educated and informed citizenry makes for a better democracy. Libraries keep inmates connected to the democratic process. Inmates lose certain rights after entering prison, but a right to information and educational resources and opportunities should not be denied.

A prison library's collection does not just contain books. It includes computers, interlibrary loan materials, movies, magazines, newspapers, handouts, bibliographies, reference resources, and legal reference material. For some inmates, the prison library is where they will encounter a computer for the first time. Helping inmates overcome the digital divide while still in prison echoes the war being waged by public libraries in communities across the nation. Modern jobs require at least some familiarity with computers. Having some sort of contact with the technology before reentering society is beneficial and adds to an inmate's social capital. Without the tools to succeed, how do we expect inmates to cope with the challenges they will face when they are released? Technology is continuously evolving and even those on the outside struggle with keeping up.

A prison library's book collection is akin to a public library's. Fantasy and science-fiction books are prevalent in fiction, as are mysteries and westerns. Self-help books are predominant in nonfiction, with books on starting a business and leadership a close second. While it may not appear as a social justice concern at face value, access to fiction and general nonfiction provides inmates reading practice and mental respite. Inmates can also teach themselves new skills or improve on the ones that they already have. Language books are another popular subject in prison libraries, and lucky libraries will even have language software on the computers.

Every prison library has a handful of dedicated patrons who come to use the book collection in a strategic way. Their interlibrary loan requests, book check-outs, and reference requests reflect what they want to do when they return to the outside. They are planners, and use their time to map out their reentry goals. The prison library can help them explore their interests and get the material they need as they develop their portfolios. Business plan books and books on being successful are of special interest and in high demand. Those interested in starting a business once released flock to the library and spend many hours using reentry resources and the nonfiction section for guidance.

Perhaps the most important component of a prison library's collection is the legal reference section. It includes resources mandated by the court that all inmates must have access to, and includes supplementary legal information resources at the librarian's discretion. Access to the court while in prison is paramount. Legal research material provides inmates the ability to challenge one's conviction. Sometimes inmates have legal counsel representation, but want to do their own research at the same time. Inmates who do not have, or cannot afford, legal counsel are called pro se. They perform legal research and submit legal documents themselves. The librarian can help them use the collection to find the resource that they need. Resources include rules of court, legal dictionaries and citation guides, boilerplate forms, reporters, case law databases, state and federal statutes and administrative codes, and legal commentaries.

Specialized Programming

In addition to physical information resources, prison libraries can provide classes and workshops on topics aimed at increasing inmates' social capital. Topics of interest include the following:

- computer literacy
- introduction to libraries
- resume writing 101
- finding a job

There are different kinds of learners; some inmates learn better when they have someone present that they can hear audibly and physically see. Sometimes a book is not enough. The librarian can answer questions that they might have in real time, instead of the inmate having to send the library a letter for more information. Special programming also allows inmates to hear what others have to say. This creates an opportunity for inmates to make meaningful connections with one another.

Those about to leave prison often seek others facing a similar situation. Inmates can experience fear and doubt as they ready themselves to return to a society that has locked them away and rejected them. Going from a strict, regimented lifestyle to an autonomous one can be jarring. Finding someone who knows what they are going through can be a morale booster and ease pre-release tension. A library's special program offerings aim to provide inmates with the little extra push that they need to succeed.

The Prison's Community

When working in a prison library, I was told all the time by people on the outside that they didn't think inmates should have books or access to movies and magazines. People complained that inmates got better X, Y and Z than those not locked up, and it wasn't fair. I was told this so much that I began tuning people out and remaining silent. This was a mistake. I should have explained, every time, why inmates should have access to information and recreational resources. The prison system is not rewarding inmates by giving them access to books, movies, and special programming. They are not getting the royal treatment. The prison system is trying to educate, rehabilitate, and keep inmates busy. The prison system is trying to provide inmates access to resources that they might not have encountered on the outside, in a society separated by socioeconomic status, and biased by race, education, and opportunity. A bored prisoner is a danger to himself and others, inside the prison and outside.

The community in which a prison resides need to understand that most of the prison's inmates will be released. Communities must ask themselves if they want released inmates walking down their streets better off than before, who have spent time reading instead of fighting; or, do they want inmates who have been socially and educationally deprived in prison, and because they had no books, programming, or educational opportunities, wasted their time and learned nothing during their prison sentence. I know the kind of inmate I would want.

Therefore, the community should step in and help prison libraries accomplish their goals. Communities have a stake in how well inmates turn out! The main way that the community can help is by donating books. Donations are a prison library's lifeblood. Donations feed the machine and keep things running smoothly. Bookstores, libraries, and citizens can all donate books to a prison. Prison librarians rely heavily on the community and petition all the time for donated material. Often communities deliver, if asked. Prison libraries do not have large budgets, and receiving a free box of books is truly extraordinary.

As mentioned above, communities have a stake in a prisoner's rehabilitation. A community that is welcoming and that consciously makes a way for those being released to succeed will have reduced levels of crime, and will help put a stop to the cycle of recidivism. It all comes down to environment and opportunity when released. What can an inmate buy with their social capital? Environment and the opportunities available will dictate how well an inmate does in the future.

Businesses and restaurants willing to hire ex-felons can contact the local prison, which can then make flyers available in dorms and the library to advertise this fact. Community colleges can offer classes at a reduced cost to ex-felons, or even better, to those still in prison. Again, would you rather have an ex-felon going to the local community college to learn a skill to be used to get a legal job, or would you rather have them committing crime and costing tax payers twenty-five thousand dollars a year?

Conclusion

Prison libraries are at the forefront of social justice, using books and creating resources to provide inmates with the ability to succeed. Prison libraries are a right, and inmates depend on them. From improving themselves, to challenging the court's decisions, the inmates use the library as a multifaceted and ever-evolving institution to meet the needs of its patrons and society at large.

Buttressed Beliefs,
Informed Action

Black Lives Matter, an Academic Library
and Building Critical Community Discourse

IAN BOUCHER

Libraries are uniquely placed for improving how people interact with one another, providing reliable information and meeting spaces to help communities get to the bottom of the complex issues that affect their lives. In the United States, American society is comprised of an extraordinary diversity of ethnic backgrounds living ostensibly together, but its history continues to be a conflicted one, especially with regard to socioeconomic inequalities for African Americans. Since 2013, this conflict has, as of this writing, become most prominent through an increasing number of headlines reporting unarmed African Americans being killed by police officers, bringing to the forefront troubling questions and debates about both the American criminal justice system and the underlying conflicts permeating American society. Significant to the conversation have been the development of the Black Lives Matter movement and the subsequent responses supporting or decrying it. Despite the media coverage, opportunities for communities to productively address or even acknowledge these questions among their neighbors free of commercial or political motivations have been in short supply. In September 2016, I implemented a Black Lives Matter discussion program at an academic library, to provide undergraduate students of all points of view with such an opportunity, to come together on the issues surrounding the Black Lives Matter movement as a community, through creative expression and research in a respectful, academic environment.

The location for this program was a small college serving students from backgrounds all over the country and the world, and about half of its student population was African American. After a tragic succession of headlines reporting killings of African Americans by police officers in the summer of 2016, I was motivated by two articles through my professional memberships about libraries bringing their communities together through reliable information and programming (Gray and Amundsen, 2016; Smith, 2016) to bring the conversation to the next level. My students could also come together, directly face a central issue in their society, and actually move forward on the conversation through their own support for one another and critical thinking.

I worked with a campus colleague to create a two-night discussion program about the issues around the Black Lives Matter movement that would meet students upon their return from summer vacation. It would be for students alone, in order to encourage them to critically engage their understandings without faculty or staff telling them what to think. My colleague and I would moderate the program, but facilitate students' experiences over our own opinions. The first night would consist of students gathering together to use crafts from the library to create and share drawings, collages, poems, or any other medium to convey their feelings, followed by reading and sharing reliable materials from a variety of sources. The second night one week later would include a discussion about a video from the library databases on educator and activist Jane Elliott's Blue Eyes/Brown Eyes exercise, as well as a reflection on a variety of real-life scenarios between police and African American citizens. The program would end with the creation of a second round of artistic representations of student understandings to display in the library or around campus, possibly even as a collective mural. The original working title was "Black Lives Matter Together," with the program summarized as:

> In light of the conflict in our country, students in our college family will come together to express themselves creatively, listen to each other regardless of point of view, read and watch objective sources, and discuss what Black Lives Matter means to all of them. We will work *together* in a respectful, constructive, supportive environment; students should feel at home surrounded by their college family. This is an opportunity to express, educate, and make an impact.

After notifying colleagues about the program, I was approached by an administrator indicating support, including arranging for a police officer or judge to speak with the students. It was also recommended that the campus counselor review the outline; we received a positive review. The administrator arranged a meeting with two criminal justice faculty, who had three primary concerns with the program outline:

- How did we know that talking about Black Lives Matter would be important to our students?
- Why were we not beginning with a program going out into the community?
- "Black" should be removed from the program title, because it may turn some people off.

I worked with my collaborator to assuage these two professors' concerns and integrate several of their ideas into a stronger program. The program was meant to provide an opportunity for students to be supported in critically engaging with an issue that was both all around them in the headlines and one that I had frequently observed on their minds. Student discussion on campus would provide a productive foundation for external action. After meeting with the professors, I strengthened discussion points about community impact for the program's finale to make this intention more specific and apparent:

- With what we've learned, what solutions could there be for our country?
- What can we do to make a difference?
- Talk about student interest and ideas for expanding this program into something further that can make a direct impact on the surrounding community.

The professors wanted me to put the program on hold while I distributed a survey to gauge student interest in library programs on social issues, but I decided to distribute the survey alongside the program. Additionally, although "Lives Matter" was a revised title I initially agreed upon, I came to the determination that I should not sugarcoat the issue, nor validate the slogans that arose to discredit others' pain. This led me to determine that what was most important for this program was to come up *with* a question for students to critically engage. Therefore, the program title was revised to "What Does 'Black Lives Matter' Mean to Us? A Conversation Among Our Students."

Concern was voiced to me about security at the event. To prepare for the worst, it was suggested to me that faculty and staff be present. Security is indeed crucial to consider for a program on a sensitive topic, and must be planned thoughtfully with the support of one's institution to ensure that the program is implemented effectively. Black Lives Matter was a sensitive topic in the headlines during my program, and there was certainly a risk that someone from on or off campus could attempt to disrupt the event. I had not considered this because my experiences with students of all ages on campus over the years—from personal discussions, to library instruction sessions, to the library movie discussion program I started earlier that summer—did not lead me to anticipate anything other than thoughtfulness, respect, and support during a library program. It was also posited to me that staff could provide extra support for students following the program. Thus, I recruited colleagues who would prioritize the students' experiences. My collaborator coordinated with the Student Government Association as enthusiastic co-sponsors. Unfortunately, I was told to tell my collaborator that although his involvement was still welcome, he was not allowed to moderate, since he did not have a degree related to the program's topic, and did not have experience researching the topic, despite his strong relationships with students and lived experience as an African American.

To prepare for the program, I curated resources from peer-reviewed journal articles of varying difficulty, Congressional Quarterly reports on controversial topics, and police department websites from different parts of the country, for students to split into the following groups, conduct research, and share their findings:

- Group A: Do U.S. Policies Contribute to Divides in Our Country?
- Group B: Police Strategies/Outreach
- Group C: Are American Laws at Their Most Effective? Are Racial Minorities Unfairly Targeted?

I also researched several real-life situations to discuss on the second night, deciding to focus on two traffic stops from the 1990s, one in which an unarmed African American man was killed, and the other in which a police officer was killed.

Although the first night was scheduled to begin at 8:30 p.m. it did not start until a bit later to give students time to arrive. Over a dozen students attended the first night, and were joined by almost as many faculty, staff, and administrators, some of whom were in addition to those I had invited. A campus security guard also happened to stop by before the program. I welcomed the students, saying that each student was present because they wanted to talk about the topic, and that due to the complexity of the issues, students might hear more than one point of view, feel a lot of emotions, and hear things with which they might not agree. I also emphasized that all were present to support each other and to come to individual understandings together, and that even if we did not all agree with everything we heard, we could at least leave with questions to think about.

Students took a few minutes to create and share powerful drawings, words, and crafts to convey what the words "Black Lives Matter" made them each think about, and why. I moved the conversation forward by asking questions for them to discuss. Here are the ones I planned with my collaborator:

- Are black lives in our country devalued? What do you think, and what have you heard from your peers/neighbors?
- Are police in our country disrespected?
- Are other races or ethnicities disrespected?
- What do the other "lives matter" movements mean?
- How do you feel about diversity on campus? Do you feel like there is a divide or not? Do we all feel safe in our daily lives in general?
- How productive are your conversations about these issues with other people, in person or online? Why?
- What do you think about our criminal justice system?

The students reflected the high academic standards of thoughtful and supportive exploration I had anticipated. Some of the staff attendees decided to participate in the discussion. When we reached the research portion, students began to leave due to the lateness of the hour and we had to end the program, but attendees, whether students, faculty, staff, or administrators, picked up the majority of the research packets to read on their own.

For the second night, administrators secured a local African American judge to speak with the students, and I moderated the discussion with these questions:

- In your experience, is race an issue in our justice system?
- How has the American justice system progressed over time? What has improved and what has not?
- What can young people do to improve any of the problems you have seen?

Student turnout was lower, and few who had attended on the first night returned. Nevertheless, the judge spoke with students in a highly engaging conversation long past the end of the scheduled time, and the attendees grew closer as a community. Many students were inspired to stay in the library after the program to discuss topics further. Students were surprised to hear a nuanced range of views from their peers, and felt that the program was an inspiring opportunity that made engaging with the topic more manageable.

The results of this program were very rewarding, as the creative expression and discussion with peers and community figures received resoundingly positive feedback from students and colleagues, and no detrimental incidents took place. The survey I distributed in print and online concurrent to the program only received 11 responses total, mostly from adult students, but still generally reflected an interest in library programs on social issues.

Directly addressing through a library program a societal issue crucial to the cultivation of diversity requires a great deal of awareness and preparation. It is important for librarians to discuss the implementation of programs like these, as there is much to collectively build upon. Like many library programs, this event involved providing a variety of craft supplies and a comfortable meeting space. For supplies, the library provided construction paper, poster board, markers, colored pencils, tape, glue, and I also brought some leftover confetti I had collected from another campus event. These supplies were distributed as evenly as possible around the room. For the location, after larger campus spaces became unavailable, we utilized a collaborative lab in the library in which we could arrange chairs in a circle, and use a projector for the video exercise that was planned for the second night. For the research packets, while it helped that I had done some previous research on this particular topic, it still took time to select the most appropriate resources for the program. I had to find materials that would be reliable introductions to different areas within the topic without being overwhelming for the students. If it is possible to do so, I would definitely recommend utilizing the expertise of colleagues or community figures in gathering research materials.

Most paramount to this program was to help students fill a societal gap in being able to address a cultural issue through building their critical thinking, research skills, and understanding in an academic environment, fostering respect and open community and minimizing any outside motivations. This was more difficult to accomplish than I anticipated. Although I think I responded constructively to the responses to my planning, I nevertheless was truly unprepared for what it meant to step into discourse about a sensitive societal issue. I had generally been left to my own ends while planning library programs, rarely garnering external notice, but the planning of this program required a great number of conversations and correspondence.

To replicate and build upon this program, a focus on building community is crucial, through yourself as well as the library resources and critical thinking you facilitate. Doing this means being aware of your entire environment, beyond the community need itself. To truly meet that need, you must be sure that your program's questions are unloaded. You must consider and welcome as many possible views about and reactions to your program as possible, so that you can respond as constructively as possible, and remain the logical and supportive force, keeping your personal understandings to yourself, whether your environment is supportive of your program or not. The planning of my program required conveying patience and empathy, as it was not only professional, but promoted respect and encouragement. Progress and education do not mean talking down to others from a bubble, but rather include listening and respecting others as people, always endeavoring to understand. In a heightened partisan environment such as the United States, where interpersonal academic discussion is obscured by media cycles validating individual biases, it is highly likely that any program about social issues will be met by concerned community members. These people need to be as welcome to their questions as students, and should be made to feel as such. Additionally, if I had the chance to do this program again, not only would I make sure to prepare my schedule accordingly, but I would also be ready to more vividly demonstrate to my concerned community members what libraries are capable of. I would explain clearly, consistently, and repeatedly, verbally and in writing, that as a library program, this program is about the students' research and discussion on a current social issue. While all views are welcome, no view is going to impose on any other, and within the program itself, it will be students driving the conversation through open-ended, neutral discussion questions. I would convey materials from other library programs in an engaging way, such as with linked infographics, to clearly convey this central characteristic of librarianship.

Although in my professional estimation, I navigated the responses to my program's planning relatively well, and I succeeded in gathering an effective collection of materials, my program ultimately did not realize what I considered to be its most crucial element—engaging students in the research portion. In addition, time did not allow the program to reach the second night's video discussion, traffic stop activity, or final reflections for future impact. While self-expression and community figures are important, understandings can only be furthered when they are buttressed with external research from a variety of sources and points of view. I believe the key to this endeavor is time.

Facilitating diversity through a program such as this requires more than a welcoming mindset and clear communication, for the support you garner will never be absolute. Additionally, there will likely also be community members responding with their own motivations, their own understanding about libraries, and their own influence over your program. I stayed as open, objective, and firm as I could in my dedication to providing this venue for students, but I have since considered two crucial points that could assist a future program in getting closer to its goal. Both of these factors relate to time. On one hand, I literally mean the time of night to begin the research portion. As a librarian, I do not always think about how starting even surface research at 10:00 p.m. would be daunting—but my students might! This is not students attending a class for a grade, but students showing interest in stepping outside their bubbles and applying themselves in real life and on their own time. Transitioning to the research or other activities immediately after the crafts and moving discussion to the end could help retain engagement. Moving the entire program to another time of day could help further; perhaps between classes and dinner, or on a weekend afternoon, would be effective, and providing meals or snacks accordingly. The most crucial element of time to consider, however, is allocation—assigning a specific amount of time to each section of the program. Therefore, no matter what is discussed, when the allotted time for that section is over, it is objectively time to move on to the research. Everything in a program like this should be above individual bias, and remain objective, measurable, and documented, and the design of this particular program is supportive for strengthening that. Of course, another question of allocation is the range of material to cover.

This experience furthered my understandings for strengthening libraries in the minds of American communities as repositories of information that can pragmatically support learning about and truly addressing life issues. Libraries, whether academic or public, are institutions like no other, where ideas can be explored and informed without fear. They are inherently about helping people guide themselves toward answers to the questions that matter to them and those around them. This attribute is not cosmetic, nor politically tinged, but core to the profession of librarianship, and is most important when life presents its most difficult questions. Libraries fulfill a unique and necessary role in culture, and need to be consciously cultivated by librarians and the communities they serve to be more apparent and embedded, because for peace to be achieved, a society must first find coexistence. Discussing conflict will always bring conflict, but the silver lining need not be obscured. Whatever societal issue librarians see an opportunity to address through their reliable information and meeting spaces, we can show people that we respect them, stick to our standards of objective information literacy and freedom of expression, and make progress together. It is also crucial that librarians share and discuss their experiences in building upon these endeavors. Championing the act of asking questions makes librarianship a difficult job, but whatever the issue being explored by librarians and the communities they serve, the reality is that there is strength in society.

Appendix: Program Materials

1. **Research Packets:**
    *   Group A: Do U.S. Policies Contribute to Divides in Our Country?
        *   Billitteri, Thomas J. (Executive Editor). "Racial Conflict." *CQ Researcher* Vol. 26, No. 2 (8 January 2016). Pages 25–48.
    *   Group B: Police Strategies / Outreach
        *   Billitteri, Thomas J. (Managing Editor). "Police Tactics." *CQ Researcher* Vol. 24, No. 44 (12 December 2014). Pages 1033–1060.
        *   "Citizens and *Police.... Friendship Through Education.*" *The City of Houston Police Department.* http://www.houstontx.gov/police/pip/.
        *   "Community Policing." *Seattle Police Department.* http://www.seattle.gov/ police/*community*-policing.
        *   Frattaroli, Shannon, Keshia M. Pollack, Karen Jonsberg, Gregg Croteau, JuanCarlos Rivera, and Jennifer S. Mendel. "Streetworkers, Youth Violence Prevention, and *Peacemaking* in Lowell, Massachusetts: Lessons and Voices from the Community." *Progress in Community Health Partnerships: Research, Education, and Action* Vol. 4, Issue 3 (Fall 2010), pp. 171–179. https://doi.org/10.1353/cpr.2010.0010.
    *   Group C: Are American Laws at Their Most Effective? Are Racial Minorities Unfairly Targeted?
        *   Beckett, Katherine, Kris Nyrop, Lori Pfingst, and Melissa Bowen. "Drug Use, Drug Possession Arrests, and *the* Question of Race: Lessons from Seattle." *Social Problems* Vol. 52, No. 3 (Aug 2005). Pages 419–441. http:// dx.doi.org/10.1525/sp.2005.52.3.419.
        *   Billitteri, Thomas J. (Managing Editor). "Racial Profiling." *CQ Researcher* Vol. 23, No. 42 (22 November 2013). Pages 1005–1028.
        *   Moore, Lisa D. and Amy Elkavich. "Who's Using and Who's Doing Time: Incarceration, the War on Drugs, and Public Health." *American Journal of Public Health* Vol. 98, No. 5 (May 2008). Pages 782–786. http://ajph. aphapublications.org/doi/abs/10.2105/AJPH.98.Supplement_1.S176.

2. **Video:**

    Anatomy of Prejudice: Jane Elliott's Seminar on Race. 2009.
    We will watch the first 15 minutes of a video from the library's databases, and I will ask students to consider what they think, if it says anything about race in our society.

3. **Real-Life Scenarios:**

    Scenario 1. A driver is pulled over by two police cars in the middle of the night, because the car is believed to be driving erratically and changing lanes without turn signals. The car has tinted windows. What would you do if you were the driver, and what would you do if you were the police officer?
    This is based on an incident in Chicago in 1999. A police officer pulled over a car with tinted windows. Two other officers joined in following, but one did not get a supervisor's approval to join pursuit of the car, and the other did not inform a supervisor monitoring the chase by radio that the windows were heavily tinted. The officers said that they tried to get the driver out of the car, and when they tried opening two doors, the

doors were locked. One of the officers broke the window and stuck in his gun into the car, and the driver struggled with the gun. The gun went off and killed the driver, who was an unarmed African American undergraduate student who was a member of the National Honor Society and a football player, days away from graduating from Northwestern University.

The officer who shot the driver was recommended a 15-day suspension, and the others, a day off without pay and a reprimand, respectively. Neither the victim's family nor the police union were satisfied with this result. In addition, the officers claimed that the driver had rammed one of the officer's cars three times and another car once. I was not able to get the race of all three police officers, but the one who shot the driver was African American.

Scenario 2. A park police officer pulls over a driver during the day near an international youth soccer tournament. What would you do if you were the driver, and what would you do if you were the police officer?

This scenario is based on an incident in Austin, TX in 2000. An African American park police officer pulled over a driver, and as he spoke with the driver, the driver shot him several times. The shooter, who had served prison time and was currently wanted by another jurisdiction for sexual assault, was spotted after the shooting by police, and after a car chase, shot himself. I was not able to get the race of the driver.

WORKS CITED

Gray, Jody, and John Amundsen. 2016. "Libraries Respond to Recent Crises: Local Libraries Help Communities Cope." *American Libraries.* 11 July. https://americanlibrariesmagazine.org/blogs/the-scoop/libraries-respond-recent-crises/.

Smith, Kelly. 2016. "Libraries Across the Country Look to Hennepin County Library for Response to Black Lives Matter." *StarTribune.* 14 July. http://www.startribune.com/libraries-across-the-country-look-to-hennepin-county-library-for-response-to-black-lives-matter/386882471/.

Improving Everyday Lives

Free Administrative Legal Assistance and Critical Trans Politics in Libraries*

ELLIOTT KUECKER

This essay proposes that libraries have an opportunity to improve the everyday lives of trans*-identified patrons through free or affordable assistance with administrative legal tasks, such as name changes, gender marker changes, finding healthcare, and gathering reliable information on how to maneuver these bureaucratic systems that ultimately impact health, employment, and all aspects of our lives that rely on gender categorization. Further, none of these legal tasks or offices work in isolation, but rather in a complex, non-linear web of disparate decisions existing at the federal, state, county, and even individual clerk levels. Inspiration for this type of public library services comes from the existing models of administrative legal assistance many public libraries offer to immigrants. While part of this proposal is practical in nature, it relies heavily on an understanding of how the United States law and the government undermine its own trans* citizens by making "trans people's lives administratively impossible..." (Spade 2015, 12) through the veil of banal and neutral policy and procedure, or rather, administrative violence.

Language may get complicated when describing this topic, so I am using the asterisk-form of the word, "trans*," to be more inclusive, a style of notation that should look familiar to librarians because of its Boolean roots. Avery Tompkins writes, "Proponents of adding the asterisk to trans argue that it signals greater inclusivity of new gender identities and expressions and better represents a broader community of individuals. Trans* is thus meant to include not only identities such as transgender, transsexual, trans man, and trans woman that are prefixed by trans- but also identities such as genderqueer, neutrios, intersex, agender, two-spirit, cross-dresser, and genderfluid (ibid.)" (Thompkins 2014, 27). While all language may be imperfect on this topic, my main point is not semantic; this is about assisting any person who would wish to accomplish changing their gender marker or name on administrative documents, not about figuring out which identities have which relationship to accomplishing these tasks.

First, one must understand that "From birth to death, the 'M' and 'F' boxes are present on nearly every form we fill out: on the identity document we show to prove ourselves and in the computer records kept by government agencies, banks, and nonprofit organizations.

Additionally, gender classification often governs spaces such as bathrooms, homeless shelters, drug treatment programs, mental health services, and spaces of confinement like psychiatric hospitals..." (Spade 2015, 77). Because of this, administrative legal changes make the stakes extremely high for trans* people, and these stakes are unique to the trans* life experience, who rely on the state to recognize their identity through driver's license, birth certificate, and other document changes. Further, each document is housed in a different branch of government under a different level of jurisdiction. The birth certificate, perhaps one of the most essential documents, is one of the most complex changes to navigate, with some states allowing one to change their name and sex identifier on their birth certificate with a completely new replacement, some allow one to amend their birth certificate with the new information, and some only allowing for certain changes under certain circumstances. In all cases, a person wishing to change this information may need a court order, a letter from a surgeon of a sex change, or other "evidence" of their transition. The question of how and if one can make edits to their birth certificate would be the perfect administrative legal intervention the library could provide, simply by providing the trans* patron with free or affordable access to a knowledgeable and trained individual.

Clearly, the trans* life experience hinges on information, as so much of the trans* identity itself is about understanding gender construction and the philosophy of personal freedom, but reliable information about the practical matters of transitioning is still difficult to find. Libraries have not fully taken on the task of providing for the information needs of trans*-identified patrons because most research and writing about trans*-identified people in LIS literature relates to collection development, so far disregarding other types of information needs. While finding reading materials that mirror one's own life experience can be valuable, it speaks only to part of the information needs of trans* patrons. Pohjanen and Kortelainen describe the multi-stage information needs of people who identify as trans*: "Early information needs are related to the causes of transgender identity, experiences of other transgender people, support groups and counseling services, and they evolve in the course of time. When the experience of an individual's own gender has become established the information needs also change. In this phase these needs are often related to public policy-related topics such as medical care, employment discrimination and transgender activism" (Pohjanen and Kortelainen 2016, 172). Their findings state that the internet is the most common source for this type of information, with personal networks and intimate relationships coming in not far behind (180). These sources can be outdated or misleading, and in the case of the internet, vocabulary barriers and insufficient county and state websites are problematic sources for info on health services and ID changes, as they will leave searchers with unanswered questions, or incorrect answers. The most reliable sources tend to be more structured personal relationships, as they note that support groups online and in-person are some of the only ways for trans* people to obtain certain types of information relevant to their transitioning process. Similarly, trans* healthcare questions showing up in Twitter discussions like #QueerAndCaringFor and #ruralqueerhealthcare, where psychological barriers related to fear and distrust of institutional sources are eliminated by asking trusted strangers for advice.

Most of the information trans* patrons may need to find relate to administrative legal changes in documentation through various government offices at the federal, state, and county level. Navigating this world is nearly impossible, which is where libraries can assist, since so many of these offices have different standards and policies. This incoherent policy framework begs for social justice and activist intervention, as "These constructs often operate in the background and are presumed as 'neutral' features of various administrative systems. The existence and operations of such administrative norms is therefore less visible than those moments when people are fired or killed or excluded explicitly because of their race or body type or gender, yet they sometimes produce more significant harm because they structure the entire context of life" (Spade 2015, 5). Meanwhile, most people are distracted from questioning these administrative and judicial offices, such as the Department of Motor Vehicles, Customs and Border Protections, the Food and Drug Administration, the Environmental Protection Agency, and more, thinking that hate crime law is where our attention should be. Problematically, while hate crime law emphasizes individual violence enacted upon another individual, it disregards the prevention of violence, aids the Prison Industrial Complex with punishment, and most importantly, diverts attention away from administrative violence from our country's institutions. Spade writes, we must "think more broadly about how gender categories are enforced on all people in ways that have particularly dangerous outcomes for trans people. Such a shift requires us to examine how administrative norms or regularities create structured insecurity" (Spade 2015, 9). Libraries must understand the way this administrative violence is enacted upon trans* people, not so we can offer a solution or a way to overthrow a deeply unjust and impossible system, but so we can help trans* people navigate the reality of these offices through assistance with information.

These documentation changes are inextricably woven into the healthcare system in the United States, which is in-turn woven into law, and ultimately this relationship may have life-or-death ramifications for the individual. Both health and the law promote a charade that argues that biology determines our sex categorization. On one hand, this trifecta of documentation/health/law dictates legal identity that then dictates healthcare: "Medicine and insurance play a part in determining sexual identities for transgender persons, but importantly, so does law. Legal institutions have traditionally understood sex as immutable, unambiguous, and fixed at birth. The law assumes that sex is binary: an individual can be a man or a woman, but not both or neither... sex is not solely defined by biological factors, but is actually 'a human-made process, often involving a legal process'" (Khan 2011, 377). Then, the state's interpretation or determination of one's legal sex ultimately determines what health rights, such as access to insurance, a trans* individual may or may not be given. This too is an urgent social justice issue, as the state has the power to determine the legal existence of an individual in a simplified two-category system, using criteria outside of just biological factors, and then doles out benefits that determine if someone lives, how long they might live, and their quality of life, based on these flawed and obscure categories.

On the other hand, medical intervention actually dictates documentation in the lives of trans* people, reinforcing the idea that one must engage in the healthcare system to change their legal identity: "For transgender populations, legal recognition is usually closely tied to medical treatment. Medical and surgical practices often drive the legal construction-and reconstruction—of sex. In most states, the sex designation on documents like birth certificates, driver's licenses, and social security cards cannot be changed without at least some evidence of gender-related medical treatment" (Khan 2011, 382). In this way, healthcare is the crux of the trans* life experience if one wants to change their gender marker on their documentation. For hormone treatment, they may need an official letter from a psychologist or counselor who says they are mentally healthy enough to undertake the task; for surgery, they may need a letter from their physician that says they have been on hormones long enough to know they are committed to this life path; to change their driver's license gender marker, they may need a letter from their surgeon stating that they had "sex reassignment surgery." Each government agency is tracking the gender marker for an individual and determining what evidence is needed to change that opinion, which is sometimes related to an official policy, but at other times merely at the call of a clerk or administrator in the office. Regardless of whether or not a trans* person would want to engage in medical intervention, if they want to change their gender marker on a document, they may have to take part in all or some of this long scenario described, and this may not even be the proper scenario depending on what state they live in. Thus accomplishing a simple documentation change requires complex research and legal advice that libraries might be able to provide.

Because of the emphasis the United States security culture places on terrorism prevention, data and documentation changes could be a matter of survival at the levels of obtaining housing, work, and other basic needs for a trans* person. The problem is exacerbated if a trans* person who has made progress changing some documents, is unable to change others, and has heterogeneous representations across documentation. Spade writes, "when a DMV compares its records with the SSA, those people whose information is inconsistent between the two agencies will be contacted with a threat to revoke their driver's licenses. When the IRS compares its data with the SSA, employers are contacted and urged to take action to rectify the conflicting information or to terminate the employee" (Spade 2015, 84). Unfortunately, most trans* people could not be stealth (the act of not being outed as trans* among a group of people or institution) with any such government or HR office due to these types of probes into data, which is one way in which the government undermines its own trans* citizen's safety. Because it is administratively impossible to change many documents simultaneously, many people have "documentation discrepancy" that often results in the loss of employment, not being hired, or other severe consequences: "A recent study found that 47 percent of trans and gender nonconforming respondents reported having experienced an adverse job outcome, such as being fired, not hired, or denied a promotion because of their gender" (Spade 2015, 80), and this act, though unethical, would be legal in the majority of states. There are numerous examples of this happening, including when the "Library of Congress's Congressional Research Service withdrew a job offer to a male-to-female transsexual woman after learning about her impending sex reassignment" (Taylor 2007, 843).

Through legal assistance, libraries can take part in assisting trans* patrons navigate administrative systems that often promote general threats to safety and outright violence, rather than protection, by utilizing a more grassroots and social justice approach of offering affordable, volunteer services. Successful implementation of such programs does involve some recognition of ideas that are well-known among activist groups: "the United States has always had laws that arrange people through categories of indigeneity, race, gender, ability, and national origin to produce populations with different levels of vulnerability to economic exploitation, violence, and poverty" (Spade 2015, 1). In the case of trans* patrons, we are talking about a varied population, that experiences suicide, depression, homelessness, violence, isolation, and numerous other hardships at higher rates than other populations. Further, we are talking about a group that we can barely call a group, because of the varying identities and life experiences that are included in the trans* label, the divergent medical or legal changes anyone in this identity may take on, and the nuanced intersections that impact their lives in other ways, such as having a history of criminal convictions, dealing with a disability, or being vulnerable based on other marginalized status. Fortunately, we may be able to mimic the amazing work many public libraries have undertaken for immigrants, who also deal with administrative violence, and sometimes have crossover into the trans* identity, as well.

Citizenship assistance mirrors my descriptions of administrative legal assistance for trans* patrons because it is not about merely providing a collection that reflects the patron's identity, nor just having people with cultural competence working in the library (though both of those things are essential), but instead emphasizing that libraries can become reliable sources of information related to administrative changes in a network of misinformation and bad help. Notably, the Hartford Public Library was awarded a grant to start The American Place to provide "citizenship workshops, English-language classes, and quarterly immigration forums" (Dankowski 2015) in addition to assisting with naturalization and other relevant applications. The Los Angeles Public Library, New York Public Library, and numerous other public libraries located in big cities known as immigration hubs provide something similar. As Kate Baker writes, "'The wrong kind of help can hurt.' This is especially true when immigrants receive incorrect information about laws and procedures" (Baker 2016). In managing this notion of "the wrong kind of help," U.S. Citizenship and Immigration Services has partnerships with numerous libraries, and even co-authored the *Library Services for Immigrants: A Report on Current Practices* report with the Institute of Museum and Library Services because of the accessibility and comfort libraries provide the population in need.

Further, many library staff have become accredited by the Board of Immigration Appeals Recognition and Accreditation (BIA R&A), from the Department of Justice, "which allows non-lawyers with approved training and the backing of a recognized non-profit organization to legally represent immigrants" (Dankowski 2015). This training utilizes time, energy, and money, but it is prioritized because the end result helps remedy the issue of misinformation or bad help with administrative procedures that are not intuitive, and it supports some libraries' priorities of being locations of accessible legal help, and hubs for social justice initiatives.

It is disappointing that libraries would not be able to partner with the Department of Justice, offices of vital statistics, or any other government agency to assist trans* patrons, given that most of the administrative procedures trans* patrons may need assistance with are determined by state or county governments, but there are other, more grassroots, options for training and partnerships. One reliable option is the Sylvia Rivera project, founded by Dean Spade, which provides legal help in New York and training anywhere. Their website states: "The Sylvia Rivera Law Project works to guarantee that all people are free to self-determine gender identity and expression, regardless of income or race, and without facing harassment, discrimination or violence" (*Sylvia Rivera Law Project* 2017). The project provides workshops that prepares allies and providers to assist trans* patrons on issues related to name change and IDs, healthcare, immigration, and interacting with law enforcement. (Regardless of what routes a library may take, the main point is that there are methods of training or partnerships to assist trans* patrons.) Additionally, there is a precedent for public libraries partnering with law schools and law professionals for more ad-hoc events, such as "Lawyers in Libraries" program held by the Maine Justice Action Group that put more than 60 lawyers in 43 libraries for those who could not normally afford legal advice (Harrison 2013).

Libraries interested in taking on this social justice initiative would have a great deal of work to do. Most likely, the first step preceding any legal assistance would be to collaborate with members of trans* communities to prepare the library environment to be one of acceptance, respect, and a place free of microaggressions. If a large portion of trans* patrons began visiting the library for new legal services, it would be essential that the staff knew the spectrum of trans* identities and experiences so as to be culturally competent. Staff who are made uncomfortable by various gender expressions or have moral or religious apprehensions about others who choose to transition might pose risks to the library's welcoming environment, thus training and education must take place before trans* patrons are invited into the library for a positive and helpful experience. Since public libraries represent their individual communities, trainings should be procured from grassroots organizations in the local communities that serve as trans* educators, especially those given by experienced professionals and members of the trans* community near the library itself. Projects like this are most successful when they are highly collaborative with the communities in need and committed to incredible levels of allyship and partnership.

After basic competency and respect training, libraries would need to decide what types of services they hope to offer, if the services would be free or low-cost, and if the services would be given by trained library staff or actual attorneys. Immigration legal advice in libraries varies in this same way; sometimes it is free, sometimes it is offered for a nominal charge; sometimes it is performed by trained library staff, while other times it is offered by attorneys. If it is offered by trained library staff, more training would be needed in federal, state, and county administrative law and trans* legal issues. If it is offered by attorneys, libraries would need to decide if they would like to pursue a partnership with a law school and set up something akin to a legal aid clinic in the library using law students, or if they would like to pursue a grant to pay for attorneys to visit on certain days of the month. These different options would form different paths for a library, and all of these options would cost some amount of money on the part of the library, or a great deal of time if the project was pursuing grant funding (which also presents the issue of being limited to the time period for which the grant was awarded).

Finally, any initiative like this poses huge political and strategic difficulties for any library. Given that public libraries are supported by local governments, libraries hoping to lead these types of initiatives would have to prepare to defend their project to their local government and taxpayers. Larger library systems with marketing departments would have an enormous advantage over smaller, more independent public libraries, as the general public is still learning what it means to be trans*, and even those committed to social justice may not yet understand the risks their fellow trans* citizens face at the hands of our own government and legal system. With proper public relations, however, a project like this could be launched by raising awareness and education about the trans* life experience and how it impacts healthcare, employment, and all other aspects of life. While the general public may understand some of the difficulties immigrants might encounter because the immigration issues are more familiar and currently affect more families, trans* issues are newer and there is no commonplace understanding of what it means to live a trans* life. In fact, the information people get about the trans* life experience from our media and current government work in opposition to the types of political arguments I have cited from activists and scholars like Dean Spade. Gaining buy-in for such a project could prove to be daunting in some cities.

All of these difficulties have been faced before on similar projects with similarly innovative initiatives, so it can be done. Drawing on libraries' willingness to engage in grassroots organizing, social justice, and defending vulnerable populations, we should address administrative violence against trans* people in the United States with our greatest tools: education and action. Libraries would have to commit to the long haul in order to reap the rewards of such a collaborative project, but ultimately, this type of work is our ethical obligation in supporting a critically underserved population.

WORKS CITED

Baker, Kate. 2016. "Public Libraries Collaborating with USCIS to Help Immigrants." *Public Libraries Online,* March 10, 2016, http://publiclibrariesonline.org/2016/03/public-libraries-collaborating-with-uscis-to-help-immigrants/.

Chung, Jeannie J. 2011. "Identity or Condition: The Theory and Practice of Applying State Disability Laws to Transgender Individuals." *Columbia Journal of Gender & Law* 21, no. 1 (2011):1–45.

Citizenship and Immigration Services. 2007. *Library Services for Immigrants: A Report on Current Practices.* July 11, 2007, https://www.uscis.gov/sites/default/files/USCIS/Office%20of%20Citizenship/Citizenshi%20Resource%20Center%20Site/Pblications/G-1112.pdf.

Dankowski, Terra. 2015. "Librarians as Immigration Lawyers." *American Libraries Magazine,* September 17, 2015, https://americanlibrariesmagazine.org/blogs/the-scoop/librarians-as-immigration-lawyers/.

Harrison, Judy. 2013. "Lawyers to Be Stations in Libraries Across State to Offer Free Legal Advice." *Bangor Daily News,* April 29, 2013, https://bangordailynews.com/2013/04/28/news/state/lawyers-to-be-stationed-in-libraries-across-state-to-offer-free-legal-advice/.

Howell, Ally Windsor. 2013. *Transgender Persons and the Law.* Chicago: American Bar Association.

Khan, Liza. 2011. "Transgender Health at the Crossroads: Legal Norms Insurance Markets, and the Threat of Healthcare Reform." *Yale Journal of Health Policy & Ethics* 375 (2011):375–383.

Marquez, Alejandro. 2017. "Supporting Transgender Individuals in Libraries: Developing Responsive Policies." *The Journal of Creative Library Practice,* 2014. Accessed November 20, 2017. http://creativelibrarypractice.org/2014/06/19/supporting-transgender-individuals-in-libraries/.

McDermott, Irene E. 2016. "How Public Libraries Can Help Syrian Refugees." *Information Today* 40, no. 2 (2016). Accessed November 20, 2017. http://www.infotoday.com/OnlineSearcher/Articles/Internet-Express/How-PublicLibraries-Can-Help-Syrian-Refugees-109501.shtml.

Pohjanen, Aira Maria, and Terttu Anna Maarit Kortelainen. 2016. "Transgender Informationbehaviour." *Journal of Documentation* 72, no. 1 (2016): 172–189.

Spade, Dean. 2015. *Normal Life: Administrative Violence, Critical Trans Politics, & the Limits of the Law.* Durham: Duke University Press.

Sylvia Rivera Law Project. 2017. https://srlp.org/.

Taylor, Jami Kathleen. 2007. "Transgender Identities and Public Policy in the United States: The Relevance for Public Administration." *Administration & Society* 39 (2007): 833–856.

Thompkins, Avery. 2014. "Asterisk." *TSQ: Transgender Studies Quarterly* 1, no. 1–2 (2014): 26–27.

PART II

Establishing Partnerships

Food for Thought

Feeding Mind and Body at Public Libraries

AMBER H. WILLIAMS, ERICA FREUDENBERGER *and* CINDY FESEMYER

As community anchor institutions, public libraries have an essential role to play in identifying and meeting the needs of the communities they serve to help them reach their aspirations. But what happens when people's dreams collide with reality? Where do public libraries step in, and how do they help move their communities forward? Three public librarians from across the country—Spokane, Washington; Columbus, Wisconsin; and the Southern Adirondacks, New York—have spent the past several years grappling with these questions. This is our story.

Librarians, as a profession, tend to be optimists and dreamers. When asked why they chose to be librarians, many describe their decision as responding to a call, choosing a vocation rather than a job (Ettarh 2018). Libraries are sacred places, devoted to the life of the mind and lifelong learning—a fantastic premise, rooted in class assumptions that too often alienate, rather than welcome.

Imagine being functionally illiterate, and passing by a library building. Most are constructed as temples to learning and are, by design, impressive examples of institutional architecture. Would a large, formidable building dedicated to words be inviting, or intimidating? Once inside, people have to navigate a complex organizational system rooted in words and numbers. To ask for assistance reveals how vulnerable you are. Add to this a frustrating experience with education, and a library is no longer a place of refuge, but refusal.

For new arrivals, struggling to make sense of a new country, customs and culture, language is only one barrier of many. Libraries are helping immigrants navigate a new landscape, including shopping for food, understanding currency, and finding ways to reweave their social fabrics to include cultures traditional and new.

How can public libraries make inroads with folk who could potentially benefit the most from what we have to offer? How do we look beyond our good intentions and embrace transformative action? One way to overcome people's anxiety and apprehension is to fulfill a fundamental human right: access to food, and inclusion in the community.

By acknowledging food insecurity, by building social capital, or by hosting a shared meal and conversation, libraries can help create profound changes not only in the lives of individuals but within whole communities. We believe that meeting people's basic physiological needs—feeding them and connecting them with resources—is the best way to build deep, long-lasting relationships that lead to vibrant and welcoming communities.

Spokane, Washington

The Deer Park Library in eastern Washington State is part of an eleven-library district. The city of Deer Park has a population of less than 4,000, but the library serves two school districts with a population more than 12,000. The Deer Park School District (DPSD) has a combined average of 57.9 percent of students qualifying for free or reduced lunch at its elementary schools (OSPI 2017). There is no funding for after-school programs, and sports are only available in middle and high school. Happily, the Deer Park Library is close to the elementary school, making the library the perfect place for children to wait for their caretakers to pick them up after the school day ends.

In 2015, the library conducted more than 100 Harwood Institute for Public Innovation–style community conversations throughout the county to determine people's aspirations for their community. In Deer Park, one interview with parents of preschool students stood out. Midway through the conversation, one mother discussed how she was not worried about her children completing their homework when she was struggling to put food on the table. When reflecting on what they had heard, library staff recounted the many times they had seen children argue over food, including fights over a thrown apple and high school students sharing discarded gas station donuts. Recognizing the need to meet the most basic human need, access to good food, Deer Park Library staff started considering ways they could help.

The staff began the process of becoming an approved afternoon snack site for the federally funded Child and Adult Care Food Program (CACFP). This funding allows the library to provide a healthy afternoon snack for children between the ages of one and eighteen at no additional cost to the library. From its start in March of 2016 to the completion of the 2017 school year, the Deer Park Library distributed 8,304 afternoon snacks. Creating a sustainable after-school snack program required library staff to recruit local volunteers from the high school and community to assist with food distribution for an hour after school. Building on the CACFP success, the library enrolled as a Summer Food Service Program (SFSP) to provide afternoon snacks during summer vacation from 3 p.m. to 4 p.m. Monday through Friday. That program now continues year-round.

Recognizing that the appetite of a three-year-old does not match that of a fifteen-year-old and that children may be hungry outside of the 3–4 p.m. window, the Friends of the Deer Park Library supplement the snack program with extra food. With their assistance, the library meets and exceeds the requirements of the CACFP and SFSP programs and, most importantly, the needs of many community children.

Staff at the library didn't stop there. Seeing so many children in a safe, supportive environment on a regular basis gave them the idea to collaborate with teachers to provide an after-school tutoring program during the school year. Now that they had met the fundamental need of food, children could opt in to receive homework help as they munched their snacks. Building on the comments gathered from the community conversation; the library was now providing access to both food and homework assistance.

On average forty-five students participated in tutoring sessions during the six-week program in 2016.

Before beginning, the program library staff expressed concerns over the possible mess of serving children food in the library. SCLD did not have a policy against food and drink in the library, so it was up to staff to address any problem that arose. After launching the project, staff concerns were proven to be unfounded. Staff asked children to clean up after themselves. They encouraged each other to follow the rules and helped one another clean up.

As a direct result of this program, library staff report that behavior issues with unattended children in the library have decreased drastically. Because the CACFP requires children to sign in to receive their snack, library staff and community volunteers are on a first name basis with all the children. Additionally, kids and families see the library as a place they want to be with services that speak to their lives.

During summer months, when the need for homework help disappears, the library began a new program. Their "Produce Swap" is a simple passive program: a table in the library has a sign in acrylic holder stating, "The food on this table is given and taken freely, nothing is for barter or sale." With that simple prompt, local citizens bring extra garden produce to the library and leave it for those in need in their community. Remaining produce is donated to the local food bank. Library staff report that the table is well used and relatively trouble-free.

Southern Adirondack Library System, New York

The Southern Adirondack Library System (SALS) is a cooperative library system comprised of 34 autonomous public libraries in Hamilton, Saratoga, Warren and Washington counties. It is one of 23 library systems in New York State, created to assist public libraries, provide free direct access, support a central library, provide interlibrary loan, outreach and literacy services, administer grants, and consult and offer professional development for library staff and trustees.

Many of the communities served by SALS are rural food deserts, defined by the USDA as "parts of the country vapid of fresh fruit, vegetables, and other healthful whole foods, usually found in impoverished areas. This is largely due to a lack of grocery stores, farmers' markets, and healthy food providers." Located in rural areas where agriculture is the predominant industry, a lack of transportation and regular employment contribute to the challenge of having a reliable food source. In 2015, the Glens Falls Hospital received a grant from the New York State Department of Health to provide access to healthy foods to communities that had at least 40 percent of students participating in the school lunch program. The hospital partnered with Comfort Food Community, a food pantry based in Washington County, New York, to create a mobile food pantry that could distribute fresh produce gleaned from local farms. The challenge for the initiative was to find locations in each of the targeted communities to distribute the produce.

The Hadley-Luzerne Public Library service area straddles two towns in two counties and serves a community that is considered both low income and low access (no grocery store within 10 miles). The nearest city is Glens Falls, 18 miles away. The only local place to shop for food is a Dollar General store or the Stewart's Shop, a gas station convenience store. In the summer of 2017, the library offered its building as a distribution site, recruiting board members and community volunteers to travel to Glens Falls to pick up produce to distribute at the library. In the course of making fresh, local produce available, the library saw an influx of new faces, many of whom entered the library for the first time because of the food program. The program changed the role of the library in the community, breaching a division between the two towns of Hadley and Luzerne, and creating an opportunity to demonstrate how the library could, in a literal and material way, transform the lives of the people it served.

Other libraries, like the Schuylerville Public Library and the Greenwich Free Library, are also responding to food insecurity in their communities. In the summer of 2017, the Schuylerville Public Library provided lunches to children during its summer reading program. The popularity of the combination of food and programming drew record numbers to the library—including adult caregivers. When the director realized that a number of the adults also needed food, she approached local businesses to fundraise to provide snacks for them. The result was more families coming to—and remaining at—the library all day long. They initially came for the snacks and children's programs, but soon saw that there was much more, including air conditioning, internet and computer access, and a wide range of resources. The library installed a "blessings box" outside of the library, where people could take or leave food or toiletries.

The Greenwich Free Library is partnering with the Comfort Food Community food pantry to create an early literacy program at the pantry. Based on the work of Betsy Kennedy at the Cazenovia Public Library, the goal of the program is to meet people where they are, and by providing early literacy programs at the food pantry, build relationships. The goal is to eventually have a robust family literacy and adult literacy program, as has happened at the Cazenovia Public Library, which now also holds parenting classes and graduation ceremonies for parents who earn their GED/TASC diploma.

Each of these rural libraries has recognized that creating a successful adult literacy program requires earning the trust of and building a relationship with their potential students. One way to do so is to meet people where they already converge, not insist that they come to the library building (or in the case of Hadley-Luzerne, provide a reason beyond books and materials to visit the library). By building social capital, they can create an inclusive atmosphere where people's needs are met, and provide them with an opportunity to think about their future.

Columbus Public Library, Wisconsin

The Upper Midwest is not a particularly diverse place, especially in the more rural areas. Nonetheless, change is happening. In Columbus, Wisconsin, a small city of 5,000, younger folks are eyeing the community as an affordable and safe place to settle and nurture a new marriage or raise a young family, while earning a good wage by commuting to nearby Madison, the seat of state government and the University of Wisconsin. Columbus has been growing steadily for the past 20 years and is fast becoming a bedroom community. While the Columbus citizenry is changing from a deeply rooted, multi-generational, agricultural and manufacturing base into a hipper place to be, more than just age and political affiliations are changing.

Columbus has historically seen immigrants settling in for a short stint or the long haul. Traditionally attracting more seasonal agricultural workers, Columbus is experiencing a rise in year-long dairy farm workers and people who work in the restaurant and hospitality industries (there is one hotel). The community has seen an increase in Spanish-speaking, Eastern European, and Asian populations. The common thread uniting these groups is the desire to learn English. English literacy is more than words. It's financial literacy and cultural literacy, too. At the Columbus Public Library, food is at the heart of all those skills.

As a long-time volunteer program of the Columbus Public Library, the Columbus Literacy Council pairs individual tutors and adult learners to raise literacy levels for special needs learners, low-literacy adults, and English as a Second Language (ESL) learners. The marked increase in ESL learners in the past five years has created the need for more than double the number of tutors than have traditionally volunteered for the program. Tutors are teaching English to people from Mexico, Honduras, Ecuador, India, Spain, Poland and more. As immigrants settle into life in Columbus, necessities are first on the list: schools, employment, housing, and food. The Literacy Council leverages its volunteers to connect ESL learners with those resources. The most fun is had by all when food is the topic of the day. In Columbus, literacy tutors and their students become friends very quickly when they bond over food.

A recent example of this is a pair of older white women who tutored an Indian family, proprietors of the local hotel. Sometimes the tutors met with the husband and wife, but more often than not, one had to work while the other was tutored, leaving a space for other family members to join in the learning sessions. The couple's 23-year-old daughter often took that empty seat, but her siblings dropped in and out of classes throughout the year. Tutoring usually took place at the hotel to simplify the learning process for the family. Occasionally, the tutors took the family on tours of the Columbus area, including stops at the library and local florists, flowers being a significant part of the hospitality industry. Then it was time to tour American grocery stores.

Taking immigrants to American groceries is a culture shock, given the large variety and brands of foods presented to shoppers. Add to that shock discomfort with both the language and the currency, and the simple act of food shopping becomes daunting. After a lesson or two centering on American money, the tutors walked the grocery store with various members of the Indian family. The family learned new words as they shopped unfamiliar aisles. They learned about American foods and were thrilled to find typical Indian spice or pre-prepared food. They ran into their neighbors and discovered that small town groceries are social places. They counted their change at the checkout counter. They learned English, money, and food in a social, American setting.

Trips to the grocery store turned into shared meals. The literacy tutors took their students to nearby Madison for trips to Indian groceries and shared meals at Indian restaurants. The family members served as experts on these trips, teaching their tutors about unfamiliar jars, cans and produce at the grocery, along with new dishes at the restaurants. The ESL students invited their tutors to their home to share meals during Indian holidays and celebrations. The tutors returned the favor, sharing their homes and meals during American holidays. True friendship, borne out of a need to learn English, turned these tutoring sessions into two-way cultural exchanges.

The Columbus Literacy Council is a formal program of the Columbus Public Library. The Library Director serves on the Literacy Council leadership committee, and the Literacy Council President sits on the Library Board. In 2017, the library provided additional physical space to the Literacy Council by giving them a dedicated office and tutoring space in an adjacent property purchased for future library expansion. Once finished, the Literacy Council will realize its dream of a full-service literacy resource classroom, meeting room and drop in study center, all located in the library. What began as a partnership between a library and a local literacy organization has blossomed into a robust literacy and cultural offering for the entire community.

Barrett (2010) defines food security as "a situation that exists when all people, at all times, have physical, social and economic access to sufficient, safe and nutritious food that meets their dietary needs and food preferences for an active and healthy life." When the United Nations released its sustainable development goals in 2016, food insecurity was identified to be so significant that the second goal was to "end hunger, achieve food security and improved nutrition and promote sustainable agriculture" (United Nations 2016).

Food insecurity isn't something that happens on distant continents; in the U.S., many rural areas are food deserts due to lack of access to whole foods. Immigrant populations, too, must overcome hurdles to learn new currency, cultural and language norms. In our experience, we recognize food security as a fundamental human right. We acknowledge that people need to have their basic needs met so that they can have the luxury of a dream, and consider more aspirational goals like self-actualization. Self-actualization leads to stronger communities of socially-connected citizens who operate from a place of empathy rather than ignorance or fear.

In Spokane, Washington, the Southern Adirondacks of New York and Columbus, Wisconsin, the link between literacy and food is clear: If you feed folk, it creates room for a more substantial discussion and relationship to evolve. If public libraries are to transform society, we must build relationships in our communities by first meeting basic needs.

WORKS CITED

Barrett, Christopher. 2010. "Measuring Food Insecurity." *Science* 327, no. 5967 (February 12, 2010): 825–28. doi:10.1126/science.1182768.

Chiu, Chung-Yi, Jessica Brooks and Ruopeng An. 2016. "Beyond Food Insecurity." *British Food Journal* 118 (11): 2614–2631. http://search.proquest.com.libaccess.sjlibrary.org/docview/1829717575?accountid=10361.

Ettarh, Fobazi. 2018. "Vocational Awe and Librarianship: The Lies We Tell Ourselves." *In the Library with the Lead Pipe.* January 10, 2018. Accessed January 28, 2018. http://www.inthelibrarywiththeleadpipe.org/2018/vocational-awe/.

"Hunger and Food Security—United Nations Sustainable Development." United Nations. 2016. Accessed January 28, 2018. http://www.un.org/sustainabledevelopment/hunger/.

OSPI. 2017. "Arcadia Elementary." Washington State Report Card. Accessed February 4, 2018. http://reportcard.ospi.k12.wa.us/summary.aspx?groupLevel=District&schoolId=2837&reportLevel=School&yrs=2016–17&year=2016–17.

"USDA Defines Food Deserts." American Nutrition Association. 2011. Accessed January 28, 2018. http://americannutritionassociation.org/newsletter/usda-defines-food-deserts.

Windisch, Hendrickje C. 2015. "Adults with Low Literacy and Numeracy Skills: A Literature Review on Policy Intervention." Paris: Organisation for Economic Cooperation and Development (OECD). doi:http://dx.doi.org.libaccess.sjlibrary.org/10.1787/5jrxnjdd3r5k-en. http://search.proquest.com.libaccess.sjlibrary.org/docview/1700398976?accountid=10361.

Partnering for Social Justice

Social Work Students' Placement at Public Libraries

Sarah C. Johnson

While the collaborative trend among professional social workers and librarians is garnering much deserved attention, literature about social work students partnering with public libraries is virtually nonexistent. Public librarians can advocate for social justice by initiating partnerships with master-level social work (MSW) students to enhance small- and large-scale programs to address the unique needs of patrons. In this essay, I highlight existing collaborations among public libraries and student social workers to raise awareness of possibilities.

Informal networking groups for social workers and librarians are growing. Whole Person Librarianship community (Zetterval 2018) currently has more than 90 members, including some who are MSW students. The skill set required of librarians has morphed, and some find that they are taking on the role of social workers. One way librarians can embrace these blurred lines is to ask budding social workers to help us forge this new path with the aim of helping patrons in need. Having worked with MSW interns in the past, former Public Library Association President Carolyn Anthony affirms "'partnerships should be encouraged, and there's so much we can accomplish by combining skills… [social workers] enable us to extend our reach and accomplish a lot more'" (Zettervall 2013).

Combining skills to meet the diverse needs of patrons by collaborating with MSW students means pairing with a profession that shares many of librarians' *Core Values* as reflected in its own *Code of Ethics* (National Association of Social Workers 2018). Pairing with social work students helps librarians implement *Core Values* of our profession by:

- working with other "organizations … to initiate and support comprehensive efforts to ensure that … libraries in every community cooperate to provide lifelong learning services to all"
- upholding our social responsibility to diversity by "providing a full spectrum of resources and services to the communities we serve"
- working to solve "the critical problems of society" (American Library Association 2004).

More thanr 64,000 MSW students are enrolled in 254 accredited programs in the United States (Council on Social Work Education 2017). Students are required to complete approximately 900 hours of fieldwork, also referred to as internships or field placements. Most social work students and educators do not consider libraries as an option for fieldwork, therefore it is crucial for librarians to promote such collaborations.

What Librarians Can Do

Though unique in their own ways, many existing partnerships tell a similar story of librarians originating partnerships with MSW programs or a third party to formalize internships, assigning students to conduct needs assessments and staff trainings, and subsequently develop or enhance micro- and macro-level library programming.

Public librarians can initiate partnerships with social work students by locating an accredited MSW program through the Council on Social Work Education and contacting the School of Social Work's Director of Field Education. If partnering with a university is not an option, connect with the local Department of Health and Human Services (DHHS) or equivalent to ascertain if MSW interns are available to partner with the library.

Examples

The trailblazing community-university partnership between San Jose Public Library and San Jose State University began when librarian Deborah Estreicher simply called "the School of Social Work, spoke to Professor Peter A. Lee, who thought a fine partnership might be had, and the rest is history" (Estreicher 2013). Recognizing an opportunity to take diversity to the next level, they developed the *Social Worker in the Library* (SWITL) model in 2007, which has since been adopted at libraries throughout the country. The University of Maryland's Graduate School of Social Work was recently awarded a prestigious grant to implement this model at three Baltimore libraries (Institute of Museum and Library Services 2017).

After completing her MLS in 2013, Sarah Preskitt returned to her hometown to work at the Anchorage Public Library. She immediately noticed the gap in services for patrons experiencing homelessness, substance abuse, and issues related to mental health, and, consequently, the stress placed on library staff. Soon after, she helped forge an internship with the University of Anchorage–Alaska School of Social Work.

Due to her outreach with the University of South Carolina, 2015 *Library Journal*'s Mover and Shaker Heather McCue helped establish an internship at the Richland Public Library for MSW students.

Long Branch Free Public Library Director Tonya Garcia built on her established relationship with Monmouth University to form an internship through the School of Social Work. Eventually, MSW student David Perez began his placement in 2015 as the first social work library intern in New Jersey.

Newark public librarian Leslie Kahn elicited the help of two Rutgers social work professors to bring on its first ever MSW intern, Kenyetta Clark, in 2017.

Georgetown public librarians in Texas also took heed and responded to "seeing more patrons who were struggling with homelessness, mental health troubles, aging-related illnesses and other [instabilities]" (Marczynski 2017). Hired as a result of a three-year grant, social worker Patrick Lloyd subsequently brought on a MSW intern from his alma mater, the University of Texas–Austin.

In Azusa, California, "the city librarian approached the [Azusa Pacific University] Social Work department to ask whether a graduate-level social worker could assist the library staff in the efforts to address a broad array of patron needs" and "for potential solutions to extend expertise and provide supportive social services to city library patrons" (Kelley et al. 2017, 112, 115).

Third Party Collaborations

When establishing an internship with a university is not feasible, some libraries arrange placements through third parties, such as the local Department of Mental Health (DMH). In such scenarios, students typically intern on behalf of the Department—not the library itself—even though they are physically situated at the library. Advantages of triaging with recognized organizations include secure relationships with the library, connection to resources, and the possibility that DMH social workers can provide student supervision.

Examples

The Los Angeles County Department of Mental Health (DMH) was awarded a one-year grant to appoint their first MSW intern in 2017 to help social workers facilitate *The Source*, a connection service for homeless patrons.

University of Alaska–Anchorage's School of Social Work joined forces with the Municipal Health Department to regularly staff a table at the main public library answering patron questions and linking them with community resources.

As an alternative to pairing with a local university, Washington, D.C. Public Library opted to team with an outside agency to do outreach to the homeless population; the activity utilized their own social work intern for about 20 hours every week.

Brooklyn Public Library indirectly hosts MSW interns from Fordham and Columbia Universities in conjunction with The Osborne Association. Students intern with Osborne to facilitate family visits through video conferencing and offering "support for re-entry after incarceration and assistance to families coping with the incarceration of a loved one" (Brooklyn Public Library 2018).

Assignments

As per requirements for field placement, MSW students must complete various tasks or assignments to align with their established learning contract and educational goals. The following suggestions are assignments MSW interns can begin with.

Needs Assessments

As every branch varies, conducting needs assessments of both staff and patrons are excellent starter assignments for MSW interns. Newark public librarian Leslie Kahn explains the aim of such assessments is to "try to figure out what are the priorities for a very diverse community and see what support we can get from that analysis" (Kearney 2017, 9).

Examples

Newark Public Library intern and MSW student Kenyetta Clark identified a service gap to pre-teens and subsequently developed programming with young patrons in mind.

At the beginning of their internship, eleven MSW students at Azusa Pacific University "worked closely with library personnel to collect data about the focal community … the library staff was considered a critical population for the community analysis" (Kelley et al. 2017, 116).

Georgetown Public Library's Community Resources Coordinator Patrick Lloyd prioritizes patron needs based on questions he receives. Typical queries at his smaller, rural library often pertain to "general financial assistance. Affordable and emergency housing are also common issues, as is the need for pro bono legal assistance" (Marczynski 2017).

Washington, D.C. Public Library conducted a staff appraisal about their experiences interacting with homeless patrons. Some survey questions included, "How's it impacting your day? What do you need from [social workers]? What do you need so that you can do your job and be helpful to these folks — and every single other customer that comes through the door?" (Jenkins 2014).

Library Staff Training

Evaluating staff concerns often highlights their desire for education and support from mental health professionals. This reflects a core value of "maintaining and enhancing our own knowledge and skills" (American Library Association 2004) in order to better meet diverse patron needs. Social work interns are often well equipped to provide basic information sessions for librarians. The content of such trainings should be tailored to the unique needs of the library community. Topics can range from mental health literacy, mandated reporting, crisis management, and how to converse with patrons who may be in need of outside services.

Examples

Los Angeles County intern Jeanette Martinez provides trainings to library staff on de-escalation techniques as a means of crisis management. Such trainings also provide excellent opportunities for interns to clarify their role at the library and manage staff expectations. Though equipped with a unique knowledge base and skill set, interns are not responsible for solving significant crises or conducting major mental health assessments. Rather, students can work to empower librarians about how to handle potentially complicated situations; how to involve additional partners if necessary such as public safety or relevant mental health professionals. Dependent on the support staff available, it is preferable that interns begin assisting with smaller tasks, program development, and addressing patrons with manageable needs.

Washington, D.C. Public Library social worker Jean Badalamenti hopes trainings can help staff "understand what it means to be homeless, what people experience when they're homeless. Just a sort of sensitivity training, but hopefully we'll be doing some other kinds of training, even around de-escalation. Identifying folks who might be in a crisis, so the library can respond and be helpful" (Jenkins 2014).

Social work students can help staff explore options for addressing the current opioid crisis. As this epidemic is now directly affecting and often occurring in public libraries around the country, staff may need assistance determining how best to respond to signs of active use and acute medical needs. Some librarians are now trained to administer Narcan and others have aligned more closely with first responders.

Once necessary services are identified, MSW interns can help enhance or develop relevant programming for patrons. Depending on the needs and capacities of a particular branch, this can be delivered on a larger, macro scale or through smaller, micro-focused services, such as referrals.

Programming: Macro

Although they may not have established formal collaborations with social work interns, many public libraries already have existing outreach services to address the diverse needs of patrons. Social work students can help enhance existing programming or develop new projects to address gaps in services as a means of bringing about social justice for marginalized patrons.

A popular outreach program for patrons experiencing homelessness is Coffee and Conversations program. This low-stakes, informal platform allows local agencies to meet patrons who are in need of community resources. Popularized by Dallas Public Library, the program is currently organized and facilitated at Kansas City and New York Public Libraries, with the help of MSW interns. Furthermore, in Los Angeles County DMH intern's primary responsibilities involve working with homeless patrons through *The Source* (Los Angeles Public Library 2018).

Based on her needs assessment of Newark Public Library, MSW Intern Kenyetta Clark identified a gap in services for teens. This allowed her to develop programs tailored to youth (Newark Public Library 2017). Likewise, teen programs created by Clark's fellow Rutgers University students are underway at New Jersey branches in Somerville and North Plainfield (TapInto Staff 2018).

At Kansas City Public Library, much of intern Amanda Landayan's work involves collaborating with the branch's Youth and Family Engagement staff, providing food for children at the Kids Cafe program, and coordinating with community agencies such as Operation Breakthrough and Front Porch Alliance (Landayan, personal communication).

Successful outreach programs at New Jersey's Long Branch Free Public Library blossomed as result of librarian Tonya Garcia noticing needs and working with MSW intern David Perez to help meet them. During his two-year placement, Perez developed Garcia's Fade to Books Barbershop Literacy program and was subsequently recognized with an Innovative Partnership award. He helped spearhead the Fresh Start Re-Entry Program to assist ex-offenders seeking employment. Perez also worked with Long Branch's Community Connects Program, a monthly event for local agencies to showcase their services for patrons in need.

Programming: Micro

Assessments often indicate a demand for individual services such as advocacy and referrals to social services. Many patrons require assistance completing online government forms and job applications. MSW interns can further "guide patrons through the state's online benefits application process, assist individuals in applying for food benefits, help applicants gather necessary documents, connect eligible families and individuals with employment and training resources, and connect with other … agencies to answer questions" (State of Delaware News 2018).

Fundamentally, social work students can help forge connections to community resources. Patrons with questions that fall outside librarians' scope can be referred to interns. They can offer to meet patrons through established office hours, walk-ins, or a basic sign-up sheet. The availability of social work interns to provide references offers a more seamless link to necessary services outside the library. Regardless of whether a branch is operating large-scale programs, interns can offer resource links to patrons who seek them.

With the help of his student intern, Community Resources Coordinator Patrick Lloyd conceptualizes his role "as distributing and gathering information, and hopefully getting that information to the people who need it—both our patrons and the community in general—to try to improve Georgetown [Texas] as a whole" (Marczynski 2017). A possible assignment attached to this information gathering could be drafting grant requests to potential funders.

As an initial exercise, librarian Sarah Preskitt had MSW students from the University of Alaska–Anchorage develop a community resource book for patrons. Subsequent interns drafted a Policy and Procedures handbook for future social work students. Another assignment involved distributing a patron questionnaire about library use. Results of this survey showed nearly one-quarter of regular library users in Anchorage are currently homeless; the library received funding to hire social worker thereafter.

As a measure of addressing social justice, interns can be of great assistance bridging the digital divide by helping patrons navigate online government forms and job applications. Such help mirrors one of our core values that information "should be readily, equally, and equitably accessible to all library users" (American Library Association 2004).

Challenges

Due to the unique nature of such partnerships, challenges may arise. First, it can be difficult to determine if students will obtain the skills and knowledge they desire at the beginning of their internships. One way to account for this is to establish a clear learning contract with both the librarian who serves as the on-site task supervisor and the social worker providing weekly social work supervision. Library placements may not be suitable for students with a strictly "clinical" focus (i.e., maintaining a minimum caseload of patrons; conducting in-depth mental health assessments). Overall, this type of placement may be better suited to generalist, policy-based students, versus those aiming for a more clinical, micro-focused path. As mentioned above, if crisis situations are commonplace in a branch, interns should not be expected to address such circumstances on their own.

It is worth considering if there will be ample tasks for the student to conduct. One way to ascertain possible workloads is establishing a clear learning contract. Such planning can help determine if a library intern is a suitable fit for a particular branch. Additionally, facilitating internships requires extra time and efforts that some libraries may not be able to afford. After considering the possibility of taking on an intern, some libraries opt out or discontinue their existing partnerships. For all its strengths and good intentions, joint ventures need to ultimately benefit patrons in need, not just the student or library staff who require extra help.

Promisingly, many pilot programs have found success: continuing and expanding current social work/library collaborations as is the case with Rutgers University and Los Angeles County. Additionally, libraries in Anchorage, Kansas City, Newark, and Azusa, California were able to fund the hiring of professional social workers.

Creativity Required

The trailblazing nature of interning at a public library requires MSW students who identify as self-starters, who are comfortable negotiating open placements with less infrastructure. While such internships have the potential to provide a great freedom, it may frustrate both students and librarians who desire established protocols.

Such original ventures also require creativity from social work educators and field placement coordinators to assist with supervision, particularly as so few libraries have a professional social worker on staff. Unless supervision is provided through a third party, placements may need to be contracted with retired or outside social workers.

Summary

Public librarians play a critical role advocating for social justice by reaching out to MSW programs and inviting budding social workers to advance tolerance for a diversity of people and needs. While professional values of both librarianship and social work have a strong overlap, librarians need to summon MSW educators, field instructors, and students to this nontraditional point of social service delivery. In turn, students can work with libraries to develop programming, strengthen outreach, and empower public librarians to advocate for social justice. If we are indeed living in the "golden age of library-social work collaboration" (Zettervall 2015), let's take advantage of this by partnering with MSW students to bring about social justice and change.

WORKS CITED

American Library Association. 2004. "Core Values of Librarianship." *American Library Association.* http://www.ala.org/advocacy/intfreedom/corevalues.

Brooklyn Public Library. 2018. "Jail & Prison Libraries: Telestory." *Brooklyn Public Library.* https://www.bklynlibrary.org/outreach/transitional-services.

Council on Social Work Education. 2017. "2016–2017 Annual Report." Council on Social Work Education. https://www.cswe.org/getattachment/About-CSWE/Annual-Reports/CSWE-Annual-Reports/CSWE-Annual-Report-2017.pdf.aspx.

Estreicher, Deborah. 2013. "A Brief History of the Social Workers in the Library Program." *Whole Person Librarianship.* May 5. https://wholepersonlibrarianship.com/2013/05/05/a-brief-history-of-the-social-workers-in-the-library-program/.

Institute of Museum and Library Services. 2017. "IMLS Grant." *Institute of Museum and Library Services.* August 10. https://www.imls.gov/grants/awarded/lg-94-17-0227.

Jenkins, Mark. 2014. "D.C. Adds a Social Worker to Library System to Work with Homeless Patrons." *The Washington Post.* August 26. https://www.washingtonpost.com/local/dc-adds-a-social-worker-to-library-system-to-work-with-homeless-patrons/2014/08/26/2d80200c-2c96-11e4-be9e-60cc44c01e7f_story.html.

Kearney, Richard. 2017. "More Essential Than Ever." *New Jersey Libraries Newsletter*, Summer.

Kelley, Alanna, Kara Riggleman, Ingrid Clara, and Adria E. Navarro. 2017. "Determining the Need for Social Work Practice in a Public Library." *Journal of Community Practice* 25 (1). Routledge: 112–25.

Landayan, Amanda. 2018, April 10. MSW Intern, Kansas City Public Library, in discussion with the author.

Los Angeles Public Library. 2018. "The Source." *Los Angeles Public Library.* https://www.lapl.org/stable-living/the-source.

Marczynski, Evan. 2017. "Georgetown Public Library Adds Services as Demand and Patron Visits Increase" *Community Impact Newspaper.* November 14. https://communityimpact.com/austin/georgetown/city-county/2017/11/14/georgetown-public-library-adds-services-demand-patron-visits-increase/.

National Association of Social Workers. 2018. "NASW Code of Ethics." *National Association of Social Workers.* https://www.socialworkers.org/About/Ethics/Code-of-Ethics/Code-of-Ethics-English.

Newark Public Library. 2017. "Student Social Worker." *Newark Public Library.* https://npl.org/event/student-social-worker/.

State of Delaware News. 2018. "Pilot Program Will Connect Library Patrons to State Services." *State of Delaware News.* January 2. https://news.delaware.gov/2018/01/02/social-workers-libraries/.

TapInto Staff. 2018. "Rutgers Social Worker Provides Assistance at Somerville Library." *Tap into Somerville.* January 28. https://www.tapinto.net/towns/somerville/articles/rutgers-social-worker-provides-assistance-at-some.

Zettervall, Sara. 2013. "An Interview with Carolyn Anthony, PLA President." *Whole Person Librarianship.* June 30. https://wholepersonlibrarianship.com/2013/06/30/an-interview-with-carolyn-anthony-pla-president/.

Zettervall, Sara. 2015. "Whole Person Librarianship." *Public Libraries* 54 (2): 12–13.

Zettervall, Sara. 2018. "Whole Person Librarianship." *Whole Person Librarianship.* https://wholepersonlibrarianship.com/.

Unidos por la Causa

Community-Driven Collection Development for Chicanx Archives

Zoe Jarocki *and* Amanda Lanthorne

Archives are in a unique position to document the history of marginalized communities. As repositories for primary source materials, their collections offer first-hand accounts of events and social movements that provide alternative perspectives not always found in published sources. In addition, by preserving the memory and history of a particular community they foster critical thinking and challenge researchers to consider alternative narratives and question dominant power structures. These collections promote inclusivity by exposing students and researchers to new cultures and identities. For students from marginalized communities, collecting these materials underscores the importance of their community's history, and reinforces that their heritage is valued and worthy of scholarship.

This essay presents a case study of San Diego State University's (SDSU) Chicana and Chicano Studies Archive Advisory Committee (CCSAAC). The committee, made up of librarians and Chicanx educators and activists, has successfully increased the diversity and depth of Special Collections and University Archives' (SCUA) holdings. Below we will detail the group's formation, history, acquisitions and outreach efforts. We will share lessons we learned and opportunities that arose from this partnership. This scalable approach is useful for institutions who seek to collect materials that document local, underrepresented groups in their own communities. For the purpose of this paper, we are using the term Chicanx as a gender-inclusive term, unless talking about individuals or referring to proper names. Chicanx is a self-selected term to describe Mexican-American identity; we also use Latinx and Mexican-American where appropriate.

History

San Diego State University's SCUA began collecting archives of marginalized groups in the mid–2000s. Although SCUA already held numerous collections documenting the women's movement and feminism, it lacked any substantial holdings pertaining to San Diego's numerous minority communities. Given SDSU's proximity to the U.S.-Mexico border and its status as an Hispanic Serving Institution, it seemed particularly egregious that we were overlooking the archival memory and history of the local Mexican-American community.

In 2007, the wife of René Nuñez, a professor and activist, approached Richard Griswold del Castillo, an emeritus professor of Chicana and Chicano Studies, to ask about donating her deceased husband's papers. Dr. Nuñez had helped to found the Mexican-American Studies (now Chicana and Chicano Studies) department at SDSU and was a prominent activist in the Chicano Rights Movement of the 1960s. His papers document these important activities. Griswold del Castillo reached out to Rob Ray, the head of SCUA, to discuss the acquisition of the collection. This major donation served as a catalyst for the formation of CCSAAC.

The committee consists of current and emeritus faculty from SDSU and surrounding community colleges, former schoolteachers and principals, community activists, and representatives from local organizations. Members of the committee, as well as numerous other people in the region, feel a strong connection to SDSU. Many CCSAAC members either attended as students or taught courses at SDSU. Indeed, SDSU's Chicana and Chicano Studies department was one of the first such departments in the country. Its faculty and students were actively involved in the Chicano Movement and the creation of significant community spaces. For example, the Barrio Logan community fought the city in 1970 to create Chicano Park, now known for its vibrant murals. It was granted National Historic Landmark status in 2017. Also formed in 1970, Barrio Station is a community center that holds after-school youth programs. The Centro Cultural de la Raza is a cultural center in Balboa Park that supports Chicanx, Latinx and Indigenous art, music, dance, theater, poetry and more. SDSU's connections to this history made it a natural home for such an archive.

The website for CCSAAC describes the mission of the Archive as an effort "to preserve the priceless records of the struggle for civil rights, and an end to second class citizenship and educational underachievement [of Chicanx people]" (Griswold del Castillo, n.d.). For the library, this archive supports the educational needs of the University, and preserves the history of a local underrepresented community previously absent from its holdings. Perhaps most importantly, as Rita Sanchez, a former professor at Mesa College and member of the committee pointed out, active community participation and engagement in documenting the Chicanx experience allowed Chicanxs to "discover and define themselves" (Rita Sanchez, pers. comm.). This partnership created a sense of empowerment and historical agency that led to the creation of a rich, powerful, and diverse archive that continues to grow.

One of CCSAAC's first projects was to create a collection development policy. This policy outlines the mission of the archive and describes its collecting priorities. The goal is to document the development of Chicanx studies at SDSU, area community colleges, and Mexican cultural centers and universities as well as related history from the Mexican and Chicanx communities that have been the subject of Chicanx studies scholarship with focus on 1968 to present. Current holdings include the *Arturo Casares Papers*, the *Chicano Federation Records*, the *Rene Nuñez Memorial Collection*, the *Carmen Sandoval Fernandez Poster Collection*, the *Gracia Molina de Pick Papers*, the *Enriqueta Chavez Papers*, the *Maria Garcia Papers*, the *Rita Sanchez Papers*, and many others. These collections contain rare photographs, reports, correspondence, newspapers, posters, realia, and ephemera.

Outreach Opportunities

After the committee's formation, members immediately began identifying potential donors and collections. Between 2008 and 2010, the committee brought in nine collections documenting a range of topics including Chicana feminism, San Diego history, higher education, and the Chicano movement. It was not enough to collect these materials—the collections needed to be made available for research and promoted.

In order to process these newly-acquired collections quickly, the committee held several fundraisers and wrote a grant. The first fundraiser, held in 2009, was a documentary film screening at Barrio Station. Funds went to the digitization of materials in the Archive. At the event, committee members were able to explain the mission of CCSAAC, discuss goals for the collections, and solicit donations. These fundraisers directly engaged the community, which was essential for obtaining community buy-in. The committee advertised the Archive and showcased its work to demonstrate the importance of collecting and preserving this history.

A year later, SCUA secured a $10,000 President's Leadership Fund grant from the University to process materials from the Archive. With this money, we were able to arrange, process, and describe eight collections and make them available for research. While this was an important step to solidifying accessibility to the Archive, promotion of the collections was just as important, both on campus and in the community.

Therefore, SCUA curated an exhibit featuring materials from the newly processed collections. *Unidos por la Causa: the Chicana and Chicano Experience in San Diego*, celebrated San Diego's Chicanx community. The exhibit consisted of five double-sided free-standing frames with curated panels featuring posters, art, and historic documents illustrating the early years of the Chicano Movement. Each panel focused on a specific issue including: higher education, the Chicano Moratorium (Chicanx-led protests of the Vietnam War), bilingual education, Chicana feminism, and Chicano Park.

It took several months to curate the exhibit with the help of numerous people. We hired a former student assistant, funded by the grant money, to help with curation. Priscilla Lopez had just graduated with a minor in Chicana and Chicano Studies and identified as Chicana. In her words,

> I never [felt] prouder of the work I was doing.... I knew that these collections were part of my identity. I felt honored to help bring forth primary source documents and photographs of the movements which had local and national impact.... In class, I had been taught about the leaders, the Barrio, the Park, and the protests. To see and hold the primary source documents brought it all to life. I understood that it was my duty to preserve them for continued empowerment of La Raza [Priscilla Lopez, pers. comm.].

We hoped her knowledge and enthusiasm would enhance the exhibit; and it did.

We also felt it was important to have the exhibit text in Spanish and English in order to make it as accessible and inclusive as possible. This was our first bilingual exhibit. Another student assistant who was interested in translation work agreed to translate the text into Spanish, his first language. Cecelia Puerto, the Spanish Language and Chicanx Studies librarian at the time, then reviewed the student's translations to ensure accuracy and quality.

The committee celebrated the opening of the Archive and *Unidos por la Causa* with a lecture by Martín Gómez, former director of the Los Angeles Public Library, followed by a reception. After remaining in the SDSU Library for eight months, *Unidos por la*

Causa then travelled to the Logan Heights Public Library, where it was also marked with a well-attended celebration. By placing the exhibit in a largely Latinx neighborhood, we were able to promote the Archive directly to the community. After special request, the exhibit moved to San Diego City College, and is now slated for display at Southwestern College.

SCUA also created a digital version of *Unidos por la Causa* to reach an even wider audience. This online component is accessible to anyone with Internet access. In many ways, the digital version is more robust, featuring oral history recordings and video footage not included in the physical display. As with the original, the digital version is bilingual. Again, the success of the exhibit as a whole was dependent on student, library, and community involvement.

In addition to this large exhibit, more recently we have been curating smaller, one-case exhibits with original materials and featuring them in the Library's Chicano Collection Room, a space in the main library that contains monographs on Chicanx history, literature, and culture. The room also serves as a study spot and community space for Chicanx students. To date, the mini-exhibits have featured Chicana feminist zines as well as an exhibit about the Chicano Park Takeover. The intent is to create a link between primary sources in the archive and the monographic collection in the space, and to expose students to the wealth of resources available for research.

Besides exhibits, SCUA librarians wrote numerous blog posts about various collections and events that were posted on the Library's main web page, including special posts on Cesar Chavez Day and during National Hispanic Heritage Month. To reach the larger community off-campus, committee members promoted the collections by talking to friends and family and hosting events to spread the word and raise funds. Members of the committee and librarians presented about the Archive at the Seguimos Creando Enlaces conference in 2017. This cross-border conference brings together U.S. and Mexican librarians to share projects and ideas. Our presentation spread the word about the project to librarians who work with largely Chicanx and/or Spanish-speaking communities in the hopes of increasing public awareness of the rich resources available at SDSU.

Furthermore, the Archive's finding aids are accessible in SCUA's Finding Aid Database, the library catalog, several research guides, and the Online Archive of California. The project itself has a stand alone website, not connected to the Library. This website is run by Griswold del Castillo, a co-chair of CCSAAC. Consequently, promotion of the Archive has been and continues to be a joint effort by the Library and the committee. Both groups have targeted different populations, and by doing so, have reached a much wider and more diverse audience.

Instruction

Another form of outreach is instruction. SCUA provides primary source instruction sessions to a variety of disciplines. We receive instruction requests from professors in History, Art, Religious Studies, Rhetoric and Writing Studies, Africana Studies, Chicana and Chicano Studies, English, and more.

A typical instruction session involves a brief introduction to Special Collections as well as a tutorial on how to find Special Collections materials in the library catalog and our finding aid database. SCUA librarians then provide a show-and-tell of materials laid out on tables that relate to the class topic. Depending on the class, students may also complete a worksheet that asks them to analyze a particular document.

Materials from the Archive are used in a range of classes in an effort to expose as many students as possible to these collections. The Chicanx community is an integral part of San Diego and California's cultural and historical narrative and is relevant to many areas of study. To date, SCUA has used materials from these collections in numerous history capstone courses; gender and sexuality classes; military history; San Diego history; Africana Studies; and others. Recently SCUA even hosted a high school class that specifically asked for an introduction to the Archive. These specialized, one-off instruction sessions have been particularly effective in promoting collections to students and faculty. The incorporation of Chicanx materials into classes integrates them into the curriculum, and invites students to explore the collections in more depth outside of class. Many come back to Special Collections and ask about related collections for use in class assignments.

Students are frequently surprised to see a flyer calling for the takeover of government land or handwritten notes from a Movimiento Estudiantil Chicanx de Aztlán (MEChA) meeting in an instruction session, because it never occurred to them that these were historical items worth preserving. This gives librarians the opportunity to expose students to marginalized narratives that require them to reconsider dominant myths and histories. By doing so, these collections foster critical thinking by providing alternatives to mainstream secondary sources. For example, when a class on gender and sexuality visits SCUA, we make an effort to include Chicana materials. These items demonstrate that the struggle for Chicanas had an added layer of racism, and that even within the Women's Movement, Chicanas and other Women of Color were often marginalized. By exploring these topics through first hand accounts, we hope students learn to make these connections. For students of color, showcasing recognizable experiences and histories in class demonstrates the relevance and influence of their community's narrative. We hope that this empowers students to take pride in their history, and inspires them, as well as their allies, to continue the fight for social justice.

The knowledge that the library uses collections to teach students is an added motivation for donors. When asked to reflect on his experience as an early donor and committee member, Arturo Casares had this to say:

> … When I was asked to be part of the archive I felt my collection of papers and photos had been carefully put away like a treasure of Chicano history…. For me it's very important for our community and for future generations to learn, know and understand the history behind institutional change. [Advances were] brought about by political changes made by students with similar backgrounds that came from barrios where they had endured prejudice and discrimination. These young men and women became the core of a political wave of change called the Chicano Movement, la Lucha, the struggle to fight and gain educational and social justice for Chicanas and Chicanos within these institutions of higher learning [Arturo Casares, pers. comm.].

For Casares, donating his papers was a way preserve his story and show future generations what he and others fought for.

Lessons and Opportunities

Perhaps the biggest opportunity has been the committee's strong ties to the community to facilitate the acquisition of materials. Committee members, not SCUA, made initial contact with donors. They drove the majority of the decision-making with their collective wisdom and expertise. The very nature of these collections required community effort—they were stored in garages, attics, and closets unknown to those without personal relationships with these potential donors. Donors often felt more comfortable working with people they knew rather than librarians and archivists. In addition, several members were active or emeritus faculty at SDSU and had a deep understanding of the research needs on campus. Consequently, the committee spearheaded all collection development and decided what subjects to collect, identified potential donors, and made the initial inquiries. SCUA's role was merely to assess collections for preservation and research value.

Fostering community-driven collection development has been invaluable, but the process was not without growing pains. For starters, SCUA was not aware it had a collection gap until faculty from the Chicana and Chicano Studies department pointed it out. This was both uncomfortable and embarrassing. Robert Ray recalls that it was important to be receptive to criticism and not get defensive about the shortcomings of the archive. By remaining open to community input, the committee helped rectify this gap in the library's holdings.

Initially, attracting potential committee members and donors was slow-going. Although the original core members had initiated the creation of the committee, some saw SCUA and the Library as an ivory tower and were skeptical. It took time to build a foundation of trust between the library, the committee, and the larger community. Before the committee had formed, a prominent educator and activist from San Diego had approached the Library about the possible donation of a collection of traditional Mexican dresses and folkloric costumes. SCUA does not have the capacity to preserve textiles and had to decline the donation. This rejection caused hurt feelings to the would-be donor. Even after the committee convened, it took time for people who felt alienated by the Library, such as this particular donor, to embrace the project. After outreach efforts by friends and fellow activists in the community, as well as attending successful fundraising events, the donor came around. In 2014, they donated their collection to the Archive. The dresses found a home at a local museum. Without the efforts of community members on the committee, this significant collection may have gone elsewhere or languished in a garage.

Another potential hurdle are group dynamics. Many of the activists on the committee have known each other for years. While this has many advantages, it can occasionally lead to disagreements. Everyone brings a wide range of experiences and diverse points of view to the table and as librarian partners it is important to realize that these can sometimes lead to differences of opinion over the allocation of funds, collecting priorities, etc.

Other obstacles include collection condition and collection content. Even though the committee has had a clear set of guidelines since its inception, they were not always enforced and collections were brought in without proper archival appraisal. As a result, some collections had mold and pest infestations that we were not aware of until they arrived onsite. Thankfully, we were able to remediate the preservation issues quickly before they became larger problems. While this issue is not uncommon to archives, in this case it served as an opportunity to educate the committee and larger public about proper storage and preservation of potential archival materials—keep them out of damp spaces and away from pests!

Collection content was also included in the collection development policy. Initially community members dropped off materials without prior notice, so content did not always adhere to policy. We also failed to distinguish the difference between museum-appropriate artifacts and archival material with broad research value. Subsequently, we received objects that we were not equipped to store and/or were better suited for a museum. Textbooks, and other non-rare, mass-produced published resources were also frequently donated. Items such as these were either incorporated into the library's main stacks, returned to the donor, or deaccessioned. These minor hiccups resulted in policy improvements. We defined terms to ensure everyone was on the same page and explained why some materials were better suited for other spaces or institutions.

Conclusion

As archivists and librarians we know it is important to collect community-specific archives in order to create as complete an historic record as possible. However, it still helps to demonstrate the relevance of these collections to both library and campus administration through statistical and anecdotal evidence. Demonstrated usage helps to obtain buy-in from the community, committee, and campus to help fund potential projects and promote resources.

To that end, SCUA has attempted to track usage of the Chicanx-related archival collections in a variety of ways—using Google Analytics, circulation and reference statistics, and anecdotal evidence. By comparing these data, we are able to determine the popularity and usage of a particular collection. Promotional and outreach efforts have paid off! Some of our Chicanx collections are among those most regularly consulted, specifically the *Arturo Casares Papers* and the *Carmen Sandoval Fernandez Poster Collection*. The term "Chican" is also the most frequently searched word in SCUA's Finding Aid Database. Furthermore, we have hosted numerous out-of-town patrons, including faculty from other universities, doctoral students, and professional historians, who visited especially for the Archive.

Comparative statistics show similar results for our local African-American collections. This evidence indicates that collections documenting marginalized communities are in high demand and justifies continued collection development and outreach targeting these groups. As Chris Taylor (2017) noted, this is part of the business imperative. We need these collections to stay relevant (Taylor 2017, 23). Yes, archives are morally obligated to document all communities, but given the high demand it makes good business sense as well.

In conclusion, community-led collection development acknowledges that archives can and should do better. Archives have neglected certain communities and populations and this neglect, whether intentional or not, has far-reaching consequences. These gaps support dominant power structures and undermine the importance and resilience of non-dominant communities. They also diminish an archive's relevance and potential audience. By ignoring the archival memory of a particular community, archives and libraries are in essence, silencing historically significant voices. In short, we need to be mindful of how we prioritize histories and cultures.

Grassroot committees that lead collection development and outreach initiatives can give communities agency to determine and preserve their own narratives. In order to successfully accomplish this, librarians and archivists must be open to criticism. It will be uncomfortable, and it will take time to build trust but the payoff is worth the effort. In our case, CCSAAC now has seventeen committee members; the Archive includes more than twenty collections with others in the works; and together we have raised more than $30,000 through events, grants, and individual donations. The intangible payoff is even greater—these collections empower students and the community, and contribute to a more empathetic, inclusive society.

We would like to conclude with a note of extreme thanks and gratitude to current and former members of the committee. This project would not be able to succeed without your dedication and hard work. Thanks to Richard Griswold del Castillo, Olivia Puentes Reynolds, Rita Sanchez, Kathleen Robles, Gus Chavez, Adelaida del Castillo, Arturo Casares, Carrie Fierro, Rob Ray, Norma Iglesias Prieto, Roberto Hernandez, Bertha Hernandez, Christian Benavides, Irma Castro, Reynaldo Ayala, Refugio Rochin and Maria Garcia.

Works Cited

Grimm, Tracy, and Chon Noriega. 2013. "Documenting Regional Latino Arts and Culture: Case Studies for a Collaborative, Community-Oriented Approach." *The American Archivist* 76(1): 95–112. Doi: 10.17723/aarc.76.1.ph222324p1g157t7.

Griswold del Castillo, Richard. Chicana/o Archive Project at SDSU. http://rgriswol.wixsite.com/chicano archive.

Taylor, Chris. 2017. "Getting Our House in Order: Moving from Diversity to Inclusion." *The American Archivist* 80 (1): 19–29.

Unidos por la Causa: The Chicana and Chicano Experience in San Diego. https://library.sdsu.edu/exhibits/2010/10/UnidosPorLaCausa/index.shtml.

PART III

Building Communities

Rethinking the Role of Libraries as Active Social Spaces

CARRIE FISHNER *and* LISA TESSIER

This paper discusses the process and results of a successful case study from The State University of New York College at Delhi (SUNY Delhi) focused on the use of an arts initiative in the library to foster conversations about diversity and inclusion. SUNY Delhi is a college of technology located near the Catskill Mountains that offers degrees in programs such as veterinary science, nursing, business and hospitality, and construction; degrees are granted from certificates through Master's, depending on the major. The campus serves a full time enrollment of 3,200 total enrollment, with about 2,000 students living on campus residentially. Students are mostly from New York State, with the greatest percentages hailing from the Metropolitan New York/Long Island, and Capital Regions. The campus is diverse with students identifying as follows: 59 percent White non–Hispanic, 19 percent African American, 17 percent Hispanic, 3 percent Asian, and 2 percent Other and Unknown (SUNY Delhi 2017).

In November of 2016 Michele DeFreece, the SUNY Delhi Vice President for Diversity, Equity, and Inclusion, announced a new initiative to encourage discussions about diversity and inclusion throughout the campus. Mini-grants would be made available to faculty, staff, and students through an application process to gain funding in support of a project that would affect diversity and inclusion across the campus. Shortly after the initial announcement, Lisa Tessier, Associate Professor in Liberal Arts and Sciences, contacted Carrie Fishner, Library Director, with an idea. Lisa wanted to use art to start a conversation; she was intrigued by the idea of one's identity and how we are often forced to put ourselves into little boxes on forms and paperwork. The idea of "I am... Check the Box" was based on this. This initial discussion led to a collaboration to capitalize on the strong physical and social resources of a campus library to build unique conversations about diversity and inclusion, and to celebrate the diversity of our campus community.

A series of six workshops (conducted at various locations as both drop-in and fixed-time sessions) brought together faculty, staff, and students using the art-making process as a vehicle for building dialogue around the topics of identity, diversity, and inclusion. Two workshops were housed in the unique physical spaces of the library, and a collective mosaic was exhibited at the library at the conclusion of the initiative. All participants and the greater campus community were invited to an Opening Celebration to reflect on the project. Participant reflections and feedback was overwhelmingly positive, and this led to this initiative being offered additional times, and as a "train the trainer" opportunity for several departments on campus including Access and Equity and the Educational Opportunity Program. Additional requests for "train the trainer" and facilitated workshops were also received for the following academic year. The program received the SUNY Delhi President's Award for Diversity and Inclusive Excellence–Best Program in 2017.

Libraries as Unique Settings

The Resnick Library at SUNY Delhi is a unique gathering spot for students throughout the day as they stop in between classes to study or print, as well as in the evenings when it becomes the primary study location. The Resnick Library sees approximately 350 student visits a day. The library is also adjacent to a small cafe and the Resnick Academic Achievement Center, which houses the campus academic support services within the same building. The strengths of different physical spaces in our library were capitalized on to facilitate this program. For one fixed-time workshop, a quiet study room was selected that provided a sense of safety that fostered reflective dialogue between the participants.

In contrast, a drop-in session was set-up at the entry of the library by the busy main circulation desk, which is also located next to the cafe. This location grabbed the attention of users who seemed to be excited and surprised to see a table for making art at the entry. This active engagement of users counters the more traditional perception of libraries as places for solitary research or study. Both types of sessions allowed users to engage in conversations with others about diversity and inclusion. Students appeared to feel comfortable coming to the library to participate in this activity, and many at the drop-in session reached out to friends to join them. Additional workshops were then held throughout the campus (i.e., the Student Union, Health Center, in a Residence Hall) to make the program as accessible as possible.

The program was designed to be interactive and to gather a diverse pool of participants. Here, the authors recognized the strong social opportunity libraries offer as physical locations that naturally bring students, staff, and faculty together outside of a formal classroom setting. The workshops in the library thus offered an ideal chance for different groups of the campus community to come together around shared dialogue about diversity and inclusion. By utilizing the library as the location for the display of the completed final projects, the authors also provided an opportunity for those community members who did not participate in the initial sessions to become involved in the initiative. Having displays of art in the library can act as a catalyst to help foster self-reflection as patrons are able to spend time observing and searching their own reactions to the display.

Workshop Design

The authors worked to create an outline that would make participants feel comfortable and form some trust within the group, which then would lead to the ability to discuss emotionally high-impact topics. Drawing on some activities often used in Student Life Development, it was decided that when delivering a fixed-time workshop, the program would begin with an icebreaker activity. The icebreaker that was chosen is one often used within diversity training; in effect, it asks the participants to indicate their own perceptions and values with respect to specific statements that are made. This is often called "Crossing the Line," and appears to have originated sometime in the early 1990's, although no definitive origin was found.

A list of statements was devised, and the authors who facilitated the workshops were given the freedom to choose which and how many prompts to use based on the group they were working with. The facilitators explained to the participants that they were to physically move to a designated part of the room (or stand up if the participants were all seated) if their answer to a prompt was "yes, they had experienced this," and if their answer was "no, they had not," then they stayed where they were (or remained seated). Participants were also told that they could choose not to answer a question, and that the responses to the activity should remain confidential after they left the room. Below is a sample of some of the question prompts used in this activity.

A participant:

- is a member of the Delhi community
- is a college student
- has earned a college degree
- enjoys reading for pleasure
- has hugged someone today
- is an oldest child
- is or was a first generation student
- speaks English as a second language
- speaks more than one language fluently
- has ever been made uncomfortable by someone's jokes
- knows little about own cultural heritage
- considers him- or herself spiritual in some way

The first questions asked are meant to be of an emotionally low impact in nature, and then the questions get progressively more impactful as the activity moves on. Facilitators were trained to debrief this exercise by encouraging discussion throughout the activity when certain questions would spark interest, and by asking participants to comment on things they were surprised by at the end of the conversation. Additionally, groups discussed what it felt like when the whole group identified with a statement, versus how individuals felt when they were the only ones to identify with a prompt. This activity was not used for the drop-in sessions; instead, the facilitators would start each participant with the individual portion of the next activity (the question sheets), before moving on to the making portion of the program.

After completing this exercise, the next portion of the program involved facilitators handing out a sheet of questions which participants were asked to consider for themselves quietly; after a few minutes of this the facilitators then went through some of these questions with the group. The questions included:

- What comes to mind when you hear "I am … check the box?" When do we see this box format used to indicate identity?
- How do you identify yourself? What does your identity look like outside, and inside (ex. values, talents, friends, interests)?

- Do you like your box? What are you proud of? Are you completely contained within it? Do you need more than one box, or a bigger box? Would you rather explode your box, or have an invisible one? What do you wonder about your box? What isn't boxed and why?
- How might others see your box? Do they see what you see? Do you see other people in boxes?

At this point in the program, participants generally felt comfortable enough with each other to share some more personal experiences and stories. Both the benefits and drawbacks of checkboxes were discussed in almost every group. For example, one young woman explained that her particular field of study is traditionally male-dominated, so for her, checking a box to identify that she is a woman is important to her personally and that this could help improve the diversity of her field. Others lamented that the choices to check from provided on applications are often too limiting and that they don't always provide a best option for expressing the complexities of how one would self-identify. One faculty member observed that having to label oneself within a box creates an artificial boundary with oneself and others, yet such boxes are a vital tool for trying to study, understand, and promote diversity at an institution. The sharing of personal stories by some often prompted other participants to share, to commiserate, or to offer support to each other. Several participants reflected in feedback surveys sent out after the end of the initiative that they were actually surprised by the emotions that they experienced as they went through this process.

During the drop-in sessions, this particular activity was not completed as described above, rather, the facilitators gave each participant the list of questions to consider on their own before moving on to the next step which involved completing the art project. Often, dialogue would start spontaneously from the participants offering commentary on their experiences or explaining their position on a question, even without the larger facilitator-led discussion opportunity. Conversations would develop organically among those present as new participants would join the session; participants would share with others they knew who passed by what they were working on, and would invite them to join the session. Students were particularly proud to share and invite their friends, even asking the authors if there would be additional sessions for their friends to attend.

After the dialogue, the facilitators prompted participants to envision what their own box looks like both inside and outside. This led directly into the art-making portion of the experience that was based upon the scholarship that suggests that the arts can play a significant role in community building, and in conversations about topics such as inclusion. Arts education is vital in building creative thinking skills; promoting self-reflection and expression; and developing an appreciation for diverse viewpoints. By creating spaces for art within libraries, patrons are allowed the opportunity to explore and reflect upon what they perceive on an individual and community basis. Topics that may be difficult to discuss through traditional conversation starters are instead able to be addressed through the process of observation and self-reflection, as well as through the lens of the art itself.

With these benefits in mind, participants were first instructed to make the same, simple, origami box and then were asked to attach it to a larger neutral paper of their choosing. Printed instructions and a demonstration were provided for participants to follow to create the initial box. Culturally-specific patterned papers (e.g., kente, molas, etc.), in both bright and neutral hues, were purchased and cut into 4 by 4 inch squares to form the starting square format for the origami. Facilitators explained to students what cultures were represented by some of the paper patterns and fielded questions as needed. People were excited when looking at the many papers to choose from and often discussed their paper choices. It was noted that some selected their paper with their culture in mind, while others selected their paper based on aesthetic appeal, or both. During this origami process, clear cues of community were seen as participants were engaging each other with questions, and often helped each other with the challenges experienced in creating the origami. The facilitators made the point of noting how the process of folding, unfolding, and refolding the paper used when making origami physically serves as a metaphor for how we may feel about sharing aspects of our identity with others at first meeting and over time.

After completing the box the participants were instructed to use the collage method to decorate their box and the neutral background paper (which had been cut into 8.5 by 8.5 squares) to represent themselves as an individual with the materials provided. A variety of supplies were on hand including maps and flag stickers, magazines for clipping out images, hand-shaped paper-punches, additional papers, batik fabric squares, sharpie markers, glue, and sparkly gems. Additionally, many participants chose to include materials that they made (drawings, symbols), or items that they brought with them (shells, pictures of loved ones). The entire work was to be designed to reflect either a portion of themselves that was indicated by a box they check, or to symbolize the self that was beyond the box and that was not represented by a simple check mark.

The number of creative "solutions" for how to construct and decorate a box was noteworthy, and demonstrated "out of the box" thinking associated with art making initiatives. Some participants described trying to portray how others perceived them, or how they present themselves differently to different groups of people. Many made the center of their boxes clear focal points, while others screened or hid their center. Some made more than one box, explaining that one box could not possibly describe or contain them. While everyone started out with similarly sized boxes and background squares, some participants expanded the size of their projects by having sections that hung down or exploded out off of the page. One observation of the authors is that the more participants, and the more they observed what others were doing, the more elaborate the art became.

Dialogue among participants evolved organically throughout the art making as people took genuine interest in each other's creations. Participants would often ask each other for help in locating particular additions to their creation (stickers or pictures in a magazine to cut out). Whenever possible, facilitators reserved time at the end of the session to allow volunteers to share their creations with the group. The conversations were moving as people shared thoughts about their love, pain, and hopes. It was fascinating to see how the final artworks evolved into much more than the simple box that was the starting seed for the project.

The authors hoped that the sharing of the final creations would be a vital part of the learning process that would promote discussion about inclusion and celebrate the diversity of our campus. The authors realize that our library offered an excellent, but underutilized exhibit space. Based upon this knowledge, the final phase was the design of a collective mosaic of 65 boxes and participant quotes. The authors designed the exhibit that took advantage of a prominent location near the entry and main circulation desk, which offered an expansive wall-surface and good lighting. This is a space that naturally brings staff, faculty, and students into proximity with one another. To further enhance the connections of this initiative to other areas of our campus, the authors coordinated with our Hospitality Management and Culinary Arts Program students led by Dean Dr. David Brower and Assistant Professor Sean Pehrsson to provide food for the Opening Reception unveiling the exhibit.

The Opening was well-attended by a diverse audience of faculty, students, and community members, and received favorable reviews. Viewers admired unique attributes of individual boxes, and it was enlightening to see how many different interpretations emerged from the same basic instructions and materials. The exhibit gave physical form to the concept of diversity on our campus, as each finished piece was uniquely about the person who created it. The exhibit was up for two weeks, and the library staff observed that the exhibit garnered patron interest up to the day it was taken down.

Conclusion

Libraries have traditionally been known as a place for academic learning, as a physical location in which to find information on specific subjects. How often do we use a library as a place not only to find concrete information, but to learn about oneself, each other, and our community? This program provided an opportunity for the community members at SUNY Delhi to be inspired by one another, and to break down barriers based on culture, language, or economic status. The exhibition of the finished artwork provided an additional benefit as those who could not participate in the art-making process were still able to become engaged through the viewing and reflection on the finished pieces.

The authors have found that the activity has resonated with almost everyone who was introduced to the project, as evidenced by the program being requested the following academic year. Each individual has to make choices on a daily basis about what to tell or show others about themselves, and this art-making process provided a way for participants to truly represent themselves as they are, and not to feel confined by society's boxes. Participants learned a lot about themselves, and about those who share their community. This was the ultimate goal of the project.

WORKS CITED

SUNY Delhi. 2017. "Fast Facts." Accessed October 4, 2017. http://www.edhi.edu/about/fast=facts/index.php.

Building Community
in an Academic Library

CAROLYN FREY *and* JAMI POWELL

The Grace Doherty Library (GDL) at Centre College, a liberal arts institution located in the rural town of Danville, Kentucky, serves as an intellectual and social hub for a campus community of 1,400 students and 500 faculty and staff. Over the past two years, the GDL has reflected on how better to connect and engage with all people who enter into this space. Reflection has resulted in new efforts guided by three fresh approaches:

1. Engage with the person of the patron (as the person of the librarian).
2. Honor traditions and get creative in making new ones.
3. Strive to be what your community needs.

Led by library staff working to make the GDL a welcoming space of inclusion, safety, respect and dialogue, our efforts are connecting us more with one another, both on campus and throughout the larger community.

Engage with the Person of the Patron (as the Person of the Librarian)

Librarians at the GDL are passionately involved with social and ethical issues at Centre College and in the surrounding community. Through our programs and our outreach, we have developed strong relationships with students and campus partners. With campus and community organizations, we strive to maintain a safe and equitable space for faculty, staff, students, and community members from the outlying area.

One of the first programs to find a home in our library was the Posse program. Posse was originally developed in New York City by Deborah Bial to encourage students from large cities to attend small, liberal arts colleges in cohorts of ten students. Centre College became a Posse partner in 2005. The librarians had a strong connection to many of the Posse students early on as these students were avid users of library services and many were employed in the library as student workers.

In 2011, the Associate Director of Library Services became a Posse mentor for nine students from Boston. In working with these students the Associate Director met and forged relationships with both older and younger students in the program. A Posse mentor meets with their ten students weekly as a group and biweekly individually. The program presents unique challenges and opportunities for both the students and the campus. Students from Boston often find it difficult to adjust to small town life and the attitudes thereof. Centre College has a history of a very uniform population in terms of diversity and experience. Involvement with the Posse program and attendance of librarians at the annual staff, faculty and student weekend-long Posse Plus Retreats have encouraged the Posse students to feel comfortable in the library and to approach library staff members for help with challenges ranging from academic issues, to mental and physical health concerns, socioeconomic challenges, and, finally, just loneliness and homesickness pangs.

Providing a listening ear for the Posse students and any other students experiencing challenges is a crucial, if unwritten, part of our daily work. An open- door policy for our students is maintained, in which they know they will receive academic and moral support, as well as a shoulder to cry on when needed.

In the mentoring role, the Associate Director was in a unique position to introduce students to other support services on campus. The Department of Public Safety, Center for Career and Professional Development, Center for Academic Services, Health Services Office, and faculty partners worked with the Posse students and their mentor to provide a network of support and care that kept these students connected and engaged with campus and academic life. Involvement with the Posse program is just one way librarians have stepped out of the typical librarianship role at Centre College.

Communication with patrons is important. But sometimes libraries can rely too heavily on policies, signs, emails and webpages as tools of communication. While those items adequately convey information to patrons, they don't generally make connections with the human beings who both use and work in the library. Staff of the Grace Doherty Library have been actively participating in two major initiatives geared toward improving dialogue and communication throughout campus and our larger community: Nonviolent Communication and Sustained Dialogue.

Nonviolent Communication (NVC) is a way of expressing ourselves more authentically by clearly saying and listening for observations (not blame), feelings (not accusations), needs (not strategies), and requests (not demands). This is an oversimplified definition, but the underlying principle is that NVC guides us through speaking, thinking, and listening more compassionately toward ourselves and others. Though the promotion and practice of this new "language" on campus is still in its early stages, interest in it is growing.

Along a similar path, Sustained Dialogue takes the concept of compassionate communication to the group level. While NVC focuses on individual reflection and expression, Sustained Dialogue (SD) addresses intergroup communication; how an individual in a group communicates with other members. Although only one SD training weekend has been offered on campus to date (geared more toward students and student groups), some faculty and staff were invited to participate, including a library staff member.

By engaging with and taking part in these campus trainings with students, library staff are building key relationships with students as both library patrons and fellow community members. Students experience and connect with a kind of library outreach that goes beyond programming or book displays. As library staff work to incorporate these dialogue initiatives within the library environment, the entire climate of the library benefits as a place of study and place of employment. We become more comfortable with engaging the uncomfortable, more effectively and compassionately managing disputes with student workers in Public Services and conflicts within the library as an office workplace.

Our mission to more deliberately and authentically engage with the human beings who gather in our library as students, employees, or whatever the identifiers are, makes the Grace Doherty Library much more than a physical place. We become a welcoming and open culture that makes an effort to speak and hear everyone with a language of compassion.

In keeping with the desire to make our library a welcoming space where important and often eye-opening discourse takes place, we began a Diversity Book Club. This event was funded, in part, by a Mellon Grant provided to the Diversity Office on campus. Our goal for the book club was twofold: to offer titles that provide a voice and perspective from a diverse author or subject area, and to promote interaction among students, faculty, and staff on our campus. Diversity is a priority on our campus at present, with a goal to increase it among the students, faculty and staff, as well as a desire to promote community and empathy among our campus constituents. We wanted to explore diversity with campus colleagues and to promote reflection and conversation regarding current political issues, while avoiding potential polarization.

The promotion of lifelong learning is a major tenet of our campus mission; the book clubs also fulfill that purpose. We facilitated three campus book clubs last academic year. Our Library Advisory Committee helped us choose the following titles for our book club: *Everything I Never Told You* (Ng 2014); *The Underground Railroad* (Whitehead 2016); *The Warmth of Other Suns* (Wilkerson 2010). To generate interest, we sent out a campus email to invite participants. We had a good response, with 35–50 attendees for each book club. Once we had participant names, we sent out Doodle polls to decide upon times to hold the meetings and provided each reader with a copy of the title to be discussed. We found that our spring book clubs were much better attended than our summer book club, due to vacation schedules.

The financial burden might be substantial if the project were not funded by a grant, due to the need to purchase books for participants. Rather than holding the book club groups at the same time in the semester, you might just purchase ten copies of a title and then make these available each month to a different book club group, on a rotating basis.

As with most of our programming, the time commitment can be substantial. The staff members involved need to read the book(s), prepare to lead the conversations, market the event, and, in our case, bake cookies or bring in snacks and drinks. We do feel that the time commitment is worth the interest and participation of campus and community partners. An interesting note on our own clubs: we found that nearly 75 percent of our participants were campus staff. This meets one of our goals of lifelong learning and is related to the fact that campus staff often do not receive the same level of professional and personal development opportunities provided to the faculty and students.

In our quest to be a safe and open space for all patrons, we believe it is crucial that we build in professional and personal development for our library staff surrounding the topics of diversity and inclusion. To that purpose, we have focused our efforts over the past year on effective workplace communication. During the summer of 2017, we read and discussed a book titled *Difficult Conversations* (Stone, Patton, Heen, and Fisher 2010). We also took a creativity assessment, which was administered by a faculty member who has studied creative problem-solving. This assessment was beneficial in allowing us to see the strengths and concerns of each staff member and how we best work together to build upon our collective interests and abilities. The assessment also highlighted the need to see every patron's individual abilities, focus, and needs. We hope this makes us more available, empathetic, and customer-service oriented.

Additionally, library staff who manage students met for an all-day training and planning session. In preparation for this session, staff members were asked to read an article titled "*What Difference Does Diversity Make in Managing Student Employees?*" (Kathman and Kathman 1998.) The managers who employ students in circulation, reference, archives, and interlibrary loan spent an afternoon planning a revamped student training day and worked on policies and procedures that would be more equitable for all students.

We have developed an extensive student employee handbook and performance evaluation form. Our effort is to provide employment experience that will help students connect what they learn in the classroom with their work in the library and in turn connect both of these experiences to their future employment goals. To that end, we began utilizing The University of Iowa's GROW (Guided Reflection on Work) assessment (https://vp.studentlife.uiowa.edu/priorities/grow/) with our student workers. The tool provides students with a reflective survey that makes connections between work and study, as well as possible future career goals and employment opportunities.

Honor Traditions and Get Creative in Making New Ones

Being a small residential college in the middle of a small rural town, Centre quickly moves from the academic pursuits of the work week into the typical weekend merry-making of a college campus. For most of the academic year, the GDL closes at 9:00 p.m. on Fridays and Saturdays. But two annual after-hours events now take place in the library, one in the fall and another in the spring, that offer an alternate option for nighttime fun and community-building for all members of the campus community.

The concept of after-hours programming in the Grace Doherty Library simply did not exist two years ago. Library staff were focused on programming events and providing a high level of library service to the campus during our regular open hours. When students from the Student Government Association proposed the library as the location for their first annual Literacy Gala, our first collective staff reaction was, "No way, are they crazy? We'll be closed then." However, after some staff reflection on the idea and reassurances from the students that they would be responsible for any and all setup, breakdown and cleanup involved with the charity fundraiser, we started thinking, "Well, why not? Why not consider new ways our library can participate in the lives of our students?" We realized that there are other spaces on our campus capable of hosting a semi-formal evening event but that students valued the place of the library as a space and resource; it was integral to the success of their event. The Gala was successful that first year and continues to be so now in its second year, enjoying active and excited student participation and generating funds for a local children's charity promoting literacy.

In fact, the success and fun of the first-annual Literacy Gala inspired another idea for after-hours programming: Library Game Night. Primarily the idea of library staff, Game Night was envisioned as an inclusive and informal event for the campus (not requiring a ticket purchase or special dress) to be held on a Friday night during the late winter doldrums. Library staff prepared hot chocolate and homemade desserts and snacks; we provided a variety of board games and arranged them on tables throughout the main floor. We also encouraged people to bring their own games and enjoy a laid-back three hours of play and socializing.

Turnout was high; students who arrived at 9:00 p.m. (the start time) ended up staying for the duration of the event, until midnight. Groups of game players formed, played, and then re-formed as different groups for different games. A few faculty and staff excitedly participated as well, adding to the festive, buzzing community of creative game-playing. As students and staff were leaving after the event, they cheered for additional Game Nights to be held in the library throughout the academic year. Many students mentioned that it was refreshing to have a non–Greek, non-alcohol, non-organization social event alternative held in their favorite place to hang out on campus.

While after-hours programming might require a little extra contribution from library staff in terms of their work schedule rearrangement, significant goodwill, excitement, and social connections were generated within our campus patron community for these non-traditional library events. We acknowledge that the library cannot become a regularly scheduled playground; in fact, we did decline a fraternity's request for an after-hours "Capture the Flag" tournament in the library. But when non-traditional ideas that align with our overall mission to be a learning community are presented, we have established a new tradition in the GDL of listening first.

Like many college campuses, we have a pronounced "town and gown" divide. Community members often view our students as privileged individuals removed from the cares and concerns of the community. For the past two years, we have partnered with the Boyle County Public Library to address this artificial division between the campus and the community at large by sharing the Human Library project. First developed in Denmark in 2010, the Human Library originated to challenge stereotypes and open up conversations around subjects often considered to be taboo or outside the norms of societal beliefs and customs, such as polyamorous couples or atheism. The Human Library consists of people who agree to have a short conversation (to be the books of the Human Library), with those who check them out for a discussion (the readers of the Human Library.) Each human book chooses a topic of interest or passion to share with his or her readers. We set the checkout time for our human books to be thirty minutes, long enough to allow the book to give some background and information on the topic but short enough that it is not interminable for either book or reader if the conversation does not flow well for them.

The Human Library was first discussed as a possibility when a student presented the idea as a project for a social justice course. He brought his idea to the library administrators and was willing to contribute his time and passion to bring the project to fruition on the Centre College campus. The Human Library does not necessarily require significant expenses but is a considerable undertaking in terms of time and marketing. For our first Human Library, held in April of 2017, we marketed the event broadly, using both campus and community marketing tools.

Social media and email blasts were utilized early in the planning process to generate interest and participation from campus community members as both books and readers. Both the local radio station and newspaper advertised the event with daily schedules and a listing of the human books available. Staff from both libraries worked together to generate personal contact with other campus and community organizations, such as veterans in Boyle County, the community group Citizens Concerned with Human Rights, churches, and elementary and secondary schools. Personal connection was crucial to encourage our human books to participate in the project. We found that many times people who had very deep and meaningful stories to share did not consider participating in the Human Library until they were approached in person.

Because the Human Library is an international organization with a patented name, permission is required to present the program locally. Information on the application process is available at humanlibrary.org and early planning is encouraged. For our first year, we applied six months in advance but did not hear back from the Human Library administrator until a few weeks before our event. There is a $59 application fee with a possibility to waive if funds are not available at the participating library. The Human Library organization requires that marketing materials include patented images, which are provided once the registration is completed, but in our case, we also gained permission from some of our human books to use their pictures on our posters and flyers, which we felt helped generate interest. Along with posters and flyers placed strategically on campus in heavily trafficked areas and in the surrounding community, we marketed in our dining services at Centre College. A popular marketing device on our campus is the use of banners that are hung in our dining services hall, as well as flyers that may be placed in the napkin holders on tables in the cafeteria. Students are a captive audience when dining and interacting with peers, so these are effective ways to reach them.

Organization on the day of the Human Library was crucial. We held the event at the campus library on Saturday from 1 to 5 p.m. a less busy day for us in terms of study times for students, and at the public library on the following Sunday. At both libraries, we devised a check-in and check-out system. The Human Library organization provides software for this process; we decided to use a notebook system instead which worked well, but later realized that a Google spreadsheet would more easily capture statistics and information. A human library book is checked out for a 30-minute conversation by the reader. We set up a table at the front of the library where the books could be checked out and sectioned off an area of the library where the books could sit and converse comfortably with each other while awaiting a check out with their eventual readers. Also provided in this space were soft drinks, coffee, and snacks, some coloring books and pencils, and a puzzle.

Our first event went very well, with 24 distinct titles, ranging in topics from a survivor of domestic abuse to a discussion of Jainism; from growing up biracial, to becoming an author. Along with capturing statistics for the number of readers, books and conversations, our library also gave each participant a survey to capture feedback about the event and to provide some reflection on the experience. Participants overwhelmingly found this to be a moving and life-changing experience, looking an individual in the eye while having a conversation devoted to a deep, personal, and often passionate story or issue from that individual's life. Here are some comments from participants regarding their experience with the Human Library:

- "Everyone has a story, you just gotta read it."
- "Authentic connecting."
- "Better understanding of other people."
- "Everyone's story is unique."
- "People are friendly if you open up"

- "I really liked the chance to get to know a member of the Centre community a little better."

We held our second annual Human Library in October of 2017 with continued success. This is an event we plan to hold annually as it draws participation from our faculty and students, and from the surrounding community.

Strive to Be What Your Community Needs

Physical space is often at a premium on college campuses. This is especially true for the small college library. After space is designated for living, eating, learning, studying and playing, there's not much real estate left for students interested in organizing themselves for community building and social awareness. At Centre, classrooms are secured shortly after the last class of the day. A few meeting rooms are available in the Campus Center (main dining hall) but are often noisy and distracting with high traffic usage. Because the GDL is the only staffed, service-oriented campus space available almost 18 hours daily, many students rely on the library's haven-like environment in the evening.

Representatives from Centre Pride Alliance, the campus LGBTQ student organization, approached the GDL for help in providing a secure and discreet space for transgender students to gather each week for one hour during the evening. We considered our available spaces and determined that a weekly one-hour booking would not present a hardship for others wishing to use the library. Stonewall @Centre now has a weekly reserved meeting in this quiet, discreet and secure space.

As Centre has initiated efforts to diversify its campus population, less effort has been directed toward providing a supportive infrastructure for those diverse students once they matriculate. Centre currently lacks a shared sacred space to meet the devotional needs of our religious students and staff. While there are plans to address this need in future construction projects, that doesn't help our current non–Christian students. Library staff were approached by the Dean of Student Life on behalf of the Muslim Student Association for assistance in creating an easily accessible temporary Dhuhr afternoon prayer space. Since our library study rooms only see heavy use after classes finish for the day at 4:00 p.m. library staff determined that a study room could be reserved daily from 1:00 until 2:30 for our campus Muslim community.

Small efforts can help foster growth and development of student groups. Adjustments to or a rethinking of existing policies can further open up the library to patron needs. We realize that the library cannot provide a reserved space for every campus group, but we can at least listen to the unmet needs of our campus community and consider ideas for possible solutions. The only librarian time commitment involved in making these two spaces available was to enter the recurring reservations within the campus online reservation system and post a sign. After this small but considered effort, students from two often marginalized and excluded groups now have a place on our campus to be who they are.

The work of promoting and fostering inclusion and social justice within the academic library requires those of us employed by institutes of higher education to show up, whenever and wherever we can, no matter the job title, no matter the pay grade. "Showing up" can manifest through a myriad of our individual passions and pursuits. It doesn't demand that we work late hours, never take a vacation, or march in the streets. It simply asks that we share of ourselves with those around us.

WORKS CITED

Kathman, Jane McGurn, and Michael G. Kathman. 1998. "What Difference Does Diversity Make in Managing Student Employees." *College & Research Libraries* 59, no. 4 (July): 378–389. https://tinyurl.com/ycytr55o.

Ng, Celeste. 2014. *Everything I Never Told You.* New York: Penguin Press HC.

Stone, Douglas, Bruce Patton, Sheila Heen, and Roger Fisher. 2010. *Difficult Conversations: How to Discuss What Matters Most.* New York: Penguin Books.

University of Iowa. Vice President for Student Life: *Iowa Grow.* N.D. https://vp.studentlife.uiowa.edu/priorities/grow/ (accessed December 12, 2017).

Whitehead, Colson. 2016. *The Underground Railroad.* New York: Doubleday.

Wilkerson, Isabel. 2010. *The Warmth of Other Suns.* New York: Random House.

Critical Librarianship in Action

Supporting Campus-Wide Dialogues

Maureen Rust *and* Aimée C. Quinn

Introduction

Students today have more to learn than previous generations partly due to technology and partly due to traditional standards in education. Academic studies across the nation showcase trends that students are learning in much different ways than previous generations (Mintz 2014). Attending classes is only one of many tasks in their busy lives as many are caregivers and work in addition to being college students. At Central Washington University, a large number of these students are first generation college students. At the same time, faculty have changed their teaching styles through a more personalized approach focused on outcomes and adaptive learning. Understanding students' individual backgrounds is essential to ensuring their academic success, the primary mission at our institution.

Civic Engagement on Today's College Campuses

Civic engagement is a rising phenomenon on college campuses in this era irrespective of partisan politics. Students of all ages are participating in public discourse and social issues in ways not seen since the 1960s. Many older Americans fear that the decline in voter participation by college age students indicates a lack of political understanding, partly due to their use of social media, when, in fact, social media brings this generation new tools to engage more readily than earlier generations (Pew 2018). Faculty engaged with these students on campus understand that the students are transcending the social norms of previous generations to pave a new path to their political voice, with social media being one measure of their participation. Students are using protests, online games, and other online tools to reach out and participate. Recognizing that each generation has new and different tools to engage with each other, we (the faculty) must let go of our preconceived ideas and theories about teaching and learning.

The Role of Critical Librarianship in Academic Libraries

The formal development of *critical librarianship*, taking: "…an ethical and political approach to library work, using critical theory to expose and question the historical, political, and social bases of our assumptions and practices" (ACRL 2017), is gaining momentum across the academic library spectrum. Libraries have a history of political engagement (Drabinski 2017, 83), evidenced in part by the American Library Association's (ALA) *Library Bill of Rights* (American Library Association 1997). The ALA's commitment to intellectual freedom and privacy illustrates how advocating for social justice and human rights was woven into the fabric of libraries from an early age (American Library Association 2007). That being said, the current rise in critical library pedagogy discussions and scholarship is a response to heightening awareness of the inequities of privilege still evident today in society, including libraries (Pagowsky and McElroy 2016, x–xi; Drabinski 2017, 76). Academic libraries are responding by expanding programming to address these inequities, give voice to marginalized citizens, and increase student exposure to engaged learning. It is imperative that libraries take this opportunity to demonstrate support for social justice and human rights and negate the notion of an atmosphere of neutrality (Elmborg 2006, 193).

Critical librarianship represents thoughtful and intentional inclusion of transformative dialogues in its teaching and learning practices and is the focus of this case study (Pagowsky and McElroy 2016, xviii). The emphasis on scholarship as conversation is a rebuttal of the "banking" practice of education called out by educator and philosopher Paulo Freire (2003, 72–73), and of the emphasis on data driven learning assessment as put forth by components of the Association of College & Research Libraries (ACRL) *Framework for Information Literacy for Higher Education* (Drabinski 2017, 77–78).

This essay discusses how the James E. Brooks Library at Central Washington University incorporates opportunities for "scholarship as conversation" to encourage student discourse on topics of human rights and social justice.

Case Study

The Student Engagement and Community Outreach Librarian and the Government Publications Librarian at the James E. Brooks Library (Brooks Library) at Central Washington University devote a considerable amount of time to library outreach, both across campus and out into the surrounding community. Central Washington University is an extremely collegial campus, and the library often partners with faculty and staff from a variety of disciplines and departments. One of these partnerships is the library's involvement in the annual Social Justice and Human Rights Dialogues series with rotating social justice themes. Through this collaboration, the library works with the campus and the community to provide civic engagement opportunities throughout the academic year.

Since the inception of the Social Justice and Human Rights Dialogues at Central Washington University in 2015, the library has maintained a seat on the Social Justice and Human Rights Steering Committee (the Student Engagement and Community Outreach Librarian and the Government Publications Librarian serve in alternating years).

One of the key tasks of the Social Justice and Human Rights Steering Committee is to integrate "teaching by doing" into the overall curriculum, including general education courses. When the Dialogues were initiated by then College of Arts and Humanities Dean Stacey Robertson, the campus was also involved in re-envisioning the general education curriculum. Dean Robertson saw an opportunity to engage students and faculty in broad campus discussions on a single topic which could be integrated into multiple courses across the curriculum alongside campus events to foster enhanced discourse and critical thinking (Central Washington University 2017). Noted scholars, authors, poets, and artists from around the world would be invited to come and share their work. The themes chosen to date are Mass Incarceration (2015–16), Migration and Immigration (2016–17), and Sustainability (2017–18).

Student Engagement and Community Outreach Efforts

Since the beginning of the Dialogues, the library has coordinated thematic programming to align with scheduled speakers and events. The library Social Justice and Human Rights task force, a team of volunteers from library faculty and staff, assembles early each academic year to plan out affiliated library programming. Examples include:

- Tabling with relevant materials available for remote circulation at speaker events, including renown social justice and human rights advocates David Fathi (director, American Civil Liberties Union) and author Eric Michael Dyson.
- Hosting quarterly book discussions with related subject matter. The books by theme were: *Orange is the New Black* (Kerman 2011) (Mass Incarceration); *The Things They Carried* (O'Brien 2009) and *American Born Chinese* (Yang and Pien 2009) (Migration/Immigration); and *A Tale for the Time Being* (Ozeki 2013) (Sustainability).
- Screening related documentaries such as *Cruel and Unusual* (Baus, Hunt and Williams 2007) (transgender incarceration) and *Belinda* (Mason and Lewis 2010) (HIV/AIDS stigma), followed by guided discussion with experts in the fields of Law and Justice, Public Health, and transgender rights.
- Creating suggested reading lists aligned with the current theme.
- Developing electronic research guides of related resources.
- Allocating money from the collection development budget for materials specific to the current theme.
- Planning large thematic exhibits and displays.

Government Publications Services Programming

Government Publications Services, the federal and state depository unit within Brooks Library, regularly participates by offering space, speaker events, and displays designed to correlate to the campus Social Justice and Human Rights Dialogues. One requirement of serving as a depository library is to engage the citizens of the area you serve through various outreach programs. Each year, the staff within Government Publications Services establishes an event calendar which outlines the displays and potential events to be held in the Maps Room, a welcoming environment suited to gatherings of up to fifty guests. Government Publications Services incorporates their schedule into the library's events calendar which is coordinated by the Student Engagement and Community Outreach Librarian.

At the Brooks Library, the Government Publications Services unit saw this opportunity as a natural extension of its regular work as it engages the campus and the surrounding community in its activities. Each year, the Dialogues theme is integrated into the area's displays and events. The physical location of the Government Publications Services unit allows for extensive displays, both two-and three-dimensional. For the first Social Justice and Human Rights Dialogue, Mass Incarceration, the unit committed to creating monthly rotating displays throughout the academic year to focus on different perspectives of "Mass Incarceration." These displays received significant attention, heightening campus awareness of Government Publications Services as a powerful research resource. Displays were a sound way to introduce Government Publications Services as a viable place to host events for the future Dialogues. Some of the displays included an in-depth look at the juvenile justice system as well as how incarceration effects families. The student reactions and questions originating from viewing these displays encouraged the staff in Government Publications Services to begin having their own series of discussions tied to the theme the following year.

The following year, "Migration and Immigration" was the chosen theme. Accordingly, Government Publications Services scheduled a series of discussions, each focused on one of the target communities: faculty and staff, students, and the community at large. Each of the events built upon the previous one and responded to topics of interest requested by the audience. The first discussion focused on issues of coming to America and the question of migration and immigration. Three faculty, each of whom came from different countries (Canada, Vietnam, and Korea) participated, bringing their first-hand experience of non-native isolation. The Government Publications Librarian was fairly new on campus as were two of these faculty, and an unexpected bond was formed. They began having regular communication with each other related to their students and their research. The other faculty members also became involved in the Dialogues and had their students attend programming for extra credit.

The second discussion focused on women in the community and women-owned businesses. Women from the community came to discuss the challenges they faced starting their businesses, especially those who came here from other countries. The third discussion was dedicated to students and an issue which came from Government Publications Services student employees: religion, freedom, and liberty. By incorporating the Dialogues into the regular events, the use of space, collections, and the service desk notably increased. The following year, students began to suggest programming they wanted to see in the space and started bringing their friends to library events. This years' theme of Sustainability has led to debates about the future of climate, more visibility of the Library in campus events, and better use of Government Publications in the community. Library student employees, both within Government Publications and from other Library areas have contributed to these discussions. For this year's theme, Government Publications Services staff are working with the Social Justice and Human Rights team on hosting a special speaker, Gina McCarthy, who is a former Administrator of the Environmental Protection Agency for President Obama. At first, they only helped set up the area and created guides. However, as the Dialogues became more established, the student employees began to contribute ideas and participated on their own time, a lovely if unexpected side benefit of library activism.

The Library as a Team Player

The Brooks Library's eager participation in and programming contributions to the Social Justice and Human Rights Dialogue is a key factor in increased civic engagement partnerships beyond the annual theme. The library frequently partners with civic-minded campus and community units including the Center for Diversity and Social Justice, the Center for Leadership and Community Engagement, the Wellness Center, the Student Medical and Counseling Clinic, Law and Justice Department, Women's Gender and Sexuality Studies Program, Lion Rock Visiting Writers Series, and the local public libraries. The library's main objective is to create an atmosphere of resource discovery and critical discussion. Partnering with scholars and other professionals serves to add complementary layers to the conversations, to the benefit of all involved (Gorham, Taylor, and Jaeger 2016, 3).

For example, Brooks Library recently partnered with the campus Wellness Center on their exhibit, "What Were You Wearing," a display created to illustrate the idea that clothes do not give consent. A staff member of the campus Wellness Center curated the contents of the exhibit held for two weeks in the library entryway. The purpose of the exhibit was to bring attention to sexual violence. The exhibit coincided with *Good Kids*, a related production by the campus theatre department. In addition to the exhibit, the library assembled relevant materials from the collection and displayed them for circulation. For World AIDS Day 2017, the library collaborated with the Wellness Center on an informal guided discussion, hosted in the Government Publications Maps Room, in which students, staff, and faculty shared the impact HIV/AIDS and its inherent stigma has had on their lives. Faculty and staff from the Wellness Center, Women's Gender and Sexuality Studies Program, Student Involvement, and the Center for Learning and Community Engagement were on hand to field important questions and share their personal stories, as well as their expertise. The welcoming and non-threatening nature of the informal discussion resulted in a rich open dialog, one the library is planning to repeat with a series of other topics.

Another example of how the library's involvement led to a human rights discussion was when the Central Washington University Office of International Studies and Programs invited the library to co-host the live webinar, "Islamophobia on Campus: From Micro-aggressions to Full-Fledged Hate Crimes and Violence," bringing a whole new contingent into the library. Following the program, the library also provided the means to stream the archived webinar for campus members unable to attend, increasing access to the materials made available and heightening awareness of the library's role in providing the information and participation in the conversation.

Additionally, as a result of the Dialogues, Government Publications Services is working with the county commissioner's office, providing information related to a new affordable housing initiative as well as solar farming. Displaying materials relevant to these initiatives in Government Publications Services promotes the space as a community resource. The library also works with the city planning department to update the cold weather shelter map online and participates on the Presidents United to Solve Hunger committee to help create and promote resources for our homeless and food-insecure students.

The ACRL Framework and the Dialogues

In 2016 the Association for College & Research Libraries formally adopted the *Framework for Information Literacy for Higher Education* superseding its predecessor, the *Information Literacy Competency Standards for Higher Education*. The intent of the Framework is to provide flexible, interconnected core values for developing information literacy curricula and for designing learning outcomes (Association of College and Research Libraries 2016). The Dialogues gave the Brooks Library the means to introduce critical literacy skills to a broader audience than was possible with its tradition instruction program. Through the introduction of civic engagement and community outreach, library faculty are able to use these Dialogues to expand their role as both faculty and librarians to integrate critical learning skills while considering how the ACRL Framework could impact their work. One of the stumbling blocks related to the Framework is how it does not help the student challenge social justice concepts for themselves; that it does not specifically address the intersection between social justice issues and information literacy education (Battista et al. 2015, 112). This challenge to the Framework is widely discussed in the critical learning literature by Seale (2016, 2–5) and Battista, et al. (2015, 112–115). In their writings, they examine how the Framework looks at specific disciplines but negates interdisciplinary instruction and engagement. The authors also caution that the Frameworks perpetuate the notion of academic authority as a subtle result of a culture of dominance. They instead encourage information literacy instruction that creates critical, engaged citizens (Battista et al. 2015, 117, 120). Explaining civic engagement through social justice is complex enough for most undergraduates to understand the societal implications. The Social Justice and Human Rights Dialogues are a path to these concepts.

Conclusion

At Central Washington University, the Dialogues themes are planned out three years in advance. As discussed above, the two librarians rotate on the steering committee and serve on various subcommittees in order to ensure that the Brooks Library has a voice in the planning and implementation of these events. Because the themes are chosen in advance, the Dialogues executive committee is able to begin planning for the coming academic year before breaking for summer intersession. At this point a new director (or co-directors) of the Dialogues is appointed, funding and budget parameters are determined, and steering committee members are confirmed. The executive committee meets to discuss potential programming, guests, and collaborative projects. Each proposal goes through several stages (proposal review, budget review, scheduling, marketing and publicity) before the final proposal comes to the steering committee. By the time the steering committee meets in the fall, there is already an initial roster of activities outline for the to start of the school year. The steering committee continues to meet throughout the school year to report on attendance and feedback on programming, and to plan further events for the academic year. The steering committee is also broken into subcommittees including faculty engagement, future themes, student engagement, funding, and community engagement. These members regularly collaborate, integrate, and reach out to serve all the communities as partners in critical engagement.

The library faculty are investigating how best to integrate the Framework as they move forward. Next year's theme is Public Engagement: Democracy, Civil Disobedience, and Youth Activism in Contemporary Times, which will offer a better opportunity to assess if using the Framework will enhance our library programming. With better understanding from the student employees plus an engaged community, Brooks Library outreach is growing stronger each year.

Not all academic libraries will have this specific opportunity for programming development and campus collaboration. However, there are many opportunities available for library involvement in planning and presenting forums for rich and rewarding conversations on civil rights and civic engagement. This participation will not only provide a valuable service to the campus and greater community but also heighten awareness of the library as an active partner and community resource.

Works Cited

ACRL Instruction Section Research & Scholarship Committee. 2017. "Five Things You Should Read About Critical Librarianship." http://connect.ala.org/node/267841.

American Library Association. 1997. "Library Bill of Rights." http://www.ala.org/advocacy/sites/ala.org.advocacy/files/content/intfreedom/librarybill/lbor.pdf.

American Library Association. 2007. "Freedom to View Statement." http://www.ala.org/advocacy/intfreedom/freedomviewstatement.

Association of College & Research Libraries. 2016. "Framework for Information Literacy for Higher Education." http://www.ala.org/acrl/standards/ilframework.

Battista, Andrew, Dave Ellenwood, Lua Gregory, Shana Higgins, Jeff Lilburn, Yasmin Sokkar Harker and Christopher Sweet. 2015. "Seeking Social Justice in the ACRL Framework." *Communications in Information Literacy* 9 (2): 111–25.

Baus, Janet, Dan Hunt, and Reid Williams, Outcast Films, Open Society Institute, New York State Council on the Arts, and Frameline. 2007. *Cruel and Unusual: Transgender Women in Prison*. New York: Outcast Films, DVD.

Central Washington University. 2017. "Social Justice and Human Rights Dialogues." https://www.cwu.edu/social-justice-and-human-rights-dialogues/.

Drabinski, Emily. 2017. "A Kairos of the Critical: Teaching Critically in a Time of Compliance." *Communications in Information Literacy* 11 (1):76–94.

Elmborg, James. 2006. "Critical Information Literacy: Implications for Instructional Practice." *Journal of Academic Librarianship* 32 (2):192–99. https://doi.org/10.1016/j.acalib.2005.12.004.

Freire, Paulo. 2003. *Pedagogy of the Oppressed*. 30th Anniversary ed. New York: Continuum.

Gorham, Ursula, Natalie Greene Taylor, and Paul T. Jaeger, eds. 2016. "Libraries as Institutions of Human Rights and Social Justice." In *Perspectives on Libraries as Institutions of Human Rights and Social Justice*, 1–11. Bingley, England: Emerald Group.

Kerman, Piper. 2011. *Orange Is the New Black: My Year in a Women's Prison*. Spiegel & Grau trade paperback ed. New York: Spiegel & Grau.

Mason, Belinda Ann, and Anne Lewis, Headwaters and Appalshop, Inc. 2010. *Belinda*. Whitesburg, KY: Appalshop.

Mintz, Steven. 2014. "Five Ways That 21st and 20th Century Will Differ." *Higher Ed Gamma* (blog), *Inside Higher Ed*, March 5, 2014. https://www.insidehighered.com/blogs/higher-ed-beta/five-ways-21st-and-20th-century-learning-will-differ.

O'Brien, Tim. 2009. *The Things They Carried: A Work of Fiction*. First Mariner Books ed. Boston: Mariner Books/Houghton Mifflin Harcourt.

Ozeki, Ruth L. 2013. *A Tale for the Time Being: A Novel*. New York: Penguin Books.

Pagowsky, Nicole, and Kelly McElroy. 2016. *Critical Library Pedagogy Handbook*. Chicago: Association of College and Research Libraries, A Division of the American Library Association.

Pew Research Center. 2018. "Demographics of Mobile Device Ownership and Adoption in the United States." *Mobile Device Factsheet.* http://www.pewinternet.org/fact-sheet/mobile/.

Seale, M. 2016. "Enlightenment, Neoliberalism, and Information Literacy." *Canadian Journal of Academic Librarianship,* 1(1), 80–91.

Yang, Gene Luen, and Lark Pien. 2009. *American Born Chinese.* First Square Fish ed. New York: Square Fish.

PART IV

Administering with Diversity

Advocacy from Within

Employees with Disabilities

JJ PIONKE

The Americans with Disabilities Act (ADA) of 1990 is the main law within the United States that governs accessibility for people with disabilities. ADA stipulates in part that people with disabilities should receive accommodations to perform their work at the same level as a non-disabled person in their position. Accommodations generally include hardware, software, or work changes that help people work with their disability to perform their job responsibilities. As an example, people with Attention Deficit Disorder might use noise-canceling headphones to help them concentrate or people with fibromyalgia might have an accommodation to work from home when they are having a disease flare. Accommodations are unique to the person and to the disability so what works for one person with that particular disability, may not necessarily work for another person with the same disability.

On paper, the process of getting an accommodation is fairly straightforward: disclose a disability to human resources, negotiate for the accommodation that is needed, try several different types of accommodations to find a best fit for all involved, try out the accommodation, and check in on how it is going after a set period of time. While the accommodation process should in theory be quick and easy, it is often wrought with anxiety, disagreement, and mounting unhappiness with procedures and fellow employees. Difficulty in the accommodation process often stems from reticence on the part of the employer not to make the accommodation requested because of any number of reasons, including administrative attitude, organizational culture, and cost (Williams-Whitt 2007, 407–408). While many libraries will work extensively with patrons with disabilities to accommodate their information needs, this may not be so for employees of libraries. This essay will focus on the need for accommodation for employees with disabilities, some practical recommendations to think about when going through the accommodation process, and a section on how advocacy for employees with disabilities who have accommodations can also improve the library for patrons with disabilities.

Literature Review

There is very limited literature about library employees with disabilities, and the articles generally focus on advocacy rather than quantitative or qualitative research. As an example of an advocacy piece, Nichols and Ercoli Schnitzer discuss the accessibility laws in the U.S. and Canada as well as some of the difficulties that patrons and employees face in libraries (2015). Crucially, they also discuss some methods for combatting stigmatization within the library: "A mental readjustment to focus on accessibility and equity and away from disability and accommodation is a shift from a problem-based model to one rooted in fairness instead. Accessibility should be at the front end of new innovations and programs, built into planning and design processes as a critical component of the model" (Nichols & Ercoli Schnitzer 2015, 21). All too often, the focus in library human resources is on accommodations rather than on creating an inclusive environment. While Nichols and Ercoli Schnitzer don't explicitly mention Universal Design, that is what they are advocating for and more importantly, that Universal Design be applied throughout the library and not just to buildings or services for patrons.

There are also a few limited academic and magazine articles about working in the library as an employee with a disability. The most notable article by Strub and Stewart is a case study that discusses an autistic library employee who does shelving and shifting of books (2010). The case study discusses the positives and negatives of working with an employee with fairly severe autism as well as tips for how to work well with such an employee. While the article is favorable towards the employee and advocates for the hiring of employees with disabilities, the employee with autism's own voice is conspicuously absent, thereby making him an object of discussion rather than a participant.

Discrimination Towards Library Employees with Disabilities

Libraries as employers don't intend to discriminate or create negative working environments for employees, especially employees with disabilities, but all too often this scenario plays out. Most libraries tend to subscribe to the medical model of disability which locates disability in individual bodies and as conditions that need to be cured through surgeries, medication, and various assistive technologies (Berger 2013, 26). However, most people who identify as having a disability subscribe to the social model which "...posits that it is not an individual's impairment or adjustment but the socially imposed barriers—the inaccessible buildings, the limited modes of transportation and communication, the prejudicial attitudes—that construct disability as a subordinate social status and devalued life experience" (Berger 2013, 27). These models are diametrically opposed, especially in terms of where the burden of access falls. In large part, the difference in understanding comes from experience. People without disabilities do not see the barriers that people with disabilities face when trying to accomplish even simple tasks. This lack of understanding far too often devolves into stigma and discrimination.

Stigma is a value judgment, typically made about people who are different in some way. To be stigmatized is to lose one's place in society and more importantly, Coleman points out that people avoid stigmatization at all costs to preserve their spot in the social order but this kind of thinking is a vicious circle that only reinforces the fears that lead to stigma in the first place (Coleman 2006, 142). For a person with a disability, being able to pass as able-bodied is a boon, especially if the disability is a mental one. Stuart, Arboleda-Florez, and Sartorious rightfully point out that "...'stigma' is often used colloquially to refer to the negative and prejudicial attitudes held by members of the public toward people with a mental illness, which has led many advocates to refocus the discourse on the more poignant issue of discrimination" (Stuart, Arboleda-Florez, and Sartorious 2012, 7). The accommodation process in part tries to eliminate job discrimination based on ability by supplying work modifications for people with disabilities so that they may perform their jobs at the same level as a person without a disability. While accommodation does nothing to address the underlying issues of stigma, accommodations do try to address discrimination. It is important to acknowledge that the underlying factor in stigma is fear, and while accommodation can help combat discrimination, it is a change in organizational culture to one of inclusion and acceptance that will help dismantle the tenet that the stigma is based on.

Why Accommodation Matters

At its core, job accommodations help employees with disabilities be better at their jobs by providing an equal playing field in which to do their work. A person with Post Traumatic Stress Disorder (PTSD) once described that being in the cube farm created a constant feeling of being like a mouse and being surrounded by the scent of cat all the time. For them, there was no sense of safety and so their hypervigilance was always active which distracted them from being able to get their work done as efficiently and thoroughly as possible. The accommodation for them was an enclosed office which helped eliminate that sense of danger by dampening sounds, sights, and smells. A successful job accommodation can help employees feel that they have job autonomy, greater job satisfaction when their need for accommodation is respected and approved, and a sense of ownership when the employee is included in the accommodation process (Balser & Harris 2008, 25). While the accommodation process is often unpleasant, if the accommodation is granted, the resulting boost to morale and relief from pain (mental or physical) typically helps the employee significantly in terms of not just attitude but also job productivity.

While successful employee accommodations can lead to increased productivity and job satisfaction, unsuccessful accommodations can have exactly the opposite effect. "…employees that have negative reactions to the accommodation may be more likely to experience a decline in organizational commitment, perceive low organizational support, leave the organization, or perceive that discrimination has occurred, all of which can affect not only the employee but the organization as well" (Balser & Harris 2008, 15). A negative reaction doesn't necessarily have to be a poor accommodation but can also be an accommodation process that takes an overly long time or a perception of resistance from administration/management to granting an accommodation to the employee. A study by Williams-Whitt on the roadblocks to disability accommodations had findings that included "…accommodated employees sensed that they were unwelcome," "Reluctance and bias were heightened where managers questioned the employee's credibility or the legitimacy of the illness," a lack of inclusion of the employee needing an accommodation in the accommodation process and the employee being included only when the process had become decidedly hostile, and a clear disconnect between what constitutes investigation into a disability versus harassment (Williams-Whitt 2007, 412–416). To say that the findings describe a hostile work environment is putting it mildly. Barriers to accommodation absolutely need to be addressed in the workplace as do attitudes towards disability and people with disabilities.

The reality in regards to accommodation is that providing them to employees that need them has a broad range of positive outcomes, including "…improved employee productivity, attendance, attitudes and coworker interaction, as well as lower stress levels, improved coworker attitudes and increased overall organizational morale.… Employees who perceive that their workplace has an inclusive climate feel higher levels of psychological empowerment on the job and higher levels of organizational support…" (von Schrader, Malzer, & Bruyere 2014, 239). When employees are happy and healthy in their work environment, the entire organization benefits.

Tips on the Accommodation Process for Employees

The process of getting an accommodation in the workplace is generally not an easy one, even though it should be, especially if you need a substantial accommodation like an enclosed room to work in when your colleagues are in a cube farm. It's not that getting an extensive accommodation is impossible, but it will be much easier going into the process with a little forethought.

- Read over the process documentation carefully. What exactly is required from you? If the documentation says that you need a letter from your medical professional—ask if they want a medical doctor or the person who is actually treating you. For example, if you have severe depression, your medical doctor might renew your prescription to your antidepressant medication, but it is your therapist who is actually treating you and knows the most about your condition and what accommodations you will need.
- Clearly articulate to the person who is going to write your letter what you need and why. If only a certain brand of noise canceling headphones will work, explain why it has to be that brand. For example, an employee has midrange hearing loss and has hyper acute hearing. When they request noise canceling headphones, they ask for the Bose brand because those headphones cover the greatest spectrum of noise without a high-pitched whine which aggravates the person's hyper acuity.
- Have patience and engage in the process. There will probably be suggestions made for accommodation alternatives. Don't be afraid to try them and give your feedback, positive or negative, about what is or is not working with that accommodation. Accommodation is often an iterative process even when you know exactly what you need. An example from the previous bullet point is trying out several different brands of noise canceling headphones before purchasing the originally requested brand.
- Ask for legal help. If the process is dragging out far longer than it should, it might be time to seek out legal representation. Do not be afraid of taking this step. There are several organizations that provide free or low-cost representation for people with disabilities. An example of a good time to reach out for representation is when the accommodation process has gotten mired for some reason and has lasted for several months. The person who needs the accommodation now has high anxiety around going to work as their work

situation is deteriorating. A legal representative can not only bring the weight of the law to the process but also help advocate for the employee, especially when the employee's voice is no longer being heard and the employee is having difficulties speaking up.

- Reach out to your support networks. The accommodation process is not easy. Absolutely contact people and organizations that are supportive. If the library has an Employee Assistance Program (EAP), don't be afraid to go to it. EAPs are confidential and can pair the employee up with a counselor or therapist to help them negotiate the hurricane of emotions that come with accommodation process.

Advocating for Yourself and Patrons

When you are an employee with a disability, especially if your disability is a hidden one, advocating for yourself is incredibly hard because you have to reveal a part of yourself that is extremely vulnerable. However, while being "out" about a disability can be difficult at times, it can also lead to important teachable moments and provides an opportunity to create a better environment for all people in the library, both employees and patrons. Here are some tips for advocacy:

- You don't have to loudly proclaim your disability everywhere you go. Letting people know that you have a disability and that you are open to discussing your experience is often far more productive. Being open to a discussion and being non-judgmental allows people who either don't have a disability or people who are new to their disabilities a safe space to ask questions and learn from your experiences.
- Disability is hard, especially because of stigmatization, don't go alone. Reach out to others in ways that help you and the library. Form a group that takes creative breaks together for fifteen minutes of coloring and chit chat or get together for coffee after work or something else. Informal discussions and fun activities can bring people together and create a supportive environment.
- When advocating for changes in the library, especially where patrons might be involved, ask them for help. The single largest advantage for advocating for change is the power of "me too" said in many voices and from many perspectives. Conduct a listening group and invite patrons to come. Ask them to tell you about the positive and negative things that they experience in the library. Then just listen to them. Do not defend the library or educate, just listen. Even if the problem that they are talking about already has a solution, the fact that they see it as a problem is a clear indication that your solution isn't working and needs to be re-evaluated.

Tips on the Accommodation Process for Employers

If you are a member of management, the following tips will help the accommodation process go much more smoothly.

- Educate yourself. As a manager, you will have received some kind of training, usually from human resources, on what the law entails in regards to accommodations for people with disabilities as well as what the procedures are in your place of work. Going a step further and really understanding the process as well as the some of the different types of accommodations available will go a long way in smoothing out the process when an employee does ask for an accommodation. The Job Accommodation Network, https://askjan.org/ is an excellent resource maintained by the US Department of Labor and is regularly used in the accommodation process.
- Create an inclusive and safe environment. Be open to having discussions about potentially sensitive topics with your employees. Creating an inclusive environment means, in part, listening to your employees concerns, being flexible with solutions, and having an open door and transparency policies. When there is a disconnect between what employees think is going on and what managers know is going on, the conditions are ripe for not only a class division but also class warfare in the library which will help and serve no one, least of all the patrons.
- Trust that your employee is telling you the truth. Also realize that they might not have to disclose the actual disability to you, only that they need an accommodation. This will vary strongly on how big your organization is and what policies are in place. You must respect the person's right to privacy and not disclose their disability or accommodation to anyone else outside of human resources. For example, after an accommodation has been granted, sending out an email to the department saying that "because of the person's issues around noise or light or insert a vague reason here, they are getting XYZ accommodation" is actually against the law. In general, for a person to disclose that they have a disability to their employer, that person's work situation has typically degraded to the point where they can't make do on their own anymore and must get an accommodation. The accommodation process is not an easy one and includes needing to have an official diagnosis, a note from the medical professional involved in the care of the disability, and disclosing the disability to multiple people in an effort to have a chance at getting an accommodation. The process alone is incredibly stress-inducing and not being believed by one's manager makes it more difficult.
- Be flexible. The employee who is asking for an accommodation knows what they need. The accommodation process is an iterative one that might mean trying several different types of accommodations out before settling on an accommodation or a series of accommodations that will help the employee with a disability. What you think they need and what they know they need are two different things. In short, the employee has the disability and knows what works best for them. The more closely the accommodation matches the employee's actual need, the more likely they are to stay, be more efficient, and be a happier employee.
- Trust that your employee knows what they need. As a manager, you might not feel comfortable with the idea of your employee working in a different part of the building as part of their accommodation or perhaps you don't believe that they are doing work at home when they say they are working from home. Trust

your employee to do their job without your direct supervision 100 percent of the time. Set up check-in meetings or emails if that will help alleviate your concern, but ultimately, by trusting your employee to use their accommodation responsibly you are signaling that the employee is valued. Not trusting the employee, signals that they aren't valued and will increase the chances that the employee is not only dissatisfied with their work but will leave when an opportunity presents itself.

Conclusion

The accommodation process, while on paper seems to be logical and pretty straight-forward, instead takes on a life of its own depending on a wide range of factors including the level of inclusivity and accessibility in the organization, attitudes of management, and the employee's own level of advocacy. Employees with disabilities are of great benefit to library organizations when they are accommodated properly. With the proper accommodations, an employee with a disability is far more likely to do better work, stay in the job, and work to improve their processes than an employee with a disability whose accommodation has been denied or an employee who is afraid to ask for an accommodation.

WORKS CITED

Balser, Deborah B., and Michael M. Harris. 2008. "Factors Affecting Employee Satisfaction with Disability Accommodation: A Field Study." *Employment Responsibilities and Rights Journal*, 20: 13–28.

Berger, Ronald J. 2013. *Introducing Disability Studies*. Boulder: Lynne Rienner Publishers.

Coleman, Lerita M. 2006. "Stigma: An Enigma Demystified." In *The Disability Studies Reader*, 2nd ed., edited by Lennard J. Davis, 141–152. New York: Routledge.

Nichols, Darlene, and Anna Ercoli Schnitzer. 2015. "Developing Inclusive Research Libraries for Patrons and Staff of All Abilities." Research Library Issues, 286: 18–26.

Strub, Maurini R., and Louann Stewart. 2010. "Case Study: Shelving and the Autistic Employee." Journal of Access Services, 7: 262–268.

Stuart, Heather, Julio Arboleda-Florez, and Norman Sartorious. 2012. *Paradigms Lost: Fighting Stigma and the Lessons Learned*. Oxford: Oxford University Press.

Von Schrader, Sarah, Valerie Malzer, and Susanne Bruyere. 2014. "Perspectives on Disability Disclosure: The Importance of Employer Practices and Workplace Climate." *Employment Rights and Responsibilities Journal*, 26: 237–255.

Williams-Whitt, Kelly. 2007. "Impediments to Disability Accommodation." *Industrial Relations*, 62: 405–430.

Healing Justice

An Approach of Caring for Intersectional LIS Professionals

Melissa Villa-Nicholas, Tonyia J. Tidline *and* Tracy S. Drake

"To reclaim our bodies and our health, is a form of resistance, a form of resilience."—Patrisse Cullors, 2015

Introduction

Underrepresented information professionals in Library and Information Sciences (LIS) often find themselves overwhelmed by juggling the needs of their patron communities and the impact of a non-diverse workplace. While the profession is currently focusing heavily on strengthening diversity and discussing issues of social justice (Roberts and Noble 2016), underrepresented LIS professionals are frequently a singular voice around diversity and social justice in the workplace, specifically those from minority communities. Addressing and transforming racial trauma through healing and self-care is essential to empowering librarians of color while confronting the continuous emotional, mental, and physical labor of existence in predominantly white spaces. Libraries can take a page from social justice groups of color by offering programming, social groups, and expanded services to promote and connect patrons to self-care, healing justice, and transformative healing practices that are both low cost and accessible.

This essay proposes that the Black Lives Matter practice of "healing justice" can be applied to encourage a practice of self-care for people of color in LIS as individuals and in community. In order to do this librarians of color must consider how these principles relate to their own individual and collaborative practice of self-care and may use healing justice concepts for this purpose. While in school, mentoring relationships may set the tone for such responsiveness and form a foundation for developing face-to-face or digital exchanges useful to support care of self and, by extension, our patrons.

The authors, as a collective, consider the work of healing justice and self-care communities from an auto-ethnographic lens. Melissa Villa-Nicholas is a Latinx woman teaching at a Library and Information Studies program; Tonyia Tidline is a Black woman who teaches library and information professionals about the intersections of social justice and librarianship; Tracy Drake is a Black woman archivist working in a public institution. The act of individual and communal self-care in this sense is practiced by a larger group of participants—those who are also professionals in the LIS field, some of whom are involved in Black Lives Matter and approach the profession from an anti-racist perspective. This work reflects our personal experience as information professionals who are educators and activists, as participants in healing communities, and as women of color navigating each of these spaces. As persons concerned with serving patrons, who, like ourselves are from of underrepresented communities the following embraces the sentiment: "before you assist others, put your oxygen mask on first."

In this essay, we will explore some of the recent trends and conversations about healing trauma and social justice self-care in relationship to librarians, and consider their application in the library setting.

Literature Review

Recent calls for intersectional approaches to LIS have motivated new formations of librarianship and information professionals. Sarah Roberts and Safiya Noble call for LIS to lead the professions with a social justice approach, acknowledging that race, gender, sexuality, and class are all integral to everyday work in LIS (Roberts and Noble 2016). Todd Honma originally named LIS as a field that is based on and built around race, racism, gender constructions, and class formation (2005); advocating that LIS professionals make race and racism especially visible in librarianship. There is an ever-growing movement in the field to bring these issues to the forefront, with such active groups as #critlib, the online movement of library workers "dedicated to bringing social justice principles into our work in libraries" through Twitter, and at conferences (about/join the discussion, critlib.org). Such discussions reveal a need for conversations about self-care for people of color and underrepresented people within LIS. We want to merge the current popular conversation of self-care with the calls of social justice and intersectionality to LIS, in order to create a stronger field that prioritizes the wellbeing of LIS professionals and their patrons. For example, scholar and transgender activist Dean Spade (2009) argues for the 'trickle-up social justice' approach that prioritizes the most underrepresented group, noting that solving problems from the bottom up will benefit everyone. We believe such aspects of healing justice thinking are applicable to librarianship and information service spaces and suggest LIS might begin to implement a trickle-up social justice outcome that will benefit all LIS educators, professionals, and patrons.

Healing Justice in LIS

We approach healing justice from both personal and communal perspectives. We emphasize care for individuals and groups within underrepresented communities that use these methods to build safe spaces of care that will also benefit LIS. The Black Lives Matter movement is key for understanding this kind of transformative effort.

Black Lives Matter (BLM)

The Black Lives Matter movement (BLM) began in the summer of 2013 after the acquittal of George Zimmerman for the murder of 17-year-old Trayvon Martin. According to Alicia Garza, co-creator of Black Lives Matter with Patrisse Cullors and Opal Tometi, it is a call to action for black people. The BLM movement is not only centered upon the idea of just activism, protest, and organizing; it has fundamentally altered the ways in which we as a community approach and think about the topic of self-care and healing justice both on the individual level and in our larger communities (Lebron, 2017).

BLM has applied "healing justice" to the Black activist movement as a way to "holistically respond to and intervene on generational trauma and violence, and to bring collective practices that can impact and transform consequences of oppression on our bodies, hearts and minds" (Hemphill, 2017). BLM has a branch of their work specifically directed towards healing and trauma. Healing justice is an approach of care that has been designed to prioritize black life. We want to be clear that our application of healing justice is an advocacy of care for all people of color in LIS, but we still centralize black lives as a movement critical to the success of LIS. Healing justice has a goal of rejuvenating the practitioner in order to continue making changes in the world towards social justice.

Personal Self-Care

The public conversation around self-care and healing justice work has recently been amplified by the use of social media. However, people of color have discussed self-care since the second wave of Feminist and Civil Rights movements. LIS students and practitioners can draw on the multitude of self-care studies and tips that are generated by women of color, especially relevant to the alarming trend of normalization of racism in the United States. We encourage self-care within our own practice as LIS professionals and within our own communities of color.

People of color have historic precedents in encouraging self-care as a radical act. Activists of color in the 1960s began to see the need for self-care, especially for people who worked in trauma-based professions and for those who worked vigorously to dismantle intersectional hierarchies such as race, gender, class, and sexuality (Harris 2017). Notably, The Black Panther Party stressed heavily the health and wellness of their members. Self-care has been encouraged since the 1960s in response to collective trauma and for people who work in trauma-based labor, both of which are relevant to library professions.

Author and children's librarian Audre Lorde noted that "Caring for myself is not self-indulgence, it is self-preservation, and that is an act of political warfare" (Mirk 2016). These early feminists of color viewed care for the mind, body, and soul as a radical act that resisted United States structures of discrimination. Chicanx activist Gloria Anzaldúa discussed care for the psyche as crucial to shifting social power structures towards equality, "The struggle is inner: Chicano, indio, American Indian, mojado, mexicano, immigrant Latino, Anglo in power, working class Anglo, Black, Asian—our psyches resemble the border towns and are populated by the same people. The struggle has always been inner, and is played out in outer terrains" (Anzaldúa, 1987 87).

The connection between self-care and social change has become more prevalent in recent social justice movements. Among library professionals, self-care has become an increasingly common topic in more popular media formats, such as blogs from librarians (Accardi 2016) and library professional organizations (ALSC blog 2016). Given the historical precedents of self-care as a radical act for women of color, pushed forward by such activist scholars as Lorde and Anzaldúa, we view self-care as paramount due to the increasingly stressful economic conditions, further tensions among race, gender, and sexuality in America's mainstream politics and social discourse, the need and use of the library for trauma-based work, and the ongoing underrepresentation of people of color in the LIS workforce.

Lisa Vallejos gives the following self-care tips, especially relevant to her work as a Professor in the university:

- saying "no" to commitment loads, especially to extra-emotional labor usually given to people of color in the workplace;
- spending time in safe environments such as trusted community spaces;
- taking action through support groups, workshops, or art that is uplifting;
- creating strong boundaries;
- getting support from friends and community in basic healing needs;
- resting from social activism;
- taking time to play [Vallejos 2017].

We also encourage practices of mindfulness such as breathing and spending time in natural settings, as a way to reset from an overwhelmingly taxing workplace. Finally, we encourage play, joy, and laughter as means of self-care for librarians of color. Isa Noyola, director of programs for Transgender Law Center, describes her form of self-care as dancing, music, and connection with others (Pozner 2016).

Incorporating the above personal self-care methods will benefit people of color, in LIS and in the community, from teaching to practice. In our own circle of LIS professionals, using our online W(h)ine time solely for laughter and joy acts as a remedy for our labor, mostly white LIS spaces that may be dismissive of our identities.

Self-Care, from Classroom to Practice

With its contemporary association with the Black Lives Matter movement, healing justice "encompasses an evolving political framework shaped by economic, racial, and disability justice … [and] seeks to transform, intervene and respond to generational trauma and violence in [socio-political] movements, communities and lives…. Healing Justice recognizes the role of collective trauma (such as the shared experience of slavery or genocide or ableism) and historical trauma (the holding and passing down of collective trauma from one generation to the next) causing or influencing community survival practices and endemic community health issues, and seeks to lift up these experiences for the possibility of resilience and transformation. Healing Justice also recognizes the role of individual and relational trauma and its impact on collective process (Healing Justice Practice Spaces: A How-To Guide 2014).

Healing justice work necessitates intervention and building relationships within and beyond community, and requires that "we begin to value care, emotional labor and resilience, not as add-ons but as central components of sustainability that restore us to life" (Hemphill 2017).

Wharton describes emotional labor as a phenomenon that reverberates throughout the work life of those in jobs requiring "interaction with others." In vocations with a "client base," like librarianship, professionals are ideally socialized with regard to the kind of emotive and impression management abilities required to preserve self and to provide service. Moreover, emotional labor "may involve enhancing, faking, or suppressing emotions to modify the emotional expression" (Grandey 2000, 95), which causes stress and burnout (99). The literature also suggests that certain types of interactive work can produce emotive dissonance and self-alienation. In other words, there is an expenditure of energy in attempting to do healing work in privileged environments demanding intervention and transformation (Hemphill 2017).

As a consequence, those who engage in healing justice work maintain a vision and plan for self-sustenance and renewal –whether this be deemed "self-" or "self-determined" care (Padamsee 2012). In this section, we consider mentorship and mindfulness as potential points on a continuum of personal care for librarians—particularly librarians of color—who choose to apply our skillset in healing justice efforts. This discussion is fluid and considers the librarian of color as both student and professional.

It is clear that mentoring is believed to have a positive benefit for students of color (Lopez 2014). Although there is no robust set of findings on specifically how this can happen, suggestions exist for developing mentoring relationships between students and faculty (whether they are faculty of color or not); between students and professionals; and in peer-to-peer arrangements. It is useful to look at mentoring in a field frequently compared to LIS, which is nursing (Douglas and Gadsby 2017), for some useful recommendations. Presumably, information professionals may benefit from the same characteristics found by nurses as indicative of effective mentorship. To produce the sense of self-efficacy required for healing justice work, students transitioning to professional status benefit from mentors who demonstrate warmth, encouragement, a willingness to listen, enthusiasm for the profession, and clarity of expectations regarding the mentor relationship (Van Dyke 2016). As recommended by those who understand emotional labor, a mentor can demonstrate and encourage a student-to-professional mentee to accept the need for self-care as a way to reinforce a sense of personal strength. Whether by means of formal mentoring programs or less formal association (López 2014), the characteristics of healthy mentoring relationships are believed to provide a model of cooperation that can be seen as essential for healing justice work.

Cooperation is stressed as a critical factor in healing justice efforts; in popular culture a debate exists about emphasis on self-care as a potential distraction from the kind of collaborative energy that the transformative effort of healing justice requires. This belief is based on noting the community-based tradition associated with healing justice (Healing Justice Practice Spaces: A How-To Guide 2014; Hemphill 2017; Padamsee 2012). However, despite some misgivings about placing an emphasis on "self" with regard to healing justice, it is undeniable that it is the work of the individual that fuels collective and collaborative ends. For this reason, an individual approach to self-care may be considered alongside a relational activity like mentoring as a way to bolster the resolve of librarians who want to be involved with healing justice. Moreover, an argument can be made for self-focus as a radical act for women of color.

The profession has started to investigate measures for self-care that librarians of color should embrace. In a recent *American Libraries* article, Ruhlmann defines and contextualizes mindfulness as "'moment-to-moment awareness of one's experience without judgment'" (2017). Mindfulness practitioners use meditation and breathing exercises to pay attention to the present moment, without letting distractions, worries, and opinions creep in. The idea is that by learning "to neither dwell on the past nor fret about the future, your mind can find peace" (Ruhlmann 2017). There has been a recent appreciation for using mindfulness techniques so that "we can serve students, faculty and other library constituencies with full focus and engagement, an open and accepting mind, and with energy and intention focused on a positive outcome" (Mastel and Innes 2013, 2). As both a practice and a frame of mind, mindfulness calls for a present moment focus and a sensibility that are related to personal and professional effectiveness. While this practice is typically associated with the process of meditation and attention to breathing, its benefits outstrip its seeming simplicity; the concept is presented here as an ingredient for successfully blending librarianship with healing justice.

In addition to the practice of meditation by focusing on the breath, mindfulness techniques include remaining in the present and accepting whatever "is" in that moment. Other examples include activities like slowly, deliberately and attentively eating a raisin or using a body scan technique that begins with grounding the feet, noticing accompanying sensations and systematically mentally moving up the body and acknowledging one's physical experience. Prayer is also noted as a longstanding practice that functions as a mindfulness technique. For all of the techniques to work it is essential to detach from their outcome, not to wonder whether or how they work. These techniques can be undertaken individually or communally.

People of Color Using Digital Spaces as Healing Communities

Much has been written about self-care practices that occur in physical spaces. However, we propose that self- care and healing justice can also occur in digital spaces. Within our larger networks, information professionals can utilize digital tools to create self-care communities. The concept of self-care communities refers to larger networks of people of color with common interests, who share stories of tragedy, trauma, and micro-aggressions. These spaces also allow information professionals to celebrate, love, and support each other. Information professionals can learn from the work being done to create healing justice circles by activists in the BLM movement and apply it to digital spaces. BLM activist Cherrell Brown refers to these spaces as "a learning space, a politicizing space, a radicalizing space" (Democracy Now, 2015). In these spaces people are allowed to be political, spiritual, radical, and uniquely themselves, unbounded by the constraints of the profession. The creation of such spaces becomes increasingly important as we consider not only the trauma and lived experiences of the people we serve but also our personal experiences in the profession as it relates to the lack of diversity in the field, feeling overwhelmed by the demands of the profession, and the stress related to the current cultural climate in the United States. Participation in these digital self-care communities happens for various reasons; each person can utilize the group for reasons specific to their concerns and still have tangible takeaways.

Carving Out Space Through the Use of Digital Tools

In our own experience there is no limit to the number of groups you can belong to or the technology that is being used to create self-care communities; only that you are familiar with the technology or have a desire to learn the technology. The impetus for the creation of digital self-care communities has plenty to do with the fact that informational professionals already exist in these spaces and are familiar with the technology; it is perhaps organically happening. Digital self-care communities can take place utilizing digital tools such as Skype, Twitter, Facebook, and various messaging apps. The ability to collectively create an outlet for people of color in marginalized fields allows for different groups to serve as different voices. By this we mean that intersectionality and diversity of concentrations in the information field allow individuals to have several identities.

Examples of Self-Care Communities

As a group, the authors participate in a digital self-care community via Skype that we have coined Online W(h)ine time. Online W(h)ine time occurs once a month, lasts one hour or longer, and includes a circle of current library and information professionals from various career paths. In this digital self-care community each person has the opportunity to speak freely about challenges, obstacles, and upcoming projects. Most importantly this space is one of love and support. Each individual is allowed time to share with the group and speak without interruption on any topic they choose; others are encouraged to respond as they see fit. Online W(h)ine time therefore becomes a space of healing, rejuvenation, and renewal. This is significant because it provides information professionals with an outlet for concerns and frustrations and prepares them to fully engage the larger communities in which they live and work.

Another example of digital self-care communities is the Black Joy Project. The Black Joy Project started on Instagram when Kleaver Cruz, a 27-year-old writer and organizer from New York, committed himself to saturate social media with positive images of black people. According to Cruz, personal concerns and movement work to affirm black lives had impacted him both emotionally and physically. Cruz began his crusade with an image of his mom smiling in front of her favorite piece of artwork and captioned the picture #BlackJoy or #BlackJoyProject. Cruz has continued his crusade and has asked others to join him in recognizing the pain of being a part of a marginalized group but also taking the time to celebrate and experience joy (Gebreyes 2016). The Black Joy Project demonstrates that experiencing joy as community is just as important as sharing pain. As it relates to information professionals of color, this can be achieved through celebrating positive interactions with patrons, flawless reference interviews, new community partnerships and successful programming.

Conclusion

As a group of LIS professionals, we want to encourage the healing justice approach that includes teaching self-care in the classroom, promoting self-care practices for librarians of color, and using digital tools to bring together people of color. Bringing together healing justice practices for individuals and communities of people of color in LIS will advocate for the well-being of library workers and LIS professionals, and will in turn provide further supportive services to library patrons. We encourage applying healing justice practices for students of color in LIS, librarians of color, LIS professionals of color, and LIS educators.

WORKS CITED

"About/Join the Discussion." Critlib: Critical Librarianship, in Real Life & on the Twitters. http://critlib.org/about/.

Accardi, Maria. 2016. "Librarian Burnout." *Librarian Burnout.* https://librarianburnout.com/about-maria/.

Ahmed, Sara. 2012. *On Being Included: Racism and Diversity in Institutional Life.* Durham, NC: Duke University Press.

ALSC Blog. 2016. Self-care Isn't Selfish. Accessed at http://www.alsc.ala.org/blog/2016/02/self-care-isnt-selfish/.

Anzaldúa, Gloria. 1987. *Borderlands, La Frontera: The New Mestiza.* San Francisco, CA: Aunt Lute Books.

Crenshaw, Kimberlé Williams, Priscilla Ocen, and Jyoti Nanda. 2015. *Black Girls Matter: Pushed Out, Over-policed, and Underprotected.* New York: African American Policy Forum and Center for Intersectionality and Social Policy Studies. Accessed March 20, 2017. http://www.atlanticphilanthropies.org/app/uploads/2015/09/BlackGirlsMatter_Report.pdf.

Democracy Now. 2015. "'Collective Healing' at National Black Lives Matter Convergence Ends with Police Pepper-Spraying Teen." YouTube video, 4:13. Posted by Democracy Now, July 27th, 2015. https://www.youtube.com/watch?v=_YPZpZdNBf8.

Douglas, Veronica Arellano, and Joanna Gadsby. 2017. "Gendered Labor and Library Instruction Coordinators." *In at the Helm: Leading Transformation.* Baltimore, Maryland: ACRL. http://www.ala.org/acrl/sites/ala.org.acrl/files/content/conferences/confsandpreconfs/2017/GenderedLaborandLibraryInstructionCo-ordinators.pdf.

Flanders, Laura. 2012. "Dangerous Rush to Legislate on Surveillance and Mental Health." *The Nation*, December 28. https://www.thenation.com/article/dangerous-rush-legislate-surveillance-and-mental-health-dean-spade-video/.

Gebreyes, Rahel. 2016. "This Project Powerfully Captures the Wonders of Black Joy: The Black Joy Project Is Elevating Depictions of Happiness, One Picture at a Time." *Huffington Post*, May 23.

Grandey, Alicia. 2000. "Emotional Regulation in the Workplace: A New Way to Conceptualize Emotional Labor." *Journal of Occupational Health Psychology* 5 (1): 95.

Green, Adrienne. 2016. "The Cost of Balancing Academia and Racism." *The Atlantic.* Last modified Jan 21, 2016. https://www.theatlantic.com/education/archive/2016/01/balancing-academia-racism/424887/.

Harris, Aisha. 2017. "A History of Self-Care." *Slate*, April 5. http://www.slate.com/articles/arts/culturebox/2017/04/the_history_of_self_care.html.

"Healing Justice Practice Spaces: A How-To Guide." 2014. https://justhealing.files.wordpress.com/2012/04/healing-justice-practice-spaces-a-how-to-guide-with-links.pdf. Accessed August 27, 2017.

Hemphill, Prentis. 2017. "Healing Justice Is How We Can Sustain Black Lives." *Huffington Post*, February 7. http://www.huffingtonpost.com/entry/healing-justice_us_5899e8ade4b0c1284f282ffe.

Lebron, Christopher J. 2017. *The Making of Black Lives Matter: A Brief History of an Idea.* New York: Oxford University Press.

López, Marissa. 2014. "On Mentoring Graduate Students of Color." *Race and Ethnicity.* https://clpc.mla.hcom-mons.org/on-mentoring-first-generation-and-graduate-students-of-color/. Accessed August 27, 2017.

Mastel, Kristen, and Genevieve Innes. 2013. "Insights and Practical Tips on Practicing Mindful Librarianship to Manage Stress." *LIBRES: Library and Information Science Research Electronic Journal* 23.1 (2013): 1.

Mirk, Sarah. 2016. "Audre Lorde Thought of Self-Care as an 'Act of Political Warfare.'" *Bitch Media.* https://www.bitchmedia.org/article/audre-lorde-thought-self-care-act-political-warfare.

Padamsee, Yashna Maya. 2012. "A Round-up and Re-frame of the Community Care Conversation." http://www.organizingupgrade.com/index.php/modules-menu/community-care/item/755-a-round-up-and-re-frame-of-the-community-care-conversation. Accessed August 27, 2017.

Padamsee, Yashna Maya. 2016. "Communities of Care, Organizations for Liberation." https://justhealing.files.wordpress.com/2012/05/communities-of-care-organizations-for-liberation.pdf. Accessed August 27, 2017.

Page, Cara, and Susan Raffo. 2017. "Healing Justice at the US Social Forum: A Report from Atlanta, Detroit & Beyond." Accessed February 20. https://www.scribd.com/document/147620375/Healing-Justice-at-the-US-Social-Forum-1.

Pozner, Jennifer. September 21, 2016. "Self Care in the Multiracial Movement for Black Lives." *Colorlines.* https://www.colorlines.com/articles/self-care-multiracial-movement-black-lives.

Roberts, Sarah, and Safiya Noble. 2016. "Empowered to Name, Inspired to Act: Social Responsibility and Diversity as Calls to Action in the LIS Context." *Library Trends* 64(3).

Ruhlmann, Ellyn. 2017. "Mindful Librarianship: Awareness of Each Moment Helps Librarians Stay Serene Under Stress." *American Libraries* 48 (6): 44–47.

Vallejos, Lisa. 2017. "Self-Care for Women of Color Experiencing Emotional Battle Fatigue." *Elephant Journal.* April 6. https://www.elephantjournal.com/2017/04/self-care-for-women-of-color-experiencing-emo tional-battle-fatigue/.

Van Dyke, Maggie. 2016. "Mentoring the Next Generation of Minority Nurses." *Minority Nurse Magazine.*

Encouraging Social Justice Professional Development

Laura Francabandera

Introduction

In *Pride and Prejudice*, Jane Austen (1918) wrote that "a man in possession of a good fortune must be in want of a wife." The meaning of this rapier-sharp witticism, she then expounds, is that regardless of whether or not the man actually desires a wife, he is often stuck within the societal structures in place at the time, simply by dint of his privilege. He is wealthy and therefore he has a duty to society to marry.

While not an exact correlation with social justice, the essence of the quote remains relatively true. People of privilege in society have a duty toward social justice, whether they want to or not. The very existence of their privilege (be it a steady job, racial or ethnic privilege, educational privilege, etc.) puts them in a place of power over others and they have a civic duty to exercise that power in a culturally and globally appropriate manner.

If librarians have power, those directing the professional training of librarians hold even more: both what you teach librarians and what you do not teach them are political and cultural statements. If a library spends its professional budget only on safe topics (communication, customer service, management exercises, etc.), that tells its library staff that only safe topics matter. If the library spends both time and budget on topics that are unconventional within the library sphere, that builds innovation and tells librarians that the library is a safe space for out of the box thinking.

What This Essay Will Cover

This essay is intended to serve as a roadmap to instituting social justice training alongside your regular library staff development training. It recognizes that the best way to encourage globally-minded and culturally appropriate staff is to start from the top and let the corporate culture trickle down within the library.

The first section of the essay will cover items that you must know before you start any social justice training with your library staff. These items include:

- how to recognize your own biases, privilege, and assumptions
- how to encourage an atmosphere of trust and openness for the training
- how to encourage staff to recognize their own biases.

These items must be part of any planning before you institute social justice training, or you may encounter resistance and even anger amongst your staff. Trust in the process and trust in each other is crucial to any successful social justice training exercise.

The second section will tell you what to expect from your library staff and introduce coping mechanisms to deal with the emotions that will result. When people encounter ideas and values that do not align with their own, they may get defensive and lash out. This section gives you a toolbox of methods to draw from for any situation that may arise in reaction to social justice training. This section also gives recommendations on how to roll out the training in order to minimize any staff backlash.

The third and final section of the essay gives you practical methods and activities that you can use to mix social justice training with your regular library staff development training. The methods include valid counseling methods, such as reflective practice and teaching the Person-Centered Approach, as well as activities like a privilege walk, ten-minute talks, and partnerships.

Unraveling the Threads of Bias

The moment you start down the path of even thinking about social justice training, it is vital that you begin with your own viewpoints and biases. The expectations of the teacher reverberate throughout the learning path, so it is important that you sit down early in the planning process and go through the same activities and exercises that you would like you staff to go through.

What we call knowledge is really just a web of intertwining experience and context (Lankes 2011), so what you believe about social justice impacts what you will teach your staff. It is vital, therefore, to actually sit down and reflect on the following items:

- *Motive.* Why are you determined to teach your staff about social justice? Is it just to tick a box on your program evaluation list? Are you actually concerned about marginalized people or is it just something you think you should do? Do you want to dismantle systems of oppression within society?
- *Expectations.* What do you expect to happen at the end of the training? Do you expect your staff to jump into activism head first? Do you expect nothing to change at all? As a leader, it is your responsibility to know your staff, how they might react, and to plan accordingly.
- *Personal Biases.* What do you personally think about some of the particular issues involved in social justice activism? What is your opinion on immigration, the school-to-prison pipeline, or First Nations people fighting the oil drillers? Why do you hold these beliefs?

Your answers to any of those questions should be written down and then reflected upon because they are a result of your personal experiences and circumstances of birth. As a part of your personal and staff reflections, it is vital to start trying to understand your biases and their origins.

Implicit Bias

Implicit bias is a subconscious mental structure about a particular group (ethnic, racial, or even based upon appearance) that you are not even aware exists (Ohio State University 2015). Implicit biases might even go against your professed opinions but still influence your actions. Take, for example, an implicit bias against dirty, impoverished people. While you likely don't go around thinking or proclaiming that you don't like poor people, the next time you pass a homeless person you might be more likely to cross the street to avoid them.

Your implicit bias gave rise to your bodily functions of fear or discomfort, which then prompted your action. Implicit biases can be slowly unlearned, but they are difficult to identify because they are ingrained in our subconscious.

Explicit Bias

Explicit biases live in our conscious thought and are in-group/outgroup borders that we've drawn up in response to some fear or stimuli (Department of Justice n.d.). If someone is worried about economic security, their explicit biases form patterns of thought and action. The perceived fear is then translated directly onto a specific group of people, like immigrants or welfare recipients. Explicit biases are regulated and give direct rise to conscious action, like discrimination, violence, or hate-speech.

When planning any sort of social justice training, it is important to address both implicit and explicit bias and to have participants reflect on how both forms of bias affect their actions. Before you include items on your agenda, it is important for you, as the facilitator, to deeply understand how your implicit and explicit biases affect your own actions as well.

What to Expect When You're Expecting

If you are planning to implement a social justice training program, it is important to understand your expectations of library staff potential reactions to the training. Because biases and values are often subconscious and motivated by fear, the instinctive reaction tends to be one of fight-or-flight. Your staff may exhibit a range of emotions, both positive and negative.

Both implicit and explicit biases form the foundation for one's belief system. Being told that she is to have "social justice" training, a staff member may often feel like her very belief system is being attacked. The fight-or-flight system often makes people fall back on reactions to defend their own belief system:

- Denial: "We don't have any problems or we don't need that kind of training."
- Avoidance: "This really isn't relevant to the library work. We don't have time for this."
- Anger: "So you're saying that you think I'm racist? I'm really offended!"
- Humor: "You know what they say, those who can't do, teach."
- Fear: "I'm the only gay person on staff, they'll all think it's about me."

Do not expect all library staff to be as excited about social justice or activism training as you might be. Sure, an occasional few staff members may care quite a bit about social justice issues, but once you place it in an official training space with their colleagues, it becomes a different situation. Suddenly, it's not just a personal decision for someone to be okay with social justice, but they're being forced to reconcile with it publicly, in front of their coworkers and colleagues whom they respect. The workplace is often fraught with competition and internal politics; adding personal beliefs to it can be explosive without proper planning.

To avoid emotional fallout, it is important that you consider hiring an outside facilitator or, at the very least, underscore the importance of trust within the trainings. It can be helpful to allow the staff themselves to come up with their own code of conduct for the trainings. They may suggest trust issues like the following:

- Trust that what you say won't be held against you in the future.
- Trust that no one will take it personally.
- Trust that no one will repeat what you say.
- Trust that everyone is trying their best.
- Trust that overcoming bias is not an easy process.

Trust is often the biggest hindrance to teambuilding and a sense of community within the workplace. Once trust is a part of your social justice training, however, it will eventually become a regular part of your workplace culture as well.

Activities and Methods for Social Justice Training

This section will give you methods and activities that promote social justice and are easily configurable based on what works best with your staff. From reflective practice to the Person-Centered Approach, methodological paths take different form than one-off activities like library displays or topical content curation. Both methodological approaches and surface activities are complementary and help scaffold learning.

Social Justice Methodologies

There are two methods that are often used in the health sciences and counseling world because they help people work through thoughts and feelings on their own. The counselor (or library trainer) is simply just a facilitator and makes no expectation of a particular end achievement. The achievement is in the process.

Reflective Practice

The first method is to institute reflective practice in your regular staff development training sessions. Reflective practice is the process of writing down an experience as you remember it, then going over and critically re-reading what you wrote. You then ask yourself questions about the experience, identify items that you learned, and think about what you would do differently next time. None of this needs to be public, but it is important to share some of the learning items with the team. Initially because if it helped you, it likely will help someone else, but also because teaching one's peers cements the learning in the one doing the teaching.

Reflective Practice Example

In the context of social justice, reflective practice could look something like this:

- Writing Prompt: Write about an experience you had in the past month that made you uncomfortable. Be sure to write about the context of the situation as well as your actions.
- Reflection Prompt: Go through and read what you wrote about your experience. Ask yourself questions as you read through it. Ask yourself questions like: Why did that make me feel uncomfortable? Was I really uncomfortable, or was there another emotion behind it, like fear or anger? Is there any place in my past or upbringing that may have encouraged behavior like this? How would someone else react in that situation?
- Synthesis Prompt: What does this tell me about my own biases? How might I overcome these biases? Are there any other places in my life where these biases show?
- Learning Prompt: How would I react differently next time in this situation? How will what I've learned here help me in my day-to-day work?

Have the participants write in a journal or something private and share some of their learning takeaways with small groups. They can share as much as they are comfortable sharing. Repeat weekly or monthly as a part of regular practice.

The Person-Centered Approach

Based off the psychologist Carl Rogers' theories and works, the Person-Centered Approach is a method of talk therapy that allows people to propose their own solutions. It hinges on the belief that people truly want what is in their own best interests and the most successful therapy results are the ones that the participant decided on their own. This approach to interaction leaves the facilitator (the therapist or the professional training leader) in mostly an active listening role. The facilitator needs to follow a set of behavioral rules to enable the participant to fully be in charge of their own therapy. The counselor needs to exhibit:

- *Non-directivity*. Being non-directive means that you are not in charge of where the session goes. You do not have an agenda or ask leading questions, but rather let the participant direct the conversation.
- *Empathy*. Different from dispassionate sympathy or pity, empathy is the ability to put yourself into someone else's shoes to experience what a circumstance might be like for them.
- *Congruence*. When all things work together for the same end, this means that your verbal and non-verbal communication need to be the same. You can't

pretend to want the best for someone if you don't actually believe it because it will come across in your body language or non-verbal cues.
- *Unconditional positive regard.* This is believing in someone's basic worth as a human being, regardless of their life choices or decisions. It can be difficult to believe in someone's worth if you disagree with their choices, but it is integral for any personal change.

The Person-Centered Approach is beneficial as a teaching methodology when you plan your social justice trainings, but it is also worth teaching in and of itself. If you teach your library staff to interact with people believing that they are people of worth who deserve the best, that is already a big step down the social justice road.

Social Justice Activities

Different from methodologies, activities give you concrete actions to put what you've learned into practice. If you've had your staff go through some reflective exercises and trainings, it is important to relate that learning to real-world scenarios. These activities can be stand-alone ones or used in conjunction with the methodologies to support learning.

- *Privilege Walk.* Have all people line up in the middle of a room and have them take a step forward or back depending on their answers to questions about privilege. Questions range in social justice areas from "Take a step forward if you've never had your electricity cut off for non-payment" to "Take a step backward if your parents did not grow up in the US." The result will usually be a generalization of how society privileges some people over others, typically with American males at the very front and women of color and disabled people nearer the back.
- *Crossing the Line.* As a part of trust exercises, this activity uses the similar questions as the privilege walk but is more focused on individualizing and humanizing stereotypes than the end result. Each item or question that you read out will result in people who feel it applies to them taking a step forward in silence. They don't do anything, but it is important to reflect on who is stepping forward and why they might feel it applies to them. They step back into line and you ask a new question, resulting in new or some of the same people stepping forward. The questions again range the gamut of social justice topics, from "Who has been subject to violence or hate speech because of your race, gender, or sexual orientation" to "Step forward if you've ever felt that you're not worthy of something." After the activity, use reflective practice so the participants can reflect on how it felt for them to recognize their own biases as well as how it felt for them to acknowledge their discrimination.
- *Peer-Teaching.* Educators know that for someone to really internalize something, the best method is to have them teach someone else. Peer-teaching can be as formal or informal as you'd like, from weekly ten-minute talks on social justice issues to informal discussions over coffee. Have your library staff teach others about a social justice topic that interests them.
- *Community Partnerships.* Social justice is never an isolated activity, but instead

requires ties to the community to be successful. As part of your social justice training, you could invite partners from the community to give talks to your library staff—from domestic violence shelters to your local LGBTQ youth advocacy group. The best way to hammer home the importance of social justice is to individualize the stereotypes and provide local ties.

Conclusion

When you want to introduce social justice training for your library staff, it is important to remember that your own staff are often personally affected by social justice issues. How you set up your training and interact with your staff is an integral part of social justice. Whichever methodologies or activities you include in the training, here are some final considerations that will help your training be as effective as possible:

- *Start slow*. Even though the topics of social justice are urgent, it is important to start your staff out slow. Don't jump right in to public protests or grand gestures. Start with small items to allow your staff time to process and reflect.
- *Be non-judgmental*. Just as you advocate for equality in society, you also need to ensure that your equality is up to par within the workplace. Do not judge your staff on what they do or do not participate in or choose to take on as their own social justice agenda.
- *Be non-prescriptive*. Allow your staff to come up with their own ideas and causes. If you bring an agenda to the program then you will have staff participating in social justice causes that they don't really believe in.
- *Feelings and experiences are valid*. Your staff may be unsettled by a social justice training program, but that is okay. Their feelings, experiences, and opinions are valid and should be actively sought and listened to.
- *Make your staff a part of the training process*. If you get your staff invested in the training process, you will increase their stake in social justice training for everyone. Allow staff the freedom to run their own seminars and be in charge of their own areas of expertise.

Above all, the most important thing to remember when trying to institute social justice training for library staff is that doing something, no matter how small, is better than doing nothing at all. Do not compare your training or staff to other library staff or training programs. Celebrate each small milestone and then keep moving on to new social justice projects. Every small step that you take to promote equality, equity, and visibility for marginalized people is a victory for your patrons, your library staff, and your community as a whole.

WORKS CITED

Austen, Jane. 1918. *Pride and Prejudice*. New York: Charles Scribner's Sons.
Lankes, David. 2011. *The Atlas of New Librarianship*. Cambridge, MA: MIT Press.
Lux, Michael, Renate Motschnig-Pitrik, and Jeffrey Cornelius-White. 2013. "The Essence of the Person-Centered Approach." In *Interdisciplinary Handbook of the Person-Centered Approach: Research and Theory*. New York: Springer.
McEwen, Celina, and Franziska Trede. 2016. "Beyond Reflective and Deliberative Practitioners." In *Educating the Deliberate Professional*. Professional and Practice-Based Learning 17. Switzerland: Springer International Publishing.

Ohio State University. 2015. "Understanding Implicit Bias." The Kirwan Institute for the Study of Race and Ethnicity.

Pennsylvania State University. n.d. "The Privilege Walk." https://edge.psu.edu/workshops/mc/power/privilegewalk.shtml.

U.S. Department of Justice. n.d. "Understanding Bias: A Resource Guide." Community Relations Services Toolkit for Policing. n.d. https://www.justice.gov/crs/file/836431/download.

Reflecting Diversity
in the *Library of Congress*
Subject Headings

Elizabeth Hobart

Library users are diverse, but the *Library of Congress Subject Headings* (LCSH) do not always reflect this diversity. Too often, subject headings fail to describe library users as they describe themselves. Headings can "other" library users, often treating white, straight, middle-class, able-bodied males as defaults. Worse, headings sometimes use pejorative terminology, either as an access point or as a "see" reference, perpetuating the use of biased terminology in the library's catalog.

This issue gained public attention in March of 2016, when the Library of Congress announced that they would replace the subject heading for "Illegal aliens" with "Noncitizens," as the phrase "Illegal aliens" is pejorative (Library of Congress 2016). On April 14, 2016, Representative Diane Black (R–TN) introduced H.R. 4926, "Stopping Partisan Policy at the Library of Congress Act," which directed the Librarian of Congress to retain the headings "Aliens" and "Illegal Aliens." As a result, at the time of this writing, "Illegal aliens" remains in LCSH.

The effect of headings like these can be significant. The effort to update the heading for "Illegal aliens" started with Melissa Padilla, a Dartmouth student who became upset when she encountered the term repeatedly in the catalog (Aguilera 2016). While Padilla chose to fight back, other patrons may disengage. Joan Nestle, the founder of the Lesbian Herstory Archives, recounts her experience conducting research at the New York Public Library in 1957: "I found the word 'Homosexual,' followed by a dash and then the words 'see Deviancy,' and next to this 'see Pathology,' with suggested subcategories of prisons and mental institutions. I never wrote that paper" (Nestle 1998, 67).

Fighting bias is a tenet of social justice, and adding biased terminology to the library's catalog risks marginalizing users. One of the seminal books on this topic is Sanford Berman's *Prejudices and Antipathies* (1971), in which he identified a number of problematic headings and offered "remedies." However, improving LCSH is often not this simple, as terms do not always have one clear, correct alternative. Terminology changes over time, so a term that is accurate today may be pejorative in the future. Users within a community may not agree as to which headings are problematic. For instance, in disability studies, the American Psychological Association advocates for people-first language (e.g., "people with disabilities"), while people with disabilities vary in preference for either people-first or identity-first language (e.g., "disabled people") (Dunn and Andrews 2015). Further, the size of LCSH makes constant maintenance virtually impossible.

Despite these challenges, librarians need to confront the biases in LCSH. To illustrate some of these problems, this essay begins by examining headings in several categories. This list is intended to be illustrative rather than exhaustive, drawing attention to some problems and encouraging readers to conduct their own investigations. The essay then examines some potential solutions, and presents advice to catalogers combating bias in subject access.

Race

Headings about race occupy a significant portion of *Prejudices and Antipathies* (Berman 1971). Some of the most egregious headings, such as "Yellow peril," have been removed. Some other terms have been canceled as headings, but persist as "see" references. For instance, "Race question" now appears as a "see" reference for "Race relations." This is only a partial solution; Berman wanted the term excised, both as a subdivision and as a "see" reference. Similarly, all headings for "Negroes" have been removed as subject terms, although they remain as "see" references for "African Americans" and "Blacks."

However, other problematic terms remain, either as headings or as "see" references. For instance, at the time of this writing, "Colored people (United States)" remains as a "see" reference for "African Americans." Berman called for the removal of this "see" reference in 1971. Surely "Colored people (United States)" cannot still be considered necessary for identification?

Along these lines, "Colored people (South Africa)" is a valid heading. This is less egregious, as "Coloured" is a term used in South Africa. The Kullid Foundation states in "The Coloured Declaration": "We are Coloureds and we are a historic and indigenous group of South Africa" (Kullid Foundation website 2017). Since some people do self-identify as "Coloured," one could argue that there is warrant for including the term in LCSH. It is not clear, however, why the Library of Congress chose to authorize this heading as "Colored people," particularly as the authority record was created in 1986. The record does not cite a source. A search in OCLC for records with the subject term "Colored people (South Africa)" shows that "Coloured" or "Coloureds" is used much more frequently in titles than "Colored," regardless of the country of publication; the author identified only nine works with "Colored" in the title, whereas "Coloured" or "Coloureds" has appeared in 56 book titles since 2001 alone. In addition, in sources examined, the preferred terminology is "Coloureds," not "Colo(u)red people." Although the term itself is used for self-identification, the form selected reflects old prejudices, rather than terminology preferred by the people who self-identify as Coloured.

Similar problems appear throughout LCSH. For instance, a search for "Latinos" directs users to "Hispanic Americans." In the words of Tatiana de la Tierra: "We hate 'Hispanic' because it is 'their' word for 'us'" (de la Tierra 2008, 96). Indigenous people of the Americas are "Indians," with "see" references from "American Indians" and "First Nations," and no reference to "Native Americans." The record includes a scope note: "Works on the inhabitants of India in general are entered under East Indians." The term "Indians," therefore, cannot be applied to people from India without a qualifier.

Worse, these headings can whitewash aspects of American history. The practice of incarcerating Japanese Americans during World War II is, in LCSH terms, "Evacuation and relocation," a sanitized description of the imprisonment of over 100,000 people. Similarly, Webster and Doyle noted problems with the Library of Congress changing the subject heading for "Indians of North America—Removal" to "Indians of North America—Relocation," which they describe as "a slap in the face" (Webster and Doyle 2008 193). Subsequently, "Indians of North America—Removal" has become a "see" reference on "Indian Removal, 1813–1903." However, "Indians of North America—Relocation" is still a heading. Apparently, "Indian Removal" is to be used only for works addressing removals between 1813 and 1903, and all others are "Relocations."

The geographical terminology for headings about indigenous people also betrays a colonizing perspective. "Indians of North America" refers only to indigenous people in the United States and Canada. Indigenous people from other countries are instead entered under the headings for "Indians of Mexico" or "Indians of Central America." All of these may then be further subdivided to specify, for example, indigenous people of Guatemala or North Carolina. This terminology assumes the territorial boundaries as defined by colonizers, rather than of the people described. At this time, no alternative exists in LCSH.

Gender

In the past, headings for women in a profession were authorized as "Women as…" This construction has been removed. Now, a work about women inventors would be given the subject heading "Women inventors." While this is an improvement, in general, male still seems to be the default for professions. For instance, a subject heading exists for "Women librarians," but men are just "Librarians." The Library of Congress does require literary warrant for subject headings; unless a work is published specifically about male librarians, the heading will not be created. However, this creates problems for biographies. A biography about Regina Anderson Andrews, for example, includes a subject heading for "African American women librarians." Melvil Dewey, on the other hand, is just a librarian.

Only a few headings treat women instead of men as the default. Searches for "Female rape victims" and "Female sexual abuse victims" redirect to the records for "Rape victims" and "Sexual abuse victims. Male victims of these crimes, however, are authorized under separate headings. As a result, a book about male rape victims could be assigned the heading "Male rape victims." A book about female rape victims, however, can only be assigned the heading "Rape victims."

In general, LCSH uses "Women" as an adjective instead of "Female." This is not a problem in itself, as preferences vary. One strange exception is certain criminal activities, such as headings for "Female gang members," "Female offenders," and "Female juvenile delinquents." However, this practice is not consistent; headings also exist for "Women murderers," "Women torturers," and "Women drug dealers," among others. Similar to the heading for "Rape victims, sex workers are female by default (both "Female prostitutes" and "Women prostitutes" are "see" references on this record), but "Male prostitutes" need to be specified.

More worrisome is LCSH's insistence that women are not criminals but offenders, although "Female offenders" is better than the earlier heading, "Delinquent woman." "Offenders" appears in only a few subject headings, including women, juveniles, people with disabilities or mental illnesses, and the elderly. "Offenders" seems minimizing, as if these groups are not capable of true crimes. At the time of this writing, the only other subject headings using the word "Offenders" represent colloquial uses, such as "Sex offenders" or "First-time offenders."

Other problems persist with headings about gender. For example, narrower terms for "Single people" differs. Narrower terms for men include "Bachelors." "Single women," however, includes "Maiden aunts" as a narrower term. "Maiden aunts" seems dated, but has been added to bibliographic records as recently as 2016.

Religion

Headings for members of faiths have improved since Berman's writing. Headings for "Mohammedans" and "Mohammedanism" have been correctly updated to "Muslims" and "Islam," and "Jewish question" has been excised (although a search for the phrase redirects users to "Jews—[place]"). However, LCSH still typically assumes Christianity as a default. For instance, the record for "Resurrection" does not have a scope note, and does not in itself specify Christian doctrine. However, "Jesus Christ—Resurrection" is the only narrower term for this heading. Headings for resurrections in other faiths are constructed as "Resurrection (Islam)" or "Resurrection (Jewish theology)," and do not have "Resurrection" as a broader term. Further, there is no heading for "Resurrection (Christian)." The tacit assumption, then, is that "Resurrection" refers only to the Christian doctrine; all others need to be separately authorized.

This problem has been somewhat ameliorated by pattern headings. For example, the heading for "Angels" formerly had similar problems. In 2004, a new heading was authorized for "Angels—Buddhism, [Christianity, etc.]," which permits catalogers to add any religion as a subdivision. This changed older headings such as "Angels (Buddhism)" to "Angels—Buddhism." As a result, catalogers are now able to use Christianity as a subdivision. While this will help moving forward, problems in already existing catalog records remain. At the time of writing, "Angels—Christianity" is used in 776 bibliographic records, whereas "Angels" without qualification is used in over 18,000.

LGBTQIA+

LCSH contains headings for both "Transgender people" and "Transsexuals," but provides little information to distinguish them. According to the GLAAD Media Reference Guide, "Transgender" is "an umbrella term for people whose gender identity and/or gender expression differs from what is typically associated with the sex they were assigned at birth," and "Transsexual" is "an older term … still preferred by some people who have permanently changed—or seek to change—their bodies through medical interventions" (GLAAD website 2017). The authority record for "Transgender people" does not reflect this definition. The first citation is Wikipedia, viewed in 2007. The article has subsequently been rewritten so the information cited is no longer present. The second citation is for the American Heritage Dictionary's definition of "transgendered," which was also consulted in 2007. At that time, the definition was: "appearing as, wishing to be considered as, or having undergone surgery to become a member of the opposite sex." Subsequently, the American Heritage Dictionary definition has been updated, stating that "Transgendered" is offensive and directing users to "Transgender," defined as "Relating to or being a person whose gender identity does not conform to that typically associated with the sex to which they were assigned at birth."

Due to the lack of a scope note and outdated references, it is difficult to distinguish "Transgender" from "Transsexual" in LCSH. This confusion is reflected in bibliographic records. Catalogers sometimes apply both headings to fully cover their bases. In some cases, both terms are appropriate to the work being cataloged. In other cases, catalogers apparently couldn't decide which term was accurate, and instead applied both. At other times, catalogers switch between the two. For instance, the bibliographic record for *At the Broken Places: A Mother and Trans Son Pick Up the Pieces* (Collins and Collins 2017) uses the heading "Transgender youth" for the son, but "Parents of transsexuals" for the mother.

As with the headings for gender, headings for homosexuality often include assumptions that are at best misleading, and at worst wrong. A search for "Homosexual prostitution," for example, directs users to "Male prostitution." This is incorrect and misleading; homosexual prostitution is not limited to male prostitutes, and male prostitutes may be hired by people of any gender identity. A work specifically about homosexual prostitution would be hidden under "Male prostitution." With current LCSH terminology, assigning a subject heading to a work about lesbian prostitution would be impossible.

Other terminology relating to LGBTQIA+ topics is dated. For instance, LCSH has a heading for "Gender identity disorders." Similar to problems described below with headings for disability, "Gender identity disorder" is an outdated term, replaced in the fifth edition of the *Diagnostic and Statistical Manual of Mental Disorders* (DSM-5) with "Gender dysphoria," which is relegated to a "see" reference on this record.

However, this area of LCSH has seen recent change. In July 2017, the heading for "Transvestites" was updated to "Cross-dressers," citing the GLAAD Media Reference Guide among other resources to demonstrate that the term "Transvestite" is now considered derogatory (Library of Congress 2017). On the same monthly list, "Transgenderism" was changed to "Gender nonconformity," and cross-references were added for "Non-binary gender" and "Genderqueer," two terms previously missing from LCSH (Thompson 2016).

Disability

In 2001, the Library of Congress replaced the heading "Handicapped" with "People with disabilities," updating the outmoded term and changing the construction to use people-first language (Library of Congress 2001). This was an improvement, but other headings for people with disabilities still need to be updated, particularly headings for certain developmental disorders. The authority record for "Autism spectrum disorders," for example, has not been updated since 2009. The references are outdated, and include a Wikipedia article that has subsequently been re-written. It also includes several narrower terms, including "Asperger's syndrome," "Autism," "Pathological demand avoidance syndrome," and "Rett syndrome." The DSM-5, published in 2013, defines "Autism spectrum disorder" (ASD) as a single disorder rather than a group of disorders, as in previous editions (Diagnostic and Statistical Manual of Mental Disorders 2013). Although the DSM-5 eliminated several of these terms as formal diagnoses, some (such as Asperger's) are still used by communities. Autism is an active area of scholarship; looking at just 2017 publications, the subject heading for "Autism spectrum disorders" appears in over 200 bibliographic records. Updating the heading to reflect current terminology, adding scope notes, and providing more current references would be beneficial to both catalogers and researchers.

LCSH also retains headings for "Mental retardation," which was a term in the DSM-IV, but has been redefined as "Intellectual disability" in the DSM-5. The subject authority record for "Mental retardation" was created in 2005. The only work cited is the website for the President's Committee for People with Intellectual Disabilities, reflecting the signing of an Executive Order renaming the committee from the President's Committee on Mental Retardation. The work cited itself states that the preferred terminology is "Intellectual disabilities," but when the record was made, "Intellectual disabilities" was relegated to a "see" reference. Nothing in the record justifies this decision.

Subject headings for physical disabilities have generally improved, although they are often slow to do so. For instance, Berman (1971) drew attention to the heading for "Idiocy" with a "see also" reference for "Epilepsy." "Idiocy" is no longer a subject heading, but it persisted until 1993 (Knowlton 2005). As a whole, however, researchers note: "In the case of the LCSH, it is fair to say that libraries have been very attentive to the needs and preferences of people with disabilities in updating their subject terms" (Adler, Huber, and Nix 2017, 128).

Conclusion

Ultimately, libraries catalog materials to make them findable and accessible. If our practices make materials more difficult to find or, worse, marginalize users, then we need to reconsider those practices. In cases where a problematic heading does have a clear alternative, catalogers should consider submitting a change proposal to the Library of Congress. However, problematic headings do not always have easy remedies. Even with full-text searching, subject headings provide valuable access points. Authors use different terminology, so relying on keyword searching is risky, and additionally problematic for translated or transliterated terms. Controlled vocabularies help ensure consistency. User-generated tagging is sometimes recommended to combat problems of bias (Moulaison Sandy and Bossaller 2016). Tagging uses natural-language terminology and allows users to participate in providing subject access. However, as with full-text searching, terminology will vary. User-generated tagging may be a good way to bolster library systems, but it is not a full solution.

Another option is to create local subjects, which may be used alone or in conjunction with LCSH or other vocabularies (Kigongo-Bukenya, Okello-Obura and State 2016). This solution has the advantage of either avoiding or supplementing LCSH, which, at root, is designed to serve a branch of the United States government. However, creating and maintaining a local vocabulary, storing it in an accessible location, and training catalogers in its use requires time and resources. In an age of shrinking cataloging departments, advancing this argument may prove difficult. In addition, locally-created headings only address the problem locally.

Catalogers may also include subject terms from outside LCSH. The Library of Congress maintains a list of other vocabularies that may be encoded in the subject field, which may be used in conjunction with LCSH (Library of Congress, Network Development & MARC Standards Office 2017). At the time of this writing, the list includes over 370 vocabularies. Again, implementing these would require time for selecting standards and training staff, but it does open possibilities of using more specific terminology developed by specialist groups, such as the Gay and Lesbian Task Force of the American Library Association and the Asian American Studies Library.

Although creating a vocabulary free from bias is impossible, admitting this bias is necessary. Acknowledging bias in systems makes it easier to recognize and, ultimately, to avoid. Jonathan Furner, writing about Dewey Decimal Classification, makes several recommendations, which are also applicable to subject cataloging: recognize bias in the system; acknowledge that neutral vocabulary does not end bias; and collect viewpoints of users who identify with the populations being described (Furner 2007). Centering users and consulting subject experts is crucial. Koford (2014), writing about disabilities studies, notes researchers felt "forced" to use terms they found insensitive or offensive. She advises catalogers to consult subject experts when developing vocabularies for fields that are unfamiliar to them. Moulaison Sandy and Bossaller (2016) also advise collaboration, stating that knowledge organization systems should "clearly include input … especially in terms of the structure of the schema and the terminology used."

Libraries catalog works to make them findable. Inaccurate subject headings can hide relevant works, and biased terminology can marginalize users. To combat bias, librarians need to acknowledge the bias inherent in our systems, center users, and consult with subject experts to determine appropriate terminology. Representing users as they represent themselves is crucial. To do otherwise risks marginalizing or minimizing their voices.

Works Cited

Adler, Melissa, Jeffrey T. Huber, and A. Tyler Nix. 2017. "Stigmatizing Disability: Library Classifications and the Marking and Marginalization of Books About People with Disabilities." *Library Quarterly* 87 (2): 117–135.

Aguilera, Jasmine. 2016. "Another Word for 'Illegal Alien' at the Library of Congress: Contentious." *New York Times*, July 22. https://www.nytimes.com/2016/07/23/us/another-word-for-illegal-alien-at-the-library-of-congress-contentious.html.

Berman, Sanford. 1971. *Prejudices and Antipathies: A Tract on the LC Subject Heads Concerning People*. Metuchen, NJ: Scarecrow Press.

Collins, Mary, and Donald Collins. 2017. *At the Broken Places: A Mother and Trans Son Pick Up the Pieces*. Boston: Beacon Press.

de la Tierra, Tatiana. 2008. "Latina Lesbian Subject Headings: The Power of Naming." In *Radical Cataloging: Essays at the Front*, edited by K.R. Roberto, 94–102. Jefferson, NC: McFarland.

Diagnostic and Statistical Manual of Mental Disorders: DSM-5. 2013. Arlington, VA: American Psychiatric Association.

Dunn, Dana S., and Erin E. Andrews. 2015. "Person-First and Identity-First Language: Developing Psychologists' Cultural Competence Using Disability Language." *American Psychologist* 70 (3): 255–264.

Furner, Jonathan. 2007. "Dewey Deracialized: A Critical Race-Theoretic Perspective." *Knowledge Organization* 34 (3): 144–168.

GLAAD. "GLAAD Media Reference Guide—Transgender." Accessed November 21, 2017: https://www.glaad.org/reference/transgender.

Kigongo-Bukenya, Isaac M.N., Constant Okello-Obura, and Eliz Nassali State. 2016. "The Correct Language of Cataloguing Local Publication in East Africa." *New Library World* 116 (9/10): 515–526.

Knowlton, Steven A. 2005. "Three Decades Since *Prejudices and Antipathies*: A Study of Changes in the Library of Congress Subject Headings." *Cataloging & Classification Quarterly* 40 (2): 123–145.

Koford, Amelia. 2014. "How Disability Studies Scholars Interact with Subject Headings." *Cataloging & Classification Quarterly* 52 (4): 388–411.

Kullid Foundation. "The Coloured Declaration." Accessed November 13, 2017: http://kullid.org.za/coloured-declaration.

Library of Congress. 2001. "Library of Congress Subject Headings Weekly List 46." November 15. Accessed November 6, 2017: https://www.loc.gov/catdir/cpso/wls01/awls0146.html.

Library of Congress. 2016. "Library of Congress to Cancel the Subject Heading 'Illegal Aliens.'" March 22. Accessed October 30, 2017: https://www.loc.gov/catdir/cpso/illegal-aliens-decision.pdf.

Library of Congress. 2017. "Library of Congress Subject Headings Monthly List 07." July 17. Accessed November 21, 2017: https://classificationweb.net/approved-subjects/1707.html.

Library of Congress, Network Development & MARC Standards Office. "Subject Heading and Term Source Codes." Accessed December 13, 2017: https://www.loc.gov/standards/sourcelist/subject.html.

Moulaison Sandy, Heather, and Jenny Bossaller. 2016. "The Moral Imperative of Subject Access to Indigenous Knowledge: Considerations and Alternative Paths." Paper presented at IFLA WLIC 2016, Columbus, OH, August 9–19: http://library.ifla.org/id/eprint/1327.

Nestle, Joan. 1998. *A Fragile Union: New and Selected Writings*. San Francisco: Cleis Press.

Thompson, Kelly J. 2016. "More Than a Name: A Content Analysis of Name Authority Records for Authors Who Self-Identify as Trans." *Library Resources & Technical Services* 60 (3): 140–155.

Webster, Kelly, and Ann Doyle. 2008. "Don't Class Me in Antiquities! Giving Voice to Native American Materials." In *Radical Cataloging: Essays at the Front*, edited by K.R. Roberto, 189–197. Jefferson, NC: McFarland.

PART V

Supporting Activism

The Archival Is Political

Archival Practice as Political Practice

ANNA J. CLUTTERBUCK-COOK *and* JEREMY BRETT

Like our colleagues in the fields of library science and public history, archivists have long wrestled with the relationship between structural oppression, political power, and the archives. Fifty years ago, historian Howard Zinn warned of "the tension between [professionals'] culture-decreed role as professionals and our existential needs as human beings." He suggested that archivists, focused on the daily task of "maintaining things as they are, preserving traditional arrangements," are in danger of reinforcing structural oppression that works against "any sharp change in how society distributes wealth and power" (Zinn 1977, 15–16).

In the five decades since Zinn's warning, archives practitioners within and without the halls of institutional power have continued to debate their role as political actors in both maintaining and challenging the status quo. Within traditional repositories, some archivists have reassessed their collection policies and priorities in a concerted effort to collect and preserve the stories of under-documented and historically marginalized communities. Community-based archives—created and maintained by the people whose histories are documented by the collections—and other initiatives have offered archival alternatives to repositories maintained by governments, corporations, and institutions of higher education. Yet overall, the archival community remains sharply divided over whether it is professionally appropriate for archivists to direct their work and their professional identities towards achieving social justice. As recently as 2013, Mark Greene wrote dismissively in *The American Archivist*—the professional journal of the Society of American Archivists (SAA)—"it isn't the job of the archivist to lead the social justice crusade." Instead, he suggested that the job of archival practitioners was, narrowly, "to pursue, acquire, and make available the records that will, among other things, allow social justice crusaders to show that injustice has occurred" (Greene 2013, 328). The myth of "archival neutrality" is a pernicious and lasting one.

Our reluctance to understand archivists as political actors, even "social justice crusaders," costs the field dearly. Too often, those of us who insist on centering what Zinn referred to as our "existential needs as human beings" ultimately choose to take their passion and talent elsewhere. "For four years, I have watched white co-workers and colleagues in this profession stay complicitly silent as state agents slaughter black people in the streets," Jarrett M. Drake wrote recently about his decision to leave his archives position in order to pursue a PhD in anthropology. "The purpose of the archival profession is to *curate* the past, not *confront* it; to *entrench* inequality, not *eradicate* it; to *erase* black lives, not *ennoble* them" (Drake 2017). Those of us who choose to remain in the archival field have a moral obligation to grapple in deep and lasting ways with this challenge to the legitimacy of our professional identities in this moment of widespread human pain.

We, the co-authors of this essay, come to this work as white, cisgender, able-bodied, neurotypical, American citizens by birth. We come from a middle class backgrounds, have advanced professional degrees, and work within institutions (a state university and an independent research library) that confer status and open doors. Jeremy studied both history and library science (1997–1999) because of his interest in the raw documentary ore that forms the historical record and allows us to understand our shared past; Anna embarked upon her graduate training in history and library science (2007–2011) out of a desire to provide equitable access to resources for learning. Neither of us encountered sustained, critical analysis of the way social inequalities were replicated and reinforced within our chosen field through our official graduate school curriculum.

We do not attempt to systematically survey all of the vital grassroots activist work being done by our colleagues; rather, we seek to share a few lessons that we have learned working through established archival bureaucracies, as well as outside of them, toward a more just community of practice.

Professional organizations such as the Society for American Archivists (SAA) and New England Archivists (NEA), the two examples we use here, not only provide a forum for archivists to learn from one another about successful social justice work, but also develop policies, issue statements, and communicate best practices to archives workers and the general public. Because of this mediating role, professional organizations are a key site for archivists to take social justice action. By creating policies, agitating for position statements, and seeking to reform organizational culture, archivists can move their professional organizations slowly but steadily in a more robustly inclusive direction.

Making change in your professional organization often requires getting involved as a volunteer. In 2010, Jeremy became a member of SAA's Issues & Advocacy Roundtable (now Section) Steering Committee, and the Roundtable's co-chair in 2012. Anna was co-founder of the LGBTQ Issues Roundtable within NEA in 2013 and two years later stepped into the role of NEA's first Inclusion and Diversity Coordinator. In both cases, our involvement as volunteers was prompted by frustration that our professional organizations were not bolder on social justice issues. Our experience working for change within these organizations highlights both the opportunities and limitations of advocating and striving for change within existing structures.

Frustrated with what he saw as SAA's bureaucratic slowness, and its focus on high-level, finance-oriented advocacy efforts rather than more specific targeted advocacies geared for immediate results, Jeremy and his colleagues tried to move Issues & Advocacy in a more responsive direction. Issues & Advocacy (I&A) took initiative and action on a number of issues—including the threatened closure of Columbia College's Center for Black Music Research; the Belfast Oral History Project at Boston College and the resulting threats to archival privilege; and the drastic downturn in resources for Library and Archives Canada. I&A also acted as a source of information for SAA at large on matters affecting particular archival institutions. However, I&A was only authorized to speak on its own behalf, rather than the entire SAA; and before long I&A was informed that anything they wrote would have to be routed through SAA higher administration. This additional layer of bureaucracy limited the possibilities for I&A to take direct and immediate action.

These limitations became apparent when SAA failed to take a public stand over the fate of Occupy Wall Street's "People's Library." On November 15, 2011, the New York City Police Department cleared the Occupy camp at Zuccotti Park, and confiscated the Occupiers' library and part of the camp's archives. Most were destroyed. The American Library Association (ALA) issued a strong protest two days later, but SAA Council took no action. Prompted by the OWS incident, I&A drafted a policy for SAA with respect to so-called "endangered archives." The policy proposed a structure modeled on ALA, consisting of two committees working together for rapid response: One would serve as SAA's advocacy arm and supplement or replace the existing Government Affairs Working Group (GAWG). The second committee would have a research and public information function. While this initial proposal was rejected by SAA Council, it may have inspired SAA to retire GAWG and establish the twin Committees on Public Policy (CoPP) and Public Awareness (CoPA) in early 2014.

These new committees were a step in the right direction: recognition of the value of archival advocacy and the need for SAA to take the lead. According to SAA's website, the Committee on Public Policy "is concerned with influencing legislative and regulatory (i.e., public policy) decisions of government at all levels" while the Committee on Public Awareness "is concerned with influencing opinions about the value of archivists and archives among the general public and stakeholder groups other than legislators and regulators (e.g., archives users, institutional resource allocators, etc.) (Society of American Archivists Committee on Public Awareness n.d.)." CoPP does now have in place a formal process through which members can initiate a call to urgent speech or action on issues that lie outside the strict confines of advocacy for the profession as a public good (Society of American Archivists Committee on Public Policy, n.d.).

In the wake of the 2016 election, it has been heartening to see SAA take a more activist stance, issuing statements on topics such as the importance of diversity and inclusion, the need for transparency in government, and its objection to the Trump Administration's call for collecting voter registration data. However, the process by which such statements are drafted, revised, and made public continues to be top-heavy: each statement must follow a lengthy approval process as the request for action is handed upwards to SAA Council. There is still work to be done.

SAA has the disadvantages of a large organization, such as multiple levels of bureaucracy, the need for a national reach, the desire to avoid offending one group of members as they respond to the needs of another, a cautious organizational conservatism—but few of the advantages, such as money or a large paid staff. Faced with these national-level roadblocks, regional associations and local affinity groups can offer nimbler opportunities to test-drive inclusive policies and strategies for shifting organizational culture. As Anna's experience volunteering as Inclusion and Diversity Coordinator (IDC) within New England Archivists demonstrates, the steady accumulation of policy changes can, over time, make a real concrete difference.

The creation of an IDC position on the NEA Executive Board began when NEA's 2010 strategic plan formally recognized the importance of diversity and inclusion for the organization's future. To act upon this commitment, NEA established a two-year Diversity Task Force to examine community needs. In their final report of June 2013, the group made a number of recommendations, among them to "institutionalize NEA's commitment to diversity and inclusion by creating a permanent body devoted to assessing and promoting the organization's progress in this area" (NEA 2013). NEA leadership also crafted a statement on inclusion and diversity, adopted in June 2014, that reads:

> New England Archivists (NEA) supports inclusion and diversity as core values in achieving its mission. NEA is committed to building and maintaining an inclusive environment where differences of opinion, beliefs, and values are sought, listened to, respected, and valued. Through inclusion, NEA is dedicated to expanding membership, participation, and leadership that reflect the broad diversity of New England [NEA 2014].

In her research on diversity work in academia, Sara Ahmed points out that "documents, once written, acquire lives of their own" (Ahmed 2012). It can be easy to dismiss statements of policy or principle as just *words* that paper over the realities of an organization that lacks the resources, or commitment of its leaders, to change the status quo. Yet policy documents, in the hands of those fighting for change, can be a powerful means by which an organization is held accountable. By itself, NEA's stated commitment to "reflect the broad diversity of New England" means little. Yet once published on the organization's website, it became a statement to which to live up.

Creating a code of conduct was the next step, to spell out consequences for those whose speech or actions made participants feel unwelcome or unsafe, and provide pathways for reporting harassment. The code of conduct went through several drafts, reviewed by the Executive Board and the organization's legal counsel, and was presented to the membership for feedback before being adopted by membership vote in November 2016. In other words, it took six years of work, by dozens of volunteers, to turn NEA's strategic goal of greater inclusion into a policy that enumerated specific rights and responsibilities required to create an inclusive organization.

The labor of documenting one's process, meeting with the relevant decision-makers, following the procedures outlined in the organization's bylaws often feel like hurdles thrown up to maintain the status quo. While those resistant to change can use these steps to slow down or halt progress, this labor can also create buy-in with key individuals and lay groundwork for more lasting change. As NEA communicated its intention to be inclusive, members came forward with ideas: gender-neutral bathrooms and lactation rooms at conferences, food options for vegans and people who eat gluten-free, preferred pronouns buttons, ASL interpretation for workshops and conference sessions. Members successfully challenged organizational practices that discriminated against low-income archivists. And, for the first time in the organization's history, a designated individual was tasked with implementing changes wherever possible. Even members who used none of these new services expressed excitement and pleasure over visible, inclusive actions.

Policy documents can also have a lasting effect beyond the organizations that create and administer them. Once New England Archivists had appointed an Inclusion and Diversity Coordinator, and adopted a code of conduct, representatives from other regional associations reached out with questions. Change in a single organization can inspire members of sister organizations to revisit their policies and processes.

The deliberative process of organizational change, however, is not always the best or only way to shift the profession. Sometimes, voices from outside organizational structures are equally, if not more important. Outsider groups like this are beholden to no overarching official structure but to the mission and organization to which they set themselves. This gives activist archivists a particular kind of freedom to speak and act in accordance with their values.

Project ARCC, for example, is a group with a simple and direct, targeted mission: "We are a community of archivists taking action on climate change. We believe that archivists have a professional responsibility to:

1. Protect archival collections from the impact of climate change
2. Reduce our professional carbon and ecological footprint
3. Elevate climate change-related archival collections to improve public awareness and understanding of climate change.
4. Preserve this epochal moment in history for future research and understanding" [Project ARCC, n.d.].

Founded in 2015, the group defines itself as "an organizing space" that provides forums for like-minded archivists to find each other and exchange ideas, information, and opportunities for action. Project ARCC also works hard to ensure that it has a presence at relevant events (i.e., the 2015 Boston Rally for Jobs, Justice & Climate), to give a public face to the activist archival profession.

Archivists for Black Lives in Philly (#A4BLiP) is another grassroots group dedicated to a specific issue (Drake 2017; Brett 2017). The group was formed in response to the activist work of Jarrett Drake, who spearheaded in 2015 the development of another independent archival organization-the community-based People's Archive of Police Violence in Cleveland, which digitally preserves artifacts and materials related to an epidemic of police violence against minorities in Cleveland (the 2014 shooting of 12-year-old Tamir Rice being the most infamous) (People's Archive of Police Violence, n.d.) Drake and his colleagues formed the People's Archive to free archival practice from the dominant and traditional narrative centered around white supremacy that obscures or erases black people's lives.

The founders of #A4BLiP have organized around the same motive for their own city of Philadelphia; the group explicitly notes that "archives are located within systems of white supremacy, also known as structural racism, in the sense that: Archives are often situated within institutions of power that historically have reinforced systemic oppression. Archives have historically been inaccessible or unwelcoming to marginalized groups. Archivists are an overwhelmingly white profession (approximately 93 percent white as of the 2004 A*CENSUS survey). Archival collecting has enshrined dominant narratives of rich, white, heterosexual, cisgender men as the most deserving of attention and preservation, while ignoring or erasing narratives of marginalized communities (Archives for Black Lives in Philly, n.d.)." These are propositions not widely accepted in the archival profession; therefore, any official professional organization would realistically not adopt them as founding principles. #A4BLiP's independence gives this group the ability to make bolder claims. Extra-official groups can also often act quickly, which can be vital in ensuring that rapidly created archives, especially those born digital (especially ephemeral), are collected and repositories found for them.

Archivists, by being present at the time events occur, can also help instill among event participants a consciousness that the materials they generate are worthy of preservation. The Women's March on Washington Archives Project, which organized rapidly to collect materials related to the 2017 series of Women's Marches across the United States, and place them in established institutions, is a notable example (Society of American

Archivists Women's Archivists Section, n.d.). The old style of archival acquisition was (and in many cases still is) passive, where archivists and archival institutions respond long after the fact to events. This is changing as more institutions move from being reactive to proactive, but still, extra-official organizations can have the necessary fluidity, dynamism, reach, and directed mission that standard archival institutions often lack.

The quick and widespread response by individual archivists and proactive institutions to the 2011 Occupy Wall Street movement offers another example of the advantages that these kinds of independent issue- or event-based groups provide to the rapid establishment of community-led archives. As the movement spread beyond New York City, a number of groups arose to ensure the preservation of the documentary record of the movement. The experience explores the range of possibilities available to activist archivists who choose to work outside (although not necessarily against) existing institutions: several community archives projects were initiated by Occupiers that aimed to collect and manage materials, from organizational records to physical ephemera to oral histories, related to the movement. Various formal institutions collected Occupy movement material, supported and provided advice to working groups of the Occupy movement in their cities, and accepted donations of some of the materials collected by the working groups.

Groups and individuals provided advice and assistance to record creators in the Occupy movement and records collectors in the aforementioned archives projects. (The most important of these was the Activist Archivists group in New York, which facilitated meetings between various groups collecting records of the Occupy movement, helped to build relationships between these groups, and provided advice and assistance for creators and collectors of records.) In addition, several groups launched projects for the collection, preservation and access to Occupy digital records, including the Occupy Archive project, established by a group of volunteers at the Roy Rosenzweig Centre for History and New Media at the George Mason University, and the Internet Archive's Occupy Wall Street Collection (Erde 2014).

Issue-based groups within the archival community can challenge the false dichotomy between neutral/professional and political/unprofessional practices. The idea of 'archival neutrality' can hamper archivists from trying to exercise their sociopolitical identities as activists within their professional identities as archivists. However, we find that by coming together as activist archivists, archives workers may express both those identities; they can explode that false 'neutrality' narrative and create a space in which they may unreservedly put their professional expertise to work serving the cause of social justice.

Our own experience organizing the Concerned Archivists Alliance (CAA) is one such effort (Concerned Archivists Alliance 2017). Formed in response to the 2016 presidential election, Jeremy put out a call for colleagues to craft a position statement that outlined our concerns as archivists about the incoming administration of Donald Trump. The situation was serious, and demanded quick action, something we were not confident we could or would get working through SAA or NEA. Jeremy and Anna, along with Hanna Clutterbuck-Cook (Francis A. Countway Library and Medical Heritage Library, Harvard University) and Katharina Hering (National Equal Justice Library, Georgetown University) drafted the statement in December 2016 and circulated it to colleagues for feedback before publicly posting it on January 15, 2017. The fact that we were a core group of four individuals, not speaking for a specific institution or organization, allowed us to be quick in our response.

Our statement eventually gathered 895 signatures from archivists around the world. We were gratified by this widespread support, and attribute it to large part to the immediacy that an extra-official organization can have. In the wake of important events, looser associations like CAA can respond more quickly to controversial or significant actions with a voice that expresses deep emotional concern. In the immediate aftermath of the 2016 election, shock and dismay were by no means confined to members of the archival profession.

Given Donald Trump's repeated demonstrations during the campaign of contempt for truth and evidence, many archivists had particular concern for what this election might mean for the future of adherence to public records laws, for the integrity of the documentary record, and for the government's commitment to the dissemination of accurate public information. Many did not want to take a wait-and-see attitude, and did not think we could afford to wait. Many wanted something of a *cri de coeur*, that the world might see that some archivists choose to think of themselves as active citizens whose engagement with social justice issues informs their identities as archivists. CAA offered hundreds of archivists a chance to express immediate support for progressive archivists' desire for change in their politics and their profession.

Since that time, CAA has maintained a social media presence, and signed on to a number of subsequent statements in opposition to administration policy and action. CAA is by design a free-form organization, and as of this writing is working towards a decentralized structure that will allow individual members of the coalition to take the lead in progressive initiatives and actions as activist archivists, rather than being dependent on a bureaucratic superstructure.

The crossroads where archival practice and social justice action meet is growing ever wider. We find it heartening to see in this historical moment of grave societal danger many younger archivists, non-traditional archivists, and minority archivists who increasingly challenge the old and harmful narrative of archival neutrality so well summed-up by Jarrett Drake (2017). Archivists are more and more finding nontraditional methods not only for doing their work but for letting their identities as activists and concerned citizens inform that work. More importantly, perhaps, we are seeing among our newer peers a shared set of beliefs that social justice is a function of our work, that we need to confront the past we curate, and that it is not enough to merely archive society but we need to question the underlying assumptions that make possible or strengthen the inequalities in society. As custodians of the documentary record, archivists have always believed that they have a special obligation to history. However, that obligation is not a passive one, or one that is independent of our private lives. Indeed, we hold that, rather, the future of archives lies with those archivists who recognize the critical importance of social justice and the mutual impact that it and records have on each other.

Works Cited

Ahmed, Sara. 2012. *On Being Included: Racism and Diversity in Institutional Life.* Durham, NC: Duke University Press.

Archivists for Black Lives in Philly. 2017. https://github.com/rappel110/A4BLiP/blob/master/20170109. Accessed January 7, 2018.

Brett, Jeremy. 2017. "#ArchivesForBlackLives: Archivists Respond to Black Lives Matter." Society of American Archivists. Human Rights Archives Section. Last modified August 7, 2017. https://hrarchives.wordpress.com/2017/08/07/archivesforblacklives-archivists-respond-to-black-lives-matter/.

Concerned Archivists Alliance. 2017. "Statement to the Archival Community." 15 January 2017. https://concernedarchivists.wordpress.com/. Accessed January 10, 2018.

Drake, Jarrett M. 2017. "I'm Leaving the Archival Profession: It's Better This Way." Last modified June 26. https://medium.com/on-archivy/im-leaving-the-archival-profession-it-s-better-this-way-d631c6d72fe.

Erde, John. 2014. "Constructing Archives of the Occupy Movement." *Archives & Records* 35, no. 2: 77–92.

Greene, Mark A. 2013. "A Critique of Social Justice as an Archival Imperative: What Is It That's All That Important?" *The American Archivist* 76(2) (Fall/Winter): 302–334.

New England Archivists. 2013. Diversity Task Force Final Report, 2 June 2013.

New England Archivists. 2014. "New England Archivists Officially Adopts a Diversity and Inclusion Statement." August 4. https://www.newenglandarchivists.org/Resources/Documents/Press%20Releases/NEA_dversity-statementPR_FINAL.pdf. Accessed December 21, 2017.

People's Archive of Police Violence in Cleveland. 2018. http://www.archivingpoliceviolence.org/. Accessed January 16, 2018.

ProjectARCC. https://projectarcc.org/. Accessed December 2, 2017.

Society of American Archivists. 2017a. Women's Archivists Section. 2017. "Project Spotlight: Women's March on Washington Archives Project" https://womenarchivistsroundtable.wordpress.com/2017/01/10/project-spotlight-womensmarch-on-washington-archives-project/. Accessed January 10, 2018.

Society of American Archivists. 2017b. Issues & Advocacy Section. https://www2.archivists.org/groups/issues-and-advocacy-section. Accessed December 21, 2017.

Society of American Archivists. 2018. Committee on Public Awareness. https://www2.archivists.org/groups/committee-on-public-awareness\. Accessed January 16, 2018.

Society of American Archivists. 2018b. Committee on Public Awareness. https://www2.archivists.org/groups/committee-on-public-policy/procedures-for-suggesting-saa-advocacy-action. Accessed January 16, 2018.

Zinn, Howard. 1977. "Secrecy, Archives, and the Public Interest." *Midwestern Archivist* 2(2):15–16.

Hip Hop and Activism

Bridging Boundaries and Healing Through Hip Hop Pedagogy

KAI ALEXIS SMITH

Documented in *Dreamer's Ally Network: Cal Poly Pomona,* as of 2016, there were 550 Dream Act students at Cal Poly Pomona and that number has only grown. Cal Poly Pomona's campus is also diverse by ethnicity, cultures, creed, and economics. Before the 2016 presidential election, student morale declined significantly. Students became concerned about their families and Dream Act status. The change was visceral. A number of faculty witnessed this change when a cohort arrived in Summer 2016. Before, the campus was lively and vibrant. However once fall/winter quarter 2016 came, the atmosphere became somber and sad. Student's anxiety levels peaked. To address this issue, Senior Assistant Librarian Kai Alexis Smith thought about harnessing the energy and creativity of a culture that many students across all the spectrums of diverse backgrounds were familiar with—hip hop. She planned the first annual *Hip Hop and Activism* series to spark new ideas, empower students and engage them in conversations around topics through the popular culture of hip hop.

The *Hip Hop and Activism* series was conducted in partnership with the African American Center. Additional collaborators included the Political Science department, Ethnic and Women's Studies department (EWS), faculty from the History department, Human Resources, and the campus hip hop student club also participated. Five events in the month of February 2016 were organized centering hip hop. Events featured discussions with faculty and students presenting on police brutality, hip hop, activism, and films such as *Slingshot Hip Hop* and *Hip-Hop: Beyond Beats and Rhymes*. After every event, a moderator (usually a faculty member) facilitated conversations that included unpacking history, concepts and ideas around race, identity, politics, policing, and socioeconomics in the United States, Latin America, the Caribbean, and the Middle East. Many times, conversations went over the allotted time. These events and discussions often resulted in students recommending practical ways to be politically active in their lives. Some students suggested attending protests, creating and editing Wikipedia pages for marginalized groups of people, getting involved with local community activism in their neighborhood, and even seeking out more socially conscious hip hop artists. In addition, Smith created an online resource guide (http://libguides.library.cpp.edu/hiphopandact)

as a companion to the series of events with recommended readings and live Twitter streams from students that were live-tweeting at the events.

The series included the following:

2/7 and 2/21, 12–2 p.m.
2 panel discussions led by faculty on the topics of police brutality and hip hop and activism
2/9 and 2/15, starting at 12 p.m.
2 films with discussions after the screening with faculty:
Film 1: *Hip Hop Beyond Rhyme and Beats*
Film 2: *Slingshot Hip Hop*
2/28, 12–1 p.m.
Spoken word performance by student group 4 Elements Hip Hop Organization

Context

Hip Hop is a culture rooted in bringing together neighborhoods and communities that started in the Bronx, New York, in the 1970s. Hip Hop is composed of four elements: MCing, DJing, breakdancing, and graffiti. It started as an outlet for economically disenfranchised youth in the Bronx as a means for social and political commentary. It has become a global movement; youth across the world have adapted hip hop culture to comment on both local and national oppressive issues and to bring about change.

According to Derrick J. Jenkins, Sr. (2012, 77) in *Hip Hop Activism in Education,* hip hop pedagogy

> refers to the style of teaching implemented by a teacher and a strategic effort by that teacher to raise the "critical consciousness" and "cultural awareness" through a social justice lens or perspective [Stovall, 2006]. Critical Hip Hop Pedagogy diverges slightly by focusing primarily on marginalized groups, as a school process for blacks, Latino, those in high poverty school environments and even teachers seek empowerment through the educational process. Gosa & Fields [2010] postulate that Critical Hip Hop Pedagogy serves three distinct functions within a curricula of empowerment: development of critical thinking within students, encouragement of the infusion of non-traditional texts and teaching tools for critique and lastly, as an emancipatory tool for connecting social ill to larger structures of oppression.

A hip hop-themed conference addressing social justice issues is not a new idea. Scholars such as Peter C. Murrell proposed to consider different types of educational approaches to reengage disenfranchised groups that integrate popular culture and as Jenkins, Sr., writes "culturally responsive pedagogies" (2002, 1). Addressing the experiences and worldview of students enhances learning and they are more likely to engage "in civil society in ways that hold schools, institutions, and politicians accountable to their interests," according to Shawn Ginwright and Julio Cammarota (2011, 15). Universities across the United States have built upon these pedagogies through hip hop conferences to frame discussions around topics related to oppression, social construction of race, activism, misogyny, and police brutality as far back as the early 2000s. Ivy league institutions like Dartmouth in 2004 and University of Wisconsin Madison in 2017 have hosted hip hop conferences to frame discussions for their predominantly white student bodies around these important issues. Universities such as Georgia State, Virginia Tech,

Hampton, Southern Connecticut State, California University of Pennsylvania, among others, have hosted these conferences. Through discussions in hip hop conferences, participants can work towards dismantling stereotypes and spark conversations around controversial topics in a safe environment. These conferences can also help change preconceived notions and educate people about racism and the true social justice roots of the culture as well as the problems hip hop culture struggles with.

Details

Planning for the *Hip Hop and Activism* series started in October 2016. The series occurred in February 2017 during Black History Month since hip hop culture's origins came out of black and Latino communities. Also, it was important to organize it soon after the 2016 presidential election.

Internal and External Partners

The idea for the *Hip Hop and Activism* series stemmed from a conversation Smith had with the coordinator of the African American Center. Smith just started her position in the library at Cal Poly Pomona and was trying to get to know campus contacts. The coordinator had experience booking local hip hop and spoken word artists on campus and was interested in a possible collaboration with another hip hop-themed event. She also informed Smith that there was a hip hop student group on campus called 4 Elements Hip Hop Organization. Smith thought about working with the cultural centers and faculty partners in her subject areas in the library for an event, but she needed to get library leaders on board. This initial conversation led to more opportunities for discussion with potential allies on campus. Smith pitched the idea to the Head of Public Services and the special events coordinator in the library. While the idea was ambitious, it was welcomed, but there were concerns about the short time frame to plan, since planning began just three months before the series' projected start date and the budget was another matter. While the series had no separate budget, the special events coordinator provided lunch and snack for a few events with support from the dean of the University Library. Smith reached out to the African American Center Coordinator and they were able to provide snacks and a lunch for a few other events in the series.

Tips:
- Start planning at least six to eight months in advance. This provides adequate time to prepare a presentation to the library dean, director or board and develop a budget to arrange for funding.
- If you ask for funding before the start of a new fiscal year, it can be budgeted in for the next year.
- This lead time is also essential to arrange for guest speakers, room reservations, coaching; it provides speakers time to prepare their presentations among other logistics.

Logistics

In November 2016, Smith worked with an informal team which included a faculty member from the EWS, the African American Center Coordinator, and the University Library's special events coordinator. In an initial meeting, a project timeline was laid out. Important 'to do" items were outlined such as determining the number of events, organizing panels, finalizing panel discussion topics, selecting the films for viewing, drafting a list of student groups for outreach, and identifying faculty on campus who could speak about hip hop and select a topic as well as guide a discussion after a film.

Within a few weeks, panel discussion topics were narrowed down and faculty were contacted. Smith booked the rooms in the library for the panel discussions and for the film viewings two months in advance. The group settled on two panel discussions that ran two hours long, two films, and two student-led events/performances. Working with the EWS faculty member became instrumental in the formation of panels. Her expertise in African American culture made her perfect to moderate discussions and speak on panels. In addition, the EWS department was instrumental in locating former Cal Poly Pomona alumni to moderate and co-present with faculty.

In order to reach peak attendance, events had to be scheduled during a time when students could participate. The films were scheduled during an open hour on campus when students didn't have classes, 12–1 p.m. Tuesdays and Thursdays. To get a student to come in during this time, Smith needed to provide food. Students will also attend events if faculty require it. Smith worked with faculty willing to have their students come to the panel discussion during class time. This situation was ideal because of the commuter nature of the student body at Cal Poly Pomona.

Tips:
- For academic or special librarians, while events in the series are public, it's best to plan them with faculty cooperation since it guarantees a core attendance.
- For public librarians and special librarians, think about the best time by considering the day of the week and time of days you get attendance. Then plan around that time frame. Try to partner with a organization or group in the community to increase attendance.

Student Groups

Because it was so important to have students involved, Smith reached out to EWS department faculty to recommend a student with public speaking experience. Faculty recommended a few alumni in the area and Smith reached out to them inquiring of their interest in participating. One student was interested and Smith spoke with her about expectations and the panel topic. While the alumna was new to moderating a panel and discussion, faculty speakers were supportive of the student and assisted when necessary.

Working with student groups has its challenges. They have busy schedules and full social lives. Therefore, it may be hard to contact them and you need to be ready for event cancellations with no or short notice. With the student hip hop group 4 Elements Hip Hop Organization, there was a similar issue of making initial contact. However, once communication began, the group was happy to work with Smith. Towards the end of the month, members of 4 Elements Hip Hop Organization performed and facilitated a discussion with participants and an open mic.

Tips:
- Reach out to students and youth leaders at least six—eight months in advance. For academic librarians, work with the faculty advisor to get students to respond. Be persistent.
- Try to set the dates for the events earlier in the semester or between midterms and finals to have faculty and students participate.
- Follow up with participants at least a week before the event.

Faculty Onboarding

It was important to reach out to faculty to reassure them that they did have the expertise to join the conversation on hip hop from their specialty and perspective. Smith reached out to faculty in various departments to inquire about their interest in speaking on a panel(s) and moderating discussion(s). Surprisingly, faculty were hesitant to participate because of their lack of expertise or lack of knowledge and biases towards hip hop culture and hip hop pedagogy. Hip hop pedagogy uses the interdisciplinary nature of hip hop culture to educate and empower students with student-centered curricula and practices. There were a few faculty members that Smith reached out to that immediately declined. Smith helped them learn more about hip hop culture and its social justice origins and explain the ideas behind the programming, the vision, and what each faculty member could contribute with their expertise using hip hop pedagogy. Once the faculty realized that they could contribute to the diverse voices in the interdisciplinary programming and understood hip hop pedagogy, they agreed to participate.

Tips:
- Identify speakers on campus in a variety of departments or in the community as potential panelists. With at least six to eight months' notice, begin reaching out to them. This provides time to discuss the event with speakers in case they are hesitant.

Outreach and Publicity

An outreach strategy was developed which included traditional advertising as well as outreach to student groups, faculty and local hip hop celebrities. The administrative assistant in the University Library office designed fliers and digital signage, which she placed around the library and in the student center. In addition, she sent information about the *Hip Hop and Activism* events series to *Poly Updates*, which is a list of events on campus for faculty. Outreach included digital signage emailed to faculty, public relations contacts, and the dorms. The Library Club, a student club composed of mainly undergraduate students interested in library activities, made *Hip Hop and Activism* buttons for further promotion. Smith reached out to a number of local celebrities in the greater Los Angeles area, but because of the short time frame she did not receive responses. Smith did not pursue celebrity outreach as aggressively as she could have.

Tips:
- Develop a communications/outreach plan. Recruit someone with graphic design skills to design advertising.
- Reaching out to local celebrities can be hard if you don't have contacts already. Create an agent list and start reaching out at least six to eight months before the event. Sometimes it can take weeks to get a response. If celebrities cannot attend the event or perform for free, as an alternative, ask them for any swag they can donate to use in a raffle or as giveaways.

LibGuide

To supplement the discussions, Smith created an online resource guide accessible through the University Library's website (http://libguides.library.cpp.edu/hiphopandact.) She researched important literature on the topic as well as the library's resources. When recommending the resources the library did not own, she provided alternative access points such as interlibrary loan and at that time LINK+, a library consortium. Smith had since updated the guide to draw upon resources from CSU+ the consortia lending program between California State University libraries. She also added links to important archives, magazines, and websites.

Tips:
- The research component might take more time that you realize. Plan ahead and work on this as early as possible.
- Reach out to speakers for recommended readings and multimedia to add to your guide.

Assessment

In order to understand if the series were successful, Smith used a variety of assessment methods. Before the series, learning outcomes were developed to benchmark assessment. Attendance was measured. Attendees had to register in advance and sign in at the door before entering the room where events took place. As with many programs, some of the registered students did not come; on the other hand, students who didn't register showed up for the panels and films. In the end, panel discussions were often full, around 45 attendees, which was near the maximum capacity of the room. Fewer students, at least a dozen, attended film screenings. Unfortunately, due to the length of these films, many students had to leave before they ended to get to classes. So there were usually only a handful of students left in the room at the end of the screening to participate in the discussion with faculty.

Live tweeting was encouraged to crowd-digest highlights from the talks and provide an opportunity for those who could not attend to participate in the discussion. A hashtag was created specifically for the series, which was #cpphiphop. However, on this campus students did not tweet at the events all that much. At the end of every *Hip Hop and Activism* series event, students were encouraged to fill out a Google form with a few questions to provide feedback about the event. The attendance at events totaled 123 and

28 attendees filled out the survey. That is 23 percent of total attendees responded to the survey which is better than anticipated.

The feedback received was constructive and positive. Every survey participant wanted more events to continue the discussion in the future. When asked: "Share your thoughts! What could be improved? What would you like to see next year?," select students responses included:

- "I really enjoyed the discussion and hope to see more of these on campus! I especially enjoy the parallels of Hip-Hop and social impact and hope to see how other forms of Pop culture can affect activism as well. I would definitely come back next year to this discussion."
- "Thanks for the organizing this series. Definitely these documentary films are very informative especially for someone out of black communities to learn more about their culture and their hardships and obstacles in fulfillment of their dreams mainly among young generations."
- "Next year there should be a workshop that teaches you how to find these underground socially conscious artists."
- "It was an amazing and empowering experience. It would be great to bring in more hip hop artists in the future."
- "I really enjoyed it; however, I could not stay for the discussion portion because it interfered with my class. It is unfortunate that not that many people showed up but perhaps it is due to conflicts with clubs, classes, and work schedules. People are usually busy during U-hour."
- "A bigger space for everyone in attendance to have a seat would be nice."

Overall, participants enjoyed the series of events and wanted it to occur again for further discussion.

Tips:
- Try to offer an incentive to encourage participants to take the feedback survey. If you get swag from local celebrities use them for raffle prizes. Enter survey respondents into a raffle for the prizes after they complete the survey. Add a section at the end of the survey for participants to add their names and contact information.
- Assess whether live tweeting is popular on your campus or in your community. Also, investigate whether another social media platform is heavily used, to encourage continuing the conversation outside the event space.

Post Mortem

Smith planned the first *Hip Hop and Activism* series in 2016. She plans to organize future *Hip Hop and Activism* events and will use the survey feedback to make adjustments for the next series. The events turned out to be more popular than anticipated. Some of the main issues Smith learned from included student behavior regarding registering for events. They rarely did this which resulted in not having enough space or food. Smith will assemble a *Hip Hop and Activism* team to brainstorm a way to avoid these and other potential issues.

To make the process more inclusive to all faculty on and off campus, Smith wants to put a call out to faculty to submit proposals. From these proposals, panels will be arranged for future events. Also, this will open up participation to off-campus contributors. A caveat is that funding will not be offered for speakers, they will be compensated with lunch. By participating in this series, faculty working towards tenure can incorporate their involvement as part of community service.

Tips:
- Draft learning outcomes for the series/events.
- Refine the assessment questions. Make the survey shorter and easier to take.
- Rethink the distribution method of the survey. Maybe, have a box with a small piece of paper with the survey questions and pencils nearby.

Conclusion

While the *Hip Hop and Activism* series was planned on short notice with very few resources, the panels, films, and discussions clearly connected with many students from diverse backgrounds on Cal Poly Pomona's campus. The series provided a platform for students to work through current issues and put them in context. In addition, students were able to explore the varied forms of activism that might work for them. While this series started in the library, it can work just as well at the University level and bring together faculty near and far to continue the conversation on social justice, information freedom, and activism.

Works Cited

Ginwright, Shawn, and Julio Cammarota. 2011. "Youth Organizing in the Wild West: Mobilizing for Educational Justice in Arizona!" *Youth Organizing for Educational Reform,* Anneberg Institute for School Reform, no. 30 (Spring): 13–21.

Gosa, Travis L., and Tristan G. Fields. 2010. *Is Hip Hop Education Another Hustle? The (Ir)Responsible Use of Hip Hop as Pedagogy.* Cornell University.

Jenkins, Derrick, Sr. 2012. "Hip Hop and Activism in Education: The Historical Efforts of Hip Hop Congress to Advance Critical Hip Hop Pedagogy Through the Urban Teacher Network." Ph.D. diss., University of Cincinnati.

Leon, Norman, Thavery Lay-Bounpraseuth, Lorena Márquez, Norma Salcedo, Dalia Garcia, Jose M. Aguilar-Hernandez, Diana Ascencio, Karen Romero and Mecir Ureta. 2016. *Dreamer's Ally Network: Cal Poly Pomona.* Pomona: Cal Poly Pomona, PDF report. Retrieved from https://www.cpp.edu/~ab540/documents/USSAC%20Report%20on%20Undocumented%20Students%20at%20Cal%20Poly%20Pomona%202016.pdf.

Murrell, Peter C. 2002. *African-Centered Pedagogy: Developing Schools of Achievement for African American Children.* Albany: SUNY Press.

Passel, Jeffrey S., and D'Vera Cohn. 2014. *Unauthorized Immigrant Totals Rise in 7 States, Fall in 14: Decline in Those from Mexico Fuels Most State Decreases.* Washington, D.C.: Pew Research Center.

Stovall, D. 2006. "We Can Relate." *Urban Education* (41)6: 584–602.

Bringing Critical Race Theory to the Library Bill of Rights

From the Past to the Future

CELESTE BOCCHICCHIO-CHAUDHRI

The principle of intellectual freedom forms the cornerstone of modern librarianship in the United States, and the Library Bill of Rights forms the bedrock for the ethical justification of that freedom. Many scholars in the field of Library and Information Science have written on the philosophical underpinnings of intellectual freedom, drawing primarily on the Western European liberal tradition as embodied by Enlightenment thinkers like John Stuart Mill and Immanuel Kant. This paper seeks to expand our understanding of intellectual freedom by putting it into conversation with the writings of Critical Race Theory (CRT) in order to ask: intellectual freedom for whom? And what is the appropriate role for librarians and other information professionals seeking to foster substantive intellectual freedom?

Critical Race Theory began among African-American legal scholars in the 1970s and has since spread to other academic fields including education and political science. Across disciplines, CRT scholars believe that racism is an ordinary part of life, rather than an exceptional act of blatant discrimination. Because American society has woven a preference for whiteness into its fabric, racism can be difficult to address. It is often subtle and unacknowledged. In this case, "whiteness" means not only skin color, but also the culture, values, and ways of thinking that have been historically developed by European and White American thinkers. Therefore, it is not enough to bring people of color into organizations without questioning the foundations of those organizations. CRT scholars also believe that because many people benefit from racism, large sections of society have little interest in combating it. Finally, CRT scholars understand race as culturally constructed, that is the meaning that people associate with different skin colors, hair textures, and other physical differences changes in different times and places (Delgado, Stefancic, and Harris 2017).

The issue of race and racism in the field of Library and Information Science is a troubling one. Despite efforts by the ALA to recruit people of color to the field, in 2013, 82.2 percent of graduates from MLIS programs were white and a mere 3.8 percent were black (Snyder, de Brey, and Dillow 2016). Indeed, Hathcock argues that the infrastructure of LIS diversity initiatives unwittingly predicts their failure. Because efforts to recruit students of color into MLIS programs focus only on adding in students from different backgrounds, it leaves undisturbed the structures that establish whiteness as the norm in Library Science (Hathcock 2015). Honma argues that the reluctance to talk openly about race and racism in favor of more limited discourse of diversity precludes any articulation of the structures of discrimination that necessitate diversity initiatives in the first place (Honma 2005). Such reluctance is a direct result of the reliance in LIS ethical theorizing on the liberal tradition, which tends to favor a supposedly color-blind neutrality that sees any mention of race and racialized experiences as inherently racist (Delgado, Stefancic, and Harris 2017, 27). Thus the emphasis in the field of LIS on neutrality severely inhibits its ability to confront the racism within the structure of the information professions.

This is not to say that scholars and professionals in the field of LIS have not argued for a more racially just vision of LIS practice. In 1976 the ALA passed a resolution on "Racism and Sexism Awareness" which urged that racism and sexism awareness training be made part of library education, that the various divisions of the ALA adopt programing to raise awareness of library users to the "pressing problem of racism and sexism," and that a plan be developed for reforming cataloging practices that perpetuate racism ("SRRT Resolution–Resolution on Racism and Sexism Awareness" 1976). However, this resolution was met with considerable opposition, framed largely in terms of intellectual freedom. The Intellectual Freedom Committee argued that the resolution should be rescinded, and the Children's Services Division argued that raising awareness among library users of any issues violated the neutrality of libraries (Horn 1977). In her defense of the Resolution, Horn argued that it "identifies what should be an obvious responsibility of librarians—to be sensitive to individuals as individuals, and to their equal rights, their need for equal treatment, and to the expansion of this democratic tenet in their work with the public"(1977, 1255). She further argues that the "new awareness of more subtle discrimination because of sex or race may have to be incorporated into the wording of a living Library Bill of Rights" (Horn 1977, 1255).

Unfortunately, such revision to the Library Bill of Rights never happened, leaving librarians who are committed to racial justice in much the same quandary that they were in the 1970s. While the Racism and Sexism Awareness Resolution was not rescinded, and remains on the website for the Social Responsibilities Round Table (SRRT), it is not findable on the general ALA website and does not seem to have had any substantial implementation. In 1978 the ALA Executive Board voted to support a model program on "racism awareness training for library personnel" (Wiegand and Davis 2015, 535). However, for the most part discussions of racism in LIS remained confined to SRRT–led preconferences, and a proposal to work with the 1983 ALA Conference Planning Committee to set aside a significant portion of conference time for anti-racist work was met with disinterest by the committee (Wiegand and Davis 2015, 536).

Certainly, the Racism and Sexism Awareness Resolution's recommendation that racism and sexism awareness training become integrated into the library school curriculum has never come to pass. Were ethical and political neutrality explicitly the guiding and overarching value of the ALA, our discussion would end here. Anti-racist work and librarianship would be considered incompatible, and individuals committed to engaging in social justice work would be advised to look elsewhere for professional opportunities. This is, however, not the case. Leaving aside for the moment the question of what kind of neutrality the ALA espouses, and how feasible it is to achieve, we also have to recognize that the Office for Intellectual Freedom is only one of the ALA's fifteen offices. The ALA also has an Office for Diversity, Inclusion, and Outreach Services that includes in its mission a commitment to "decenter power and privilege by facilitating conversations around access and identity as they impact the profession and those we serve. We use a social justice framework to inform library and information science workers' development of resource" ("Office for Diversity, Literacy, and Outreach Services" 2016). While it is significant that race and racism are not specifically mentioned in this mission statement, the focus on decentering power and privilege and the stated commitment to social justice frameworks provides librarians interested in addressing racism both inside and outside the library with substantial professional backing.

Unfortunately, this aspect of the ALA's core values is not as integrated into LIS education as the Library Bill of Rights is. Shockey argues that the privileging of "technocratic managerial theories over the concern for human and social welfare" in mainstream LIS education is caused by the ALA's insistence on "maintaining an organizational commitment to embedding a neutrality-focused conception of intellectual freedom with LIS education" (Shockey 2016, 108). This brings us back to the way in which the focus on neutrality prevents the field from addressing its own racism. Why is the Office of Intellectual Freedom privileged over the Office for Diversity, Inclusion, and Outreach services? Why does the field of LIS feel compelled to put intellectual freedom and racial justice on opposite sides of the debate?

In writing about regulation of hate speech on college campuses, Charles R. Lawrence III warns that "by framing the debate as we have—as one in which the liberty of free speech is in conflict with the elimination of racism—we have advanced the cause of racial oppression and put the bigot on the moral high ground" (Lawrence 1993, 57). In other words, by privileging the racists' right to speech over the person of color's right to be treated as an equal in society, we transform the perpetrator of verbal violence into a victim of censorship, and the injured person of color is rendered an insignificant actor in the battle for free speech. The conflict becomes one not between the racist and the person they maligned, but one between the racist and the institutional censor (be it university or library) that seeks to limit racist hate speech.

Of course, part of the problem is that the initial conflict is framed as one between an individual racist and an individual person of color, rather than one between institutionalized white supremacy and people of color as a group. If we privatize it, we ignore "the greatest part of the injury" (Lawrence et al. 1993, 8). That injury is not only to the person who heard, read, or saw the racist message: the injury is primarily to the group which understands the message to one of their continued subordination, and ultimately to all of society as we slip away from the vision of equality toward which we profess to aspire. If we see racist hate speech as the bad speech of radical individuals, then it makes sense to think that more good speech from mainstream, nonracist, society will cure the ills caused by racist speech. However, if we see episodes of racist hate speech as symptomatic of a larger structural racism within the culture of the United States as a whole and LIS in particular, then it makes sense to take a more active role in working to dismantle that structure.

The field of LIS has been long divided on the role of libraries in the larger society. The Social Responsibility Round Table was formed in 1969 to promote social responsibility as a core value of the profession, but its continued marginalization with ALA is attested to by its own description of the SRRT newsletter as "a constant source of alternative viewpoints on libraries and their role in society since 1969" ("SRRT—About Us" n.d.). While the continuity is impressive, one way of reading this statement is that SRRT has failed to convince the ALA as a whole that libraries should be agents for social change for over forty years. This response is a bit glib, of course, and fails to acknowledge the ways in which SRRT has influenced ALA policy.

The idea that librarians have any sort of social responsibility has been severely criticized for decades. *Library Journal* reprinted some of the foundational articles of the debate in its 1993 edition of Library Classics, including David Berninghausen's 1972 article "Social Responsibility vs the Library Bill of Rights," and excerpts from "The Berninghausen Debate" in which several prominent librarians of the time responded to Berninghausen's article. David Berninghausen argued that focusing on social problems had eroded the ALA's focus on issues of librarianship thereby weakening that institution. He went as far as to warn that the emphasis on social responsibility "if it continues, might sever the link of common purpose which is the reason for the existence of this organization" (Berninghausen et al. 1993, S2). The balanced collection is, for Berninghausen, antithetical to the idea that librarians should seek to educate their patrons.

In his rebuttal, Summers argues against the idea of the balanced collection, naming it an abstraction that only exists in the minds of writers of collection development manuals. "Libraries do not, and cannot," Summers argues, "present all sides of controversial questions. Some sides of every question are stupid, unscholarly, anti-intellectual, and incoherently expressed" (Berninghausen et al. 1993, S6). While it may be tempting to follow Summers and simply declare racist viewpoints "stupid" or "incoherent," such labels are unlikely to convince anyone.

That the debate around the Library Bill of Rights, social responsibility, and racism has continued without real resolution for almost half a century indicates that the current terms of the debate are unproductive. The LIS field is stuck in a loop where values of intellectual freedom clash with values of equality and it seems like we must let go of one or the other.

Instead, I propose we change the terms of the debate.

Critical Race Theorists emphasize legal indeterminacy over absolutism. That is, "one can decide most cases either way by emphasizing one line of authority over another or interpreting one fact differently from the way one's adversary does" (Delgado, Stefancic, and Harris 2017). We have seen this kind of indeterminacy at work within LIS: depending on which of the core values of the ALA you choose to emphasize, you can come out on different sides of the intellectual freedom/social responsibility debate. Some librarians have even used the Library Bill of Rights itself to justify a social responsibility stance (Wedgeworth and Summers 1993). Given that the ALA's understanding of intellectual freedom stems from the First Amendment of the United States, taking legal indeterminacy seriously means looking at the various ways in which speech has been categorized as either protected or not protected through different interpretations of the First Amendment.

One of the most important and familiar civil rights cases in the history of the United States is generally not considered to have anything to do with the First Amendment. The 1954 decision in *Brown vs. Board of Education* is most commonly interpreted as narrowly concerned with the integration of physical spaces; legal scholar Charles R. Lawrence III makes a compelling case that *Brown* actually recognized segregation as a form of injurious *speech*, thus setting a precedent for regulating racist hate speech. I quote extensively from his chapter in *Words That Wound: Critical Race Theory, Assaultive Speech, and the First*

Amendment because, in addition to being a foundational text for critical race theory, it cogently articulates the relationship between speech and deed inherent in American racism:

> *Brown* held that segregation is unconstitutional not simply because the physical separation of Black and white children is bad or because resources were distributed unequally among Black and white schools. *Brown* held that segregated schools were unconstitutional primarily because of the *message* segregation conveys—the message that Black children are an untouchable caste, unfit to be educated with white children [Lawrence 1993, 59].

A common argument against this line of reasoning, and against considering hate speech to fall under the rubric of unprotected speech, is that Critical Race Theorists too easily conflate words with deeds, since all actions contain some sort of message. Lawrence argues that the distinction between segregation and other acts that also have an expressive component is where the central purpose lies. If the expressive content is secondary to the action, then the action should be regulated as action and not speech. But if the message expressed through the action is primary, then the conduct itself becomes a form of speech:

> Racism is both 100 percent speech and 100 percent conduct. Discriminatory conduct is not racist unless is also conveys the message of white supremacy. Likewise, all racist speech constructs the social reality that constrains the liberty of nonwhites because of their race. By limiting the life opportunities of others, this act of constructing meaning also makes racist speech conduct [Lawrence 1993, 62].

Lawrence argues that the Supreme Court's decision to declare segregation inherently in violation of the equal protection clause of the Fourteenth Amendment, in contrast to earlier court decisions that had sought only to equalize the separate accommodations made for Black Americans, indicates that the Court understood segregation as being primarily intended to convey the message of white supremacy. Thus in *Brown,* the Court decided that in weighing the requirements of the First Amendment with the requirements of the Fourteenth, the provisions of the Fourteenth were more important. Lawrence reiterates that the purpose of segregation is to label and define black people as inferior to white people. It communicates a message and it is that message that causes lasting harm to black Americans (Lawrence 2001).

More recently, Delgado and Stefancic argue that hate speech utterance are performative rather than referential (Delgado et al. 2017, 154). Hate speech does not refer to reality; it does not communicate anything and thus has no value in the marketplace of ideas. Instead, hate speech actively recreates the social reality of the speaker and the victim. Like Lawrence, Delgado and Stefancic believe that the equal protection clause in the Fourteenth Amendment provides a legal framework for regulating hate speech. By making the Fourteenth Amendment central "the defenders of offensive speech are required to show that the interest in safeguarding such speech is compelling enough to overcome the preference for equal personhood" (Delgado and Stefancic 2018, 25).

Of course, librarians are not lawyers nor are most of us legal scholars. Making decisions about what is legally protected and unprotected speech is quite beyond our expertise and professional purview. However, the Library Bill of Rights is not a legal document, nor are there any laws mandating that librarians behave in one way or another in regard to providing access to information, as long as they don't violate anti-discrimination laws. This gives information professionals considerable leeway in how we choose to approach our dual commitments to informational freedom and equity of access.

Critical Race Scholars argue that the incremental change inherent in liberal ideology is insufficient to address the profound historical and current harm of racism. Because racism as a structure is so deeply embedded in the institutions, laws, and culture of the United States, radical measures are necessary, "otherwise the system merely swallows up the small improvement one has made, and everything goes back the way it was" (Delgado, Stefancic, and Harris 2017).

Evidence for this assertion can be seen in the fact that American public schools are more segregated now than they were in 1968, despite the ruling in *Brown vs. Board of Education* ("Segregation Today" n.d.). The failure of the incremental approach can also be seen in the dismal success rates of programs to diversify the field of LIS. Consequently, it is time for a radical re-interpretation of the Library Bill of Rights in order to support a substantive understanding of intellectual freedom that does not pit freedom of speech against the right to equal treatment.

In speaking of the recent controversy over Scholastic's decision to pull the picture book *A Birthday Cake for George Washington* from publication due to concerns about its depictions of slavery, author Daniel José Older defends the decision from free speech advocates by changing how we think about censorship:

> Pulling a book because it's historically inaccurate and carries on the very American tradition of whitewashing slavery is classified as "censorship," while maintaining an ongoing majority white industry that systematically excludes narratives of color is just business as usual [Older 2016].

We are unused to thinking about publishing decisions as a form of censorship. After all, publishing companies are private entities and definitions of censorship most often limit themselves to action taken by government entities. However, if we take the lack of diversity within publishing seriously, as we should, then we must confront Older's definition of such racial exclusion as a form of censorship more injurious than opting not to keep a racist book on our library shelves.

Article II of the Library Bill of Rights states that libraries "should provide materials presenting all points of view on current and historical issues." This article has a more positive framework than others; that is it creates an obligation for librarians to actively seek materials from various perspectives. However, the standard interpretation only asks librarians to agree to purchase potentially controversial materials from the typical mainstream publishers.

A more radical approach to Article II would encourage librarians to actively seek out voices and points of view that are typically excluded from mainstream publishing. Digital and print-on-demand self-publishing and small presses could both be sources for these materials. The Cooperative Children's Book Center at the University of Wisconsin maintains a list of small presses that produce multi-cultural literature, most of which are owned by people of color or First Nations people ("Small Presses Owned/Operated by People of Color and First/Native Nations" 2016). However, these books are held by very few libraries. A WorldCat search for one of them, Cedar Grove Publishing, returned only four results. A thorough study of the library holdings of juvenile materials published by small presses is an important further avenue of study. Given the lack of small press materials reviewed by industry journals and the increasing reliance on vendors for collection development, it is unlikely that many libraries have an active policy to collect materials from smaller presses.

Instead of asking how and whether anti-racist work by librarians, including choosing not to include racist material in our collections, goes "against the integrity of other interests implicated in the status quo," like our current understanding of intellectual freedom, we should ask "how these traditional interests and values serve as vessels of racial subordination" (Lawrence et al. 1993, 6). A Library Bill of Rights that enables, or perhaps even necessitates, the continued subordination of people of color violates the Fourteenth Amendment's equal protection clause. Library policies that value the Office of Intellectual Freedom over the Office of Diversity, Outreach, and Inclusion uphold the structures of institutional racism that keep the profession primarily white and middle class.

WORKS CITED

Berninghausen, David, Robert F. Wedgeworth, F. William Summers, Patricia Glass Schuman, Jane Robbins, Clara S. Jones, Ervin J. Gaines, Arthur Curley and Andrew Armitage. 1993. "Social Responsibility vs. the Library Bill of Rights." *Library Journal*, 1993.

Delgado, Richard, and Jean Stefancic. 2018. *Must We Defend Nazis?: Why the First Amendment Should Not Protect Hate Speech and White Supremacy*. Reprint edition. New York: NYU Press.

Delgado, Richard, Jean Stefancic, and Angela Harris. 2017. *Critical Race Theory*. 3rd edition. New York: NYU Press.

Hathcock, April. 2015. "White Librarianship in Blackface: Diversity Initiatives in LIS." *In the Library with the Lead Pipe*, October. http://www.inthelibrarywiththeleadpipe.org/2015/lis-diversity/.

Honma, Todd. 2005. "Trippin' Over the Color Line: The Invisibility of Race in Library and Information Studies." *InterActions: UCLA Journal of Education and Information Studies* 1 (2). http://escholarship.org/uc/item/4nj0w1mp.

Horn, Zoia. 1977. "The Library Bill of Rights vs. the 'Racism and Sexism Awareness Resolution.'" *Library Journal* 102 (11): 1254.

Lawrence, Charles R. 1993. "If He Hollers Let Him Go: Regulating Racist Speech on Campus." In *Words That Wound: Critical Race Theory, Assaultive Speech, and the First Amendment*, 53–89. New Perspectives on Law, Culture, and Society. Boulder: Westview Press.

Lawrence, Charles R. 2001. "Segregation Misunderstood: The Milliken Decision Revisited." In *In Pursuit of a Dream Deferred: Linking Housing and Education Policy*, edited by John A. Powell, Gavin Kearney, and Vina Kay, 183–207. New York: Peter Lang, International Academic Publishers.

Lawrence, Charles R., Mari J. Matsuda, Richard Delgado, and Kimberlé Crenshaw. 1993. "Introduction." In *Words That Wound: Critical Race Theory, Assaultive Speech, and the First Amendment*, edited by Charles R. Lawrence, Mari J. Matsuda, and Kimberlé Crenshaw, 1–13. Boulder: Westview Press.

"Office for Diversity, Literacy, and Outreach Services." 2016. Text. Offices of the American Library Association. June 3, 2016. http://www.ala.org/offices/diversity.

Older, Daniel José. 2016. "The Real Censorship in Children's Books: Smiling Slaves Is Just the Half of It." *The Guardian*, 29 January 2016, sec. Books. https://www.theguardian.com/books/2016/jan/29/smiling-slaves-the-real-censorship-in-childrens-books.

"Segregation Today." n.d. Teaching Tolerance—Diversity, Equity and Justice. Accessed August 3, 2016. http://www.tolerance.org/supplement/segregation-today.

Shockey, Kyle. 2016. "Intellectual Freedom Is Not Social Justice." *Progressive Librarian*, no. 44 (Spring): 101–10.

"Small Presses Owned/Operated by People of Color and First/Native Nations." 2016. Children's Cooperative Book Center. July 2016. https://ccbc.education.wisc.edu/books/pclist.asp.

Snyder, Thomas D., Cristobal de Brey, and Sally A. Dillow. 2016. "Digest of Education Statistics 2014, NCES 2016-006." *National Center for Education Statistics*.

"SRRT—About Us." n.d. Accessed August 2, 2016. http://libr.org/srrt/about.php.

"SRRT Resolution—Resolution on Racism and Sexism Awareness." 1976. http://libr.org/srrt/resolutions/1976-1-racism.php.

Wedgeworth, Robert S., and F. William Summers. 1993. "The Berninghausen Debate." *Library Journal* 118 (15): S3.

Wiegand, Wayne A., and Donald G. Davis, Jr. 2015. *Encyclopedia of Library History*. New York: Routledge.

Collaborative Justice

Gender-Based Activism in the University Library

CARRIE MORAN *and* LEANDRA PRESTON-SIDLER

Introduction

The core value of librarianship is to provide equitable access to information to anyone who needs it. It is a profession founded on social justice; in an academic setting, the library is a natural partner for Women's and Gender Studies (WGST) departments. University libraries are typically centrally located, well-trafficked, and hold nostalgic value for their users. This combination of factors provides an ideal setting to support gender-based activism. At the University of Central Florida (UCF), a collaborative partnership between the library and the WGST program kicked off when a proudly feminist librarian became their liaison.

The WGST program was excited to have a librarian who understood their content and mission. This relationship thrived as we created opportunities to bring attention to library spaces and resources, as well as Women's and Gender Studies' programming. The primary goal of everyone involved was to create events emphasizing action around intersectionality and the often-painful reality that such identities entail. Events such as open mics, film screenings, and a full day "WomanFest" create safe spaces for the campus community to share, learn, and process social justice issues.

Climate

The partnership was initiated in March 2016, during a time when the American public was becoming increasingly divisive on myriad topics in response to the upcoming presidential election. Although the UCF campus has spaces and services for diverse populations, there were few events or spaces that allowed the campus community to come together to express the challenges they faced without fear of heated debate.

Libraries have always been safe spaces for their communities. Public libraries in major metropolitan areas often employ social workers and offer classes on diverse topics. Academic libraries are typically the most well-trafficked buildings on campus other than student unions and dining halls. Students visit their campus library to study, meet, use computers, print, play games, do research, among other activities. Some libraries house other campus offices and services, like tutoring and writing assistance.

The importance of the academic library as a third space, between the dorm and the classroom, cannot be overstated. If students do not feel safe to be themselves in their library, they will miss opportunities to use these resources. Library building and service design can impact the way students feel in a space. Gender-neutral bathrooms, universally accessible spaces, inclusive signage, and staff trained to work with diverse populations are a few examples of what this looks like in practice. Not every library can implement these design choices due to budgetary and other constraints, but almost all academic libraries have some sort of classroom or gathering space. Offering programming that supports a social justice mission is a cheaper, quicker, and more flexible option for moving toward creating a safe environment for the campus community.

Collaboration

The WGST faculty and librarian are all committed to bringing their activism to their work on campus; this mutual dedication was crucial in forming the foundation of a sustainable partnership. The first event that resulted from this partnership was a screening of the documentary *Wonder Women!: The Untold Story of American Superheroines* (Guevara-Flanagan, 2012) followed by a panel discussion for Women's History Month in March 2016. This program was well attended, and highlighted student interest in events tackling gender-based issues. This initial success, coupled with a desire to give students a safe space to gather for discussion, generated the idea to launch an ongoing series of events.

The WGST librarian was also the President of UCF's Pride Faculty & Staff Association (PFSA). She took on this role two weeks before the Pulse tragedy, one of the worst mass shootings in American history that greatly impacted the UCF and greater Orlando community. She was a speaker at many campus events that occurred in the wake of Pulse, and worked with students, faculty, and staff to connect them to support resources on campus. Pulse made the diverse communities within Orlando and UCF unite in a way they hadn't before, and highlighted a need for more spaces and venues on campus to discuss these issues.

As PFSA President, the librarian was able to foster connections across campus with the offices and programs supporting diverse communities, and the individuals on campus most likely to support programming on diverse topics. The WGST program has a network of affiliates on campus who teach in or support gender-based learning and programming. These networks proved invaluable in the promotion and success of all future events. In "Mobilization among Women Academics: The Interplay between Feminism and the Profession" (Hart 2008), emphasizes the power of collaboration to make change. She writes, "Creating powerful networks can be a significant tool to provide support and improve the climate within academe [as it is] only through collective strength can any movement achieve its goals" (Hart 2008, 5). This is particularly true for traditionally marginalized groups, which is what both WGST and PFSA represent.

Open Heart Open Mic

The Open Heart Open Mic series was born during a summer planning meeting with the WGST Librarian, the WGST Program Director, and two full-time WGST faculty.

Although much of the collaboration between the library and the WGST program is accomplished virtually, regular face to face meetings were a crucial part of fostering the creative energy necessary for dynamic, collaborative projects. When reflecting on the success of the "Wonder Women" film screening, the team generated ideas for programming for the 2016–17 academic year. Creating a yearly event during Women's History Month was a clear priority, but the team felt that a regularly scheduled, ongoing event was necessary.

In the previous academic year, the Library partnered with the Student Accessibility Services office to offer an open mic night. The WGST librarian, who is also a poet, helped bring this event to the Library. The event was well attended; diverse stories were shared. An open mic series seemed to be ideal for creating a safe space for students to discuss the wide range of issues they were facing, and to process the unsettling political climate.

For the initial round of the series, one open mic event centered around a theme was scheduled each month. The subjects for the first three events were Hispanic Heritage Month (September), LGBTQ History Month (October), and Indigenous Peoples Month (November). The rationale for selecting a subject was to help tie in with other campus events honoring those themes, and to provide a focus for selecting pieces to share.

To inspire a community spirit at the events, refreshments were served and attendees were encouraged to bring their own food to share. The first three open mics were scheduled in evenings and located in a large library classroom. Many institutions are experiencing scheduling challenges as enrollment grows faster than campus space. Academic libraries can help meet this challenge for hosting events due to their central location and the ease of booking library classrooms.

The series was marketed through various channels, including the library website, the WGST program website, social media, the campus events calendar, and via email to the network of WGST program affiliate faculty. The WGST faculty also announced the series to their classes, and encouraged attendance. We chose the title "Open Heart Open Mic" because it reflected the emphasis on the events being a safe space to share emotions, not just words.

Lessons from Fall 2016

The first semester of Open Heart Open Mic events had challenges and successes. Each month's events had students, faculty, and staff in attendance. Many events external to the classroom are aimed at only one of these audiences, or are not interactive in any meaningful way. Each of the WGST faculty and the WGST Librarian prepared materials ahead of time that spoke to the theme. They also shared personal work and stories to kick off the event. This was crucial in helping students feel comfortable in the space, and also recognize that they could find commonalities with faculty and staff they might not have been expecting.

Is it possible to create a safe space without first gaining the trust of your users? In a 2016 talk at the Library Instruction West Conference, Donna Lanclos stated "How do you become trustworthy? Not as individuals, but structurally? What makes it make sense for students or faculty to come to you? To the Library? Where else is the library? Does the persistent question, "why don't they come to us?" make sense if we are all supposed to be part of the same community?" (Lanclos 2016). These important questions cannot be answered without some degree of vulnerability, both in planning for spaces and services, and in the implementation of those spaces and services. For the open mic series, this trust was garnered by the development of an event outside the traditional experience of an academic library, and by sharing personal stories during the event.

This vulnerability enabled attendees, particularly students, to feel comfortable enough to participate. The first semester had a few special moments that demonstrated this trust. During the October event, focused on LGBTQ History Month, a student who is a singer-songwriter chose to attend because she was seeking others in the LGBTQ community at UCF. She performs in many local venues, but shared that she was not out to her family, and that they attended all of her performances. She wrote a song about a relationship she had with another woman, and before playing the song she stated "I've never been able to play this song with the correct pronouns before." Her willingness to share this story and song would not have happened in a space that did not feel safe for her.

That same evening, another student shared that she attended the event because she identified with the community, but didn't expect to perform her poetry because she didn't think any of her poems fit the theme. After hearing others share a wide variety of stories, poems, and songs, she felt comfortable to share her work. This story informed planning for the Spring semester, as we gathered feedback that the selection of a theme could be a barrier to attendance and participation if a person didn't identify with the chosen community of focus. That event was also the first event with another campus partner, the Wellness and Health Promotion (WHPS) program.

The library established a relationship with this program in the previous year. WHPS had been a regular participant in the library's Campus Connections program that provided space for other campus organizations to set up an informational table in the library lobby. In Fall 2015, they asked if they could use their table to run a campaign called "To Knights with Love." This ongoing campaign provides students with materials to write and decorate anonymous letters of support which are later distributed on campus in a variety of ways.

WHPS also holds regular "make and take" mini craft tables on campus, and the library quickly became a space where they offered both of these initiatives to students. The WGST Librarian was the main point of contact for this partnership, and she asked if WHPS would be willing to attend events and offer these opportunities to attendees. For the October event, they brought mini flag templates with a chart of the various LGBTQ flag designs for students to create their own. They also brought supplies for folks to write support letters.

This interactive activity was very popular with attendees. They were able to connect while making crafts, and have something to take home after the event. The crafts and letter-writing activities created a supportive environment, and gave a tangible outlet for self-expression that did not require attendees to share with the entire room. The first open mic didn't have these activities, so when there were no longer any willing participants, the event ended earlier than scheduled. The addition of the crafting area helped extend the length of the event, and even prompted more sharing after the first round of participation.

One of the challenges in any event is scheduling. UCF is a largely commuter-based campus, and many of the people who stay on campus after 5pm are attending an evening class or working in some capacity. We staggered the first semester event hours and scheduled two hours in the space. The experience in the first semester informed a decision to hold Spring semester open mics during the day.

Planning for Spring 2017

The Library and the WGST program found great value in the Open Heart Open Mic series. The Library attracted new students, and established or strengthened relationships with campus organizations and academic departments. The WGST program was able to market their courses and study abroad opportunities to a new set of students, and provide a space outside the classroom for students to process what they were learning in their WGST courses. Attendance at the first semester events was mixed between students who found out about the program through their courses, and those who found out through other means.

One of the most successful marketing techniques was distributing information through campus housing. Even though UCF is a primarily commuter campus, one of the initial motivators for hosting this series in the evening was to provide cultural activities to students living on campus. Each of the first semester events attracted these students, and several brought friends who did not live on campus. UCF also has a centralized events calendar for the entire campus. The main campus calendar populates daily and weekly emails to the entire UCF campus community.

In Spring 2017, the WGST Librarian engaged in research with transfer students about their interaction with and use of the library. In questions focused on library events, a majority of survey respondents and interviewees reported using this calendar and/or their email to find out what was happening on campus. They also typically looked for events on the day before or of the event, and were primarily looking for things to do during time periods between classes or other campus activities. This reinforced the value of the calendar system, and of switching the event times to the lunch hour.

The open mic series for Spring 2017 was scheduled during an intersession planning meeting between the WGST program faculty and librarian. Several of the lessons learned during the first semester influenced changes for the Spring. No theme was assigned, and a line was added to marketing materials that read "You are welcome to bring a story, poem, song, or any other vocal presentation to share—on any topic." We placed events on Facebook, and sent a direct invitation to an on-campus spoken word club. The increased attendance at Spring open mic events reflected the value of these changes.

Another discussion focused on the ways to preserve the creative works of the very talented students sharing original poems and songs during the events. At the April open mic event, student Grace Cristiani shared her poem "Nevertheless, She Persisted." After the event, she gave the WGST program permission to publish it on their website. Starting in Fall 2017, students who share work at open mic events are invited to submit their work to the UCF Library's institutional repository STARS (http://stars.library.ucf.edu). The Library also started holding writing contests in April 2017, and these became a cross-promotional tool for the open mic events.

WomanFest 2017

Our ultimate collaborative accomplishment is WomanFest, which brings students, faculty, and the community together for a series of events spanning an entire day. The first WomanFest was held in March 2017. A section of WST 3603: Introduction to Gender Studies course was offered from 10:30 a.m. to 11:45 a.m. on the same day as a section of WST 3460H: Honors Women, Race & Struggle course which took place from 1:30 p.m. to 2:45 p.m. WomanFest was scheduled to span the two class periods, with an open mic in the middle. The faculty teaching each of these sections took the lead planning the programming that would occur during their course period. For the morning class, we decided to focus on women in leadership.

The American Association of University Women (AAUW) has a UCF chapter. We reached out to them to provide speakers for a panel discussion on women in leadership. UCF student Layla Ferris covered this event, and wrote about the panel: "Three extraordinary women represented the AAUW-Orlando/Winter Park branch at the panel: Christine Mouton, president of the branch and director of UCF's Victim Services; Rana Tiwari, appointed officer for the branch's legal advocacy fund; and Jean Bubriski who is currently teaching English for international students at Seminole State College. Each woman shared stories of success and failure, empowering the audience of about fifty people" (Ferris 2017). Each panelist told her story, then engaged in discussion with students.

Each element of the day was thoughtfully planned, from the content of the agenda to the hot pink WomanFest water bottles provided to participants. The WGST Program Director and librarian both contributed to a campus-wide planning effort centered on creating programming for Women's History Month. This opportunity informed decision-making on what to offer at WomanFest and provided a channel to promote the event more widely.

The open mic portion of the event was more emotional than any prior ones. Attendees shared more than just poetry or music; several shared their life stories. One student spoke about the stigmatization she experienced due to her Colombian heritage, and openly wept in front of the crowd. This inspired another student with Colombian heritage to disclose personal details about her struggles with identity. Students spoke about mental health issues, fears about the political climate, but also talked about strength and comfort they gained sharing these issues with others. The bond created during this experience extended throughout the semester, as the WST 3603 class returned to the library for a private zine workshop, and invited the WGST librarian to come to their final class of the semester—a classroom open mic.

The last portion of WomanFest focused on alternative media with a zine presentation and workshop. Zines are self-produced booklets "filled with diatribes, reworkings of pop culture iconography, and all variety of personal and political narratives, […] an example of participatory media created by consumers rather than by the corporate culture industries" (Piepmeier and Zeisler 2009, 2). Students in the Women, Race, and Struggle course were provided a plethora of materials to create their own zines for a class assignment focusing on issues relevant to the course. Beyond that, in the spirit of zines, there were no guidelines or constraints around the content.

A WGST faculty member who specializes in Third Wave Feminism led the workshop, which included a presentation focusing on the herstory, structure, and function(s) of zines, so students had a better foundation on which to create their own. The Library's Head of Special Collections set up a display of zines created by UCF students to provide examples and raise awareness about Special Collections. The workshop was both fun and informative, allowing students to interact with one another and faculty/staff in ways often limited by classroom structure and space.

Students were also invited to contribute their creations to Special Collections, providing an opportunity for their own media creation to become part of larger conversations. In *Girls Make Media,* Mary Celeste Kearney writes about young women's media production as a form of activism elevating female voices and bringing them out of private spaces into public spheres Kearney asserts that the expansion of girls' access to media-making tools enables marginalized voices to take a more central role in media production, noting that "Contemporary girl made media extends beyond their producers' bedrooms, long understood as the primary location for girls' creative endeavors" (Kearney 2006, 3). The Library is a space with unlimited possibilities, not just for media consumption, but to encourage media production, as well.

Lessons Learned from WomanFest

WomanFest 2017 was an incredibly successful event in terms of attendance and the experience created for participants. It would have been impossible to create that experience without collaboration between multiple partners internal and external to the library. Within the library, the WGST librarian worked with outreach librarians, the library's Art Specialist, the Special Collections and University Archives department, the Circulation department, the Reference department office manager, and the LibTech department. Library administration provided a larger budget for this event than any other to-date, and even purchased a microphone and speaker set because the event proved so successful.

Outside the library, the WGST faculty relied on their network of affiliates to promote and even attend the event. The WGST librarian made use of her other role as president of a campus diversity organization to partner with the Office of Diversity and Inclusion. This office donated funds that enabled the purchase of custom WomanFest water bottles. These giveaway items were purchased through a local, alumni-owned company who donated stickers free of cost to support this event. Making a commitment to activism is like planting a tree, you never know how the roots or branches will grow, but they often transcend their origins in unexpected ways.

The outreach and communication channels established during the promotion of open mic events worked well for this event. WomanFest was promoted through the campus-wide marketing of Women's History Month. Future events might garner more attendance if they are also directly marketed to campus offices and organizations that work to support diversity and inclusion efforts.

Looking Ahead

The WGST librarian who established these programs accepted a position at California State University San Marcos in July 2017, but wanted to ensure programming would continue. Although a new librarian was assigned to the program, the library's reference department office manager was tasked with partnering on event planning. She was instrumental in the success of WomanFest, and her personal interest in feminism and social justice is part of the key to success. Before the WGST librarian left, she and the office manager met with the WGST program faculty to plan events for the entire

2017–18 academic year to allow for a smooth transition and highlighted the collaborative nature of events, from planning to implementation.

Open Heart Open Mic events were scheduled for the Fall semester, and a date has already been selected for WomanFest 2018. The magic of these events transcends physical spaces; the former WGST Librarian was able to FaceTime the October open mic event to share her poetry and tears as other participants read their work. She is planning to continue virtual attendance at these events, and hopes to initiate some at her new library. There is also infrastructure in place with the Special Collections and University Archives department to continue holding zine workshops, and to allow for students donate their zines to the library's zine collection. The fact that students can contribute to a collection of work to be seen and shared provides reinforcement that their voices matter and validates the value of their creations.

Conclusion

The library is an essential space for universities to meet the academic needs of students and faculty, but, as our efforts demonstrate, it can provide so much more. The events discussed here serve as examples of a library utilized to its full potential through collaboration, connection, and creativity. Our open mic events, film screenings, discussion panels, and media workshops also emphasize that education and activism take many forms. With committed librarians and faculty working together, libraries can be not-so-quiet safe spaces for students to explore information, expand their minds, and pursue passions.

Works Cited

Brown, Sarah, and Katherine Mangan. 2016. "What 'Safe Spaces' Really Look Like on College Campuses." *The Chronicle of Higher Education*, 8 September 2016: 63–66.

Ferris, Layla. 2017. "UCF Celebrates Women's History Month with Womanfest 2017." *NSM Today*. Accessed October 5, 2017. http://www.nicholsonstudentmedia.com/news/ucf-celebrates-women-s-history-month-with-womanfest/article_9248f08a-03b3-11e7-b4b3-3b8eecddd46e.html.

Guevara-Flanagan, Kristy. 2012. *Wonder Women! The Untold Story of American Superheroines*. Directed by Kristy Guevara-Flanagan. Newburgh, NY: New Day Films. DVD.

Hart, Jeni. 2008. "Mobilization Among Women Academics: The Interplay Between Feminism and Professionalization." *NWSA Journal* 20, no. 1: 184–208.

Kearney, Mary Celeste. 2006. *Girls Make Media*. New York: Routledge.

Lanclos, Donna. 2016. "Teaching, Learning, and Vulnerability in Digital Places: Library Instruction West." *Donna Lanclos—The Anthropologist in the Stacks*. Accessed November 23, 2017. http://www.donnalanclos.com/teaching-learning-and-vulnerability-in-digital-places-library-instruction-west-2016-keynote/.

Piepmeier, Alison, and Andi Zeisler. 2009. *Girl Zines: Making Media, Doing Feminism*. New York: New York University Press.

PART VI

Generating Programming

Creating Communities
Through Living Books

The Human Library Experience
at Southern New Hampshire University

HEATHER WALKER-WHITE *and* JOSHUA BECKER

Communities of all stripes are initiating Human Libraries as a means to confront intolerance and to promote an awareness of diverse life experiences. Unlike traditional libraries, in a Human Library the "books" are individuals who volunteer their time to tell their story. These "books" are "checked out" by users. The individuals who check out these books are considered readers. "Books" and "Readers" will then converse over a set period of time.

A book shares a key aspect of their personal history. As the Human Library organization states: "The Human Library is a place where real people are on loan to readers. A place where difficult questions are expected, appreciated and answered" (Origin of the Human Library 2017). These conversations between book and reader regularly examine sensitive topics. Through these conversations visitors can achieve a greater understanding of social diversity.

The Human Library movement originated in Copenhagen, Denmark in 2000 (they were known as "Living Libraries" until 2010). Since that time, Human Libraries have received a fair share of international recognition. In 2003, the Human Library concept was formally endorsed by the Council of Europe (Dreher and Mowbray 2012, 11). Over nearly twenty years this movement has gradually spread to over eighty countries (Granger 2017, 20).

The first Human Libraries were held in the United States in 2008 (Wentz 2012, 38); New Hampshire had its first Human Library event in 2013 (Gamtso, Mannon, and Whipple 2017, 189). In the United States this movement has become increasingly popular in both community and academic settings. While colleges and universities are frequent sites for Human Libraries, school libraries have also become popular venues. Although Human Libraries may differ markedly in both audience and tone, their basic premise ensures that these events will provide meaningful vehicles for campus and community outreach in the future.

Upon visiting a Human Library event, users will be given a catalog and be able to choose among the available books. The range of different personal experiences usually focus on the difficulties of being part of a specific subculture or minority group. There may be many different types of books in each event with topics ranging from religion, ethnicity, gender, and careers, among others. After checking out a book, users will be given a list of possible conversation prompts to help begin a thoughtful discussion.

Although any organization can hold this type of event, the term Human Library is trademarked. To use that term as an event title, your organization must register with humanlibraries.org and pay a licensing fee. In return, you have the right to use the Human Library name and licensed images (Granger 2017, 21). Registered organizations will also receive digital information packets with downloadable fliers, logos, questions, and other materials that will help facilitate the event.

A Human Library event is often marketed using both print and digital means. The Human Library organization will also promote the event via Facebook for registered organizers. Many libraries have used social media to raise awareness of these events. Academic libraries often set up an online presence and library guides (i.e., libguides) to promote these events. Sometimes these resources become very elaborate and remain accessible long after the conclusion of the event. The Augustana Campus at the University of Alberta began offering Human Libraries annually in 2009 (Augustana Human Library 2017, 13). In these situations, the online presence will expand every year, allowing other institutions to leverage these guides as they establish their own events.

The structure and themes of Human Libraries allow for significant variety. Some organizations choose to have their events centered around a common theme (i.e., "Build Bridges," "Creating Community," and "Chains of Freedom"). However, this practice is by no means universal. Some organizations don't have a unifying theme; instead, they choose to include any willing book that has an interesting story to tell.

Although the original intent of Human Libraries was to encourage individuals to have stark conversations about difficult realities, many libraries have chosen to differ from this approach. Rather than place individuals outside of their comfort zone, some organizations choose to stress cultural richness through the unique stories of each book. Specifically, some academic libraries use this event to focus on a variety of experiences as a means to enrich the lives of their students (Gamtso, Mannon, and Whipple 2017, 196).

The selection of books will vary significantly based on the setting and potential audience. In an academic setting, Human Library books are usually recruited among students, faculty, staff, and alumni. For community organizations, local residents make up the largest group. In some instances Human Libraries travel to different communities or academic institutions. In the United States, Human Libraries have formed a repository of individuals willing to serve as books at other events (Granger 2017, 23).

These events can range from a couple of hours on a single day to multiple days. Many Human Libraries may be run by the libraries but sponsored by larger civic and community organizations. In academic libraries, partnerships and collaborations are often formed with other on campus organizations (diversity, student affairs, wellness, etc.) or specific courses offered during that semester (Gamtso, Mannon, and Whipple 2017, 197). A few organizations choose to host Human Libraries remotely or as a "Traveling Human Library" (Dreher and Mowbray 2012, 30).

There are other variations as well. Book checkout times are often between ten minutes to half an hour, although longer times occasionally occur. While Human Libraries generally involve one individual checking out one book, sometimes a book has a conversation with a small group (Dreher and Mowbray 2012, 42). After the checkout time has ended, books are frequently given a short break, before speaking to the next reader(s).

For Human Libraries to be successful, both as annual or seasonal events, a strong structure is often needed. Due to the time, effort, and logistics required to set up these events, many organizations have scaled back their efforts. Some academic institutions have had success by scheduling Human Libraries as part of a broader range of events (i.e., University festival). Similarly, some public libraries choose to hold Human Libraries during themed events such as National Library Week (Gamtso, Mannon, and Whipple 2017, 191).

Research studies suggest that there are several tangible effects that spring from these events. Human Libraries have produced broad understanding among different communities. Attendees report significant benefits in participating. These events, "tend to facilitate a more interactive, two-way process of conversations in which Readers may disclose as much as Books" (Dreher and Mowbray 2012, 55). In another study books mentioned, "I learned from them as much as I hope they learned from me" (Dobreski and Huang 2016, 2).

Despite strong attendance at Human Libraries, coupled with positive user feedback over many years, limited quantitative research exists that measures the direct impact of Human Libraries on users. That may be changing. A recent study surveyed sixty-nine books from four Human Libraries about their experiences. Participants noted eight different levels of benefits. Some of the most prominent benefits included, "learning, self-expression, reflection, therapeutic benefits, and personal enjoyment" (Dobreski and Huang 2016, 2).

Southern New Hampshire University (SNHU) is the largest educational institution in the Manchester area; the campus is located in the city of Manchester (population 110,000). The city is the largest in northern New England and is among the most diverse urban centers in the region. Manchester is also home to a refugee resettlement area. The refugee resettlement initiative began in the 1970s and has long been the largest in the state (Refugee Resettlement 2009–2016). The region is economically and politically diverse, marked by significant affluence coupled with urban poverty. This area has been severely affected by the current opioid epidemic. In this diverse landscape Shapiro Librarians wanted to introduce a Human Library.

SNHU is a private non-profit institution that was founded in 1932. The institution offers degrees ranging from Associates to Doctoral. Its main campus in Manchester, NH serves nearly 4,000 undergraduate and graduate students. Most students attending the main campus live in residential housing, although there is also a sizable commuter population. (SNHU's online college has a very large enrollment. As of this writing, the online college was not involved in our Human Library events.) SNHU's campus is also marked by economic and cultural diversity. More than 90 percent of campus students receive financial aid. International students come from more than sixty-seven countries, and their numbers, both graduate and undergraduate, have grown significantly in the last decade.

Shapiro Library is housed inside the Wolak Library Learning Commons (WLLC). This building is also home to several key campus offices including the Learning Center and Information Technology Services. It also has a large café area, set apart from the library, for students and faculty to meet. This setting provided the ideal backdrop for our intended event.

Despite the increase of Human Library events worldwide over the past two decades, only a handful of events have taken place in northern New England in recent years. The Human Library movement was first brought to our attention by an event held at another local university, and our interest was piqued after we learned more about the movement at a conference. Taking into consideration the diversity of our campus and the surrounding community, as well as wishing to offer more programming, we thought that a Human Library would be the perfect event to bring to our campus. Our aim in hosting a Human Library was threefold: to provide an opportunity for community members to connect in a new and different way; to broaden our users' perceptions and experiences of the Shapiro Library; and to offer more social programming in the library.

Our first event was planned for mid–October of 2017. This part of the semester was chosen as it allowed sufficient time to introduce the Human Library concept to the campus, recruit books, and promote the event; it also did not conflict with midterm examinations. Recruitment of books was done solely among SNHU community members. Books were recruited in person, and through email invitations to offices identified as serving users who may have a particular interest in volunteering to be books (e.g., the Office of Diversity Programs, the International Student Services office, etc.). Framed as "creating community through conversation," our event sought to bring together the diverse peoples of our learning community in a safe space where conversations could occur freely and comfortably.

In the spirit of the Human Library movement, attention was drawn to the "outsider" aspect of books. However, this proved to be intimidating to potential volunteers, and contributed to lower than expected number of sign-ups. Despite significant efforts to explain the concept of a Human Library, there was some reluctance among people to volunteer as books. Though people appreciated the idea of individuals who have experienced marginalization, prejudice, or other stigma sharing their stories, they were not yet comfortable having their stories be the focus of conversations. Interestingly, potential books were also confused by the concept of the Human Library, with some individuals expressing their "understanding" that they were to dress as a character from their favorite book. Ultimately, book titles included a variety of topics such as *minority women in STEM, experience of an international student in America, Muslim physical disability, so you want to be a global citizen*, and *published author*, and feedback of the event was positive.

A libguide was created for the event, including a description of the Human Library movement, the purpose of our event, and a link to an online volunteer book sign up form. Books provided their own title and description that were not altered by event organizers in any way. This information was used for the print catalog listings for readers to peruse prior to checking out a book. Promotion of the event was done via the Shapiro Library's social media channels, in person, and via targeted emails to university departments which were thought to serve community members who may have a particular interest in our Human Library.

In an effort to create awareness of the event, on campus marketing was engaged, and a video about our Human Library was created and shared via on campus social media channels. Unfortunately, this coverage was not completed until after our event had occurred, but it did serve as a vehicle for helping organizers continue to introduce the Human Library concept to the broader SNHU community and hopefully generate support and enthusiasm for any future events.

Our first Human Library was scheduled to begin during the Wednesday weekly free period, a seventy-five minute time period set aside when there are no classes. However, as such, it was one of several campus activities taking place at the same time as a variety of club meetings, athletic practices, and faculty meetings. Despite competing demands on users' schedules, we felt that the weekly free period presented the best opportunity to introduce the Human Library to the SNHU community. Our Human Library was held in a section of the WLLC's café which offers flexible seating, and the seating arrangement provided ample space between readings to allow for privacy between book and reader.

Our Human Library ran for two hours, for a total of six sessions. Sessions lasted fifteen minutes with five minute breaks scheduled between readings designed to allow the books time to rest and regroup prior to the beginning of the next session. Readers received a print catalog with the title and description supplied by the books, but no names or other identifying information was listed in an effort to encourage readers to engage with someone based solely on the book's description, rather than existing relationships with the book. Readers signed up for timeslots during which they would check out their selected book(s), and then waited for their session to begin. Booklets containing information about the Human Library movement (and our event in particular), guidelines for readers, and conversation prompts were handed out to each reader. Prior to the start of each session, event organizers made every effort to escort readers to their selected books and make personal introductions. Time warnings were given at five and one minutes prior to the end of each session to alert both books and readers that their time together was nearly over.

Readers were offered the opportunity to provide feedback via a brief paper survey at the end of their session(s), and it was overwhelmingly positive. Nearly all respondents had never heard of the Human Library, nor had they ever attended such an event. Almost all said that they would attend a similar program again. One reader expressed surprise and delight about her newly deepened connection with someone whom she believed she already knew well. Her initial purpose in attending our Human Library was to support her friend (and the event), but it ultimately resulted in a deeper appreciation for the book's experiences and his willingness to share his story in the Human Library format. Following her session, she was eager to have another, this time with a book completely unknown to her.

Research indicates that the benefits of being a human book range from altruistic to personal. Volunteer books report satisfaction not only with helping or teaching readers by sharing their experiences, but also through reflecting upon their personal experiences (Dobreski and Huang 2016, 2). This was repeatedly observed among our participants. Throughout our Human Library event, books also had the opportunity to sit and read each other. This can be a serendipitous side effect of Human Libraries and one for which books from our and other local events have shared their enthusiasm and appreciation. Additional feedback from books included delight at being able to engage with each other in a forum unlike any other on campus, and pleasure from the opportunity to connect with people from various units of the SNHU community.

Overall, our first Human Library event was considered a success. Though turnout was lower than anticipated, both books and readers made meaningful connections. We were pleased that difficult conversations took place in a safe space where books and readers felt comfortable enough to allow themselves the vulnerability necessary to bridge gaps and work towards creating understanding. Participants—books and readers alike—

were largely positive about the event, and expressed interest in taking part in future Human Libraries on campus.

We took the lessons learned from our first event and eagerly began to think about hosting a second Human Library. While planning, organizers took a critical look at elements from our first event and explored how to enhance them. In particular, the recruitment of books, promotion of the event, and increasing participation were identified as areas for improvement.

Our second Human Library event was planned for mid–March of 2018, and retained the same theme of "creating community through conversation." This time, the Human Library would be held the week following spring break, and, again, did not conflict with midterm exams. Though organizers discussed whether or not to change the time of day the event would be held, the Wednesday free period was again determined to be the most appropriate time for our second Human Library. In an effort to provide a broader perspective, we decided early on not to limit the pool of potential books to SNHU community members. Recruitment included invitations to individuals who had previously volunteered as books in other local Human Library events. This approach nearly tripled the number of book participants, and titles included *Sick and Tired of Being Sick and Tired, Traumatic Brain Injury, Women Veteran,* and *Tiny White Box/Great North Woods,* among others. This also helped create momentum for the event. Not only did the books from the broader community increase the variety of content available to readers, they helped with promotion of the event through their personal social networks.

As with our first Human Library, promotion was done via the library's social media channels, and included the creation of a hashtag, #SNHUmanLibrary, which was used in all social media posts promoting the event. Going forward, this hashtag will be used to promote all future Human Library events hosted by the Shapiro Library. Word of mouth and targeted emails also played a significant role in event promotion. More offices, as well as more individual university personnel, were identified as recipients for email blasts; on campus marketing provided additional assistance with email blasts and social media posts. An increase in Humanities department programming in the library over the course of the academic year also led to those individuals spreading the word about our event to their students. These three elements: more prominent promotion by individual books, the creation of the hashtag, and broader digital promotion increased overall online engagement for the event.

A library website reorganization required us to convert the libguide created for our first Human Library event into a webpage associated with the Shapiro Library homepage for our second (and subsequent) events. New additions to our Human Library's online presence included the creation of an FAQ about Human Libraries, which can be queried from the FAQ search box on the library's homepage, as well as the creation of an online catalog. This was published a week prior to the event and allowed potential readers to peruse book titles and descriptions in advance of our second Human Library. As in our first event, readers could also choose among books from a print catalog available on the day of the #SNHUmanLibrary.

Engaging with more student organizations was identified as a means to increase awareness of, and attendance at, our second event. Specifically, the Student Government Association's (SGA) Penmen Pride program was used to induce student participation. The Penmen Pride program assigns points to on campus events, which students can accrue to earn prizes. Applying for the #SNHUmanLibrary to be a Penmen Pride event proved to be advantageous for the event itself, as well as for future planning. The student government representative assigned to cover the Human Library (and thus award points to student participants), who is also a writer for the campus newspaper, the Penmen Press, succeeded in convincing editors to cover our event. Organizers also asked the SGA representative and campus paper staff for their input about how to better promote our Human Library and received thoughtful responses which will inform our event planning going forward.

Our second Human Library proved to be measurably more successful than our first, with total book and reader participation increasing by more than 50 percent, and increased online engagement and promotion of the event. Participant feedback was entirely positive, with one reader commenting that she felt as though her "heart expanded" during the course of the event, and several other readers commenting on the unique nature of the Human Library and their desire, and willingness, to attend future events. Overall, library administration is pleased with the program's initial successes and has identified it as one of the Shapiro Library's "signature events" going forward.

In planning future Human Library events, we will continue to focus on strengthening relationships with SNHU community partners. It is our hope to engage more effectively with on campus offices (Office of Diversity Programs, International Student Services, Women's Center, and others) to recruit both books and readers, and to cultivate co-sponsorship opportunities for our Human Library events. Such co-sponsorships will not only aid in the promotion of the #SNHUmanLibrary, but will generally benefit the library's outreach efforts. Additionally, we hope to identify teaching faculty who will incorporate the #SNHUmanLibrary as a graded component of their course assignments. Lastly, it is our hope to bring the #SNHUmanLibrary to our many online SNHU community members, enabling participation of our online students, faculty, and staff as both books and readers.

Future promotional efforts will include broader engagement with on campus marketing. Organizers also propose to employ more basic PR methods in addition to established online marketing efforts, as student feedback indicates that fliers posted on bulletin boards and sandwich board advertising around campus are effective. Broader promotion within the Manchester, NH community is desirable, as well, and it is likely efforts will be made to draw attention to our Human Library events via local print, digital, and broadcast media.

In early 2017, we first considered bringing the Human Library movement to the Southern New Hampshire University campus. In a matter of months, organizers successfully introduced the concept to the SNHU community, implemented a new program, established and strengthened relations with a variety of units on campus, and, most importantly, created community through conversation. Along the way, successes and areas for improvement were identified and, much like a Human Library itself, the #SNHUmanLibrary became a living program that will continue to evolve in each iteration. We hope our story will inspire other organizations to bring the Human Library movement to their communities as a way to actively create connections.

Works Cited

"Augustana Human Library." 2017. *American Libraries* 48: 12–13. http://ezproxy.snhu.edu/login?url=http://
    search.ebscohost.com/login.aspx?direct=true&db=eft&AN=125343840&site=eds-live&scope=site.
Dobreski, Brian, and Yun Huang. 2016. "The Joy of Being a Book: Benefits of Participation in the Human

Library." *Proceedings of the Association for Information Science and Technology* 53 (1): 1–3. doi:10.1002/pra2.2016.14505301139.

Dreher, Tanja, and Jemima Mowbray. 2012. *The Power of One on One: Human Libraries and the Challenges of Antiracism Work*. UTSePress.

Gamtso, Carolyn, Melissa Mannon, and Sandy Whipple. 2017. "The New Hampshire Human Library Project: Breaking Barriers and Building Bridges by Engaging Communities of Learners." In *The Experiential Library: Transforming Academic and Research Libraries Through the Power of Experiential Learning*, edited by Peter McDonnell. 1st ed., 187–201. Cambridge, MA: Chandos Publishing.

Granger, Liz. 2017. *If These Books Could Talk: Patrons Check Out People at Human Libraries*. American Library Association.

"New Hampshire Department of Health and Human Services Office of Health Equity Refugee Resettlement 2009–2016." New Hampshire Department of Health and Human Services. Accessed April 12, 2018. https://www.dhhs.nh.gov/omh/refugee/documents/ytd-1.pdf.

"The Origin of the Human Library." Human Library. Accessed April 12, 2018. http://humanlibrary.org/about-the-human-library/.

Wentz, Erin. 2012. *The Human Library: Sharing the Community with Itself*. American Library Association.

Check(Out) Your Privilege, or:
How We Learned to Stop Worrying
and Love Putting on a Diversity Event

Damon Campbell, Lydia Harlan *and* Rachel Lilley

The University of Oregon Libraries' well-established Library Diversity Committee adopted a newly energized tone when a new Dean of Libraries joined the institution and assumed the responsibility of chairing the committee. Inspired by the sense of urgency in her leadership, our committee recognized the need to move conversations surrounding diversity into action which, ultimately, resulted in a public program focused on privilege. Mia McKenzie (2014), Lambda Literary Award-winning author and creator, Director, and Editor-in-Chief of Black Girl Dangerous Press, said this of privilege: "The bottom line here is that if you acknowledge your privilege and then just go ahead and do the same things anyhow, you have done absolutely zero things differently from people who don't acknowledge privilege at all. Because the outcome is exactly the same…. I suggest we stop talking about 'acknowledging' it, and start focusing seriously on 'pushing back against it.'"

To this end, the Diversity Team chose to put on a "stacks crawl"—traditionally defined as a staff-guided tour of a Library's stacks and facilities designed to acquaint patrons with the library, its physical spaces, programs, services, and collections—as a means of familiarizing our community (and ourselves) with the library's resources on diversity and privilege. Our committee quickly agreed that white privilege was essential to the discussion, since we understood this topic to be a polarizing one, and since the student population of the University of Oregon in the fall of 2016 identified themselves as 59.87 percent white (University of Oregon n.d.), while the makeup of the overall population of the area surrounding Eugene was reported at 85.8 percent white according to the latest available census (United States Census Bureau n.d.). The initial concept of the event generated excitement among the members, and over the course of several months evolved into a powerful and timely public program, *Check(Out) Your Privilege: Library Stacks Crawl and Facilitated Diversity Discussion*, held on November 2, 2016. This essay will discuss the ways this idea evolved, the strategies employed to bring it to fruition, and the lessons learned.

The Nucleus of the Idea

Discussions about putting on a diversity event began in January 2016. While the practical components of the event continually evolved, we settled on two objectives that remained unchanged. The event was intended to: 1) raise awareness of issues related to privilege, and allow attendees to discuss these issues in a safe, open space and 2) raise awareness of the library collections (specifically as they relate to privilege), and allow attendees to interact with the collections. In order to efficiently manage the logistics of the event, and provide staffing on the day of the event, a sub-committee, the Stacks Crawl Working Group, was formed. This group was comprised of three co-leads, Damon Campbell, Lydia Harlan, and Rachel Lilley, as well as four additional library staff. We were given a $1000 budget to cover marketing and catering costs.

Originally, we imagined the event as a series of stacks crawls, each covering an area of privilege. The crawls would be held in branch libraries around campus, and the series would close with a panel discussion in the main library after the last crawl. As we worked through the details of how this would work logistically, we realized that the idea of a multi-day event was too unwieldy, as it would be difficult for the Stacks Crawl Working Group to maintain both the working capacity and enthusiasm required for such a program. Further, we eventually ruled out the idea of holding discussions in the stacks, as these had the potential to disrupt the study and work of patrons and staff, and might inhibit an in-depth discussion of the resources and issues at hand. In addition, we wanted to partner with campus and community experts in different areas of research to help us deepen our understanding of privilege, and felt that active discussions with these experts would not be easily accomplished while exploring the stacks. Rather, we felt a sit-down discussion, inspired by the idea of a traditional stacks crawl, would make for a more productive and focused discussion, and would allow attendees to more freely share their experiences on the emotionally and politically charged topic of privilege. We decided to host the "crawls" and panel on the same day, with each "crawl" presented as a breakout session in a separate room in the main library building. Attendees, library facilitators, and expert panelists would break into groups, proceed to their designated rooms, and discuss the available information resources and their experiences with their chosen area of privilege. The concluding panel would bring all the attendees back together in the main room, and would give them an opportunity to share what they'd learned, any experiences they'd had in confronting privilege, and workshop dialogues for dealing with privilege in the real world. We created a scope statement to track the goals and scope of the event, and we referred to this document often in the course of our planning to ensure we remained on task.

The ultimate timing of the event was the result of a few factors, including: the academic calendar, faculty and staff professional development schedules, and the then-upcoming presidential election. Hosting the event during the academic year would ensure that most of the campus community would have the opportunity to join us. Equitable access to the event was paramount; we wanted to give as many people the opportunity to attend as possible, while recognizing that the topic we'd chosen could be seen as a divisive one. Hosting an event about an issue like privilege during a difficult political season ran the risk of creating polarizing conversation and alienating some members of the campus community. Yet it also provided an opportunity we felt we could not ignore: the opportunity for an engaged and moderated discussion about privilege in a safe space.

In order to further maximize attendance, we decided to host the event in the early afternoon, as we received suggestions that attendees and participants would likely be more able to take an afternoon away from work versus the morning. Additionally, hosting the event in the afternoon allowed the planning committee to deal with any last minute preparations or issues that arose in the morning to ensure the event's success. These revisions to the structure and timing of the event were concluded by March 2016, and were approved by both the Dean of Libraries and the Division of Equity and Inclusion.

Not an Exact Science

We turned our attention back to content, and selected five facets of privilege to be highlighted: cisgender (a term used to describe someone whose personal gender identity and biological sex match) privilege, economic privilege, male privilege, straight privilege, and white privilege. A Stacks Crawl Working Group Member was assigned to each area of privilege as a library facilitator, and they accepted a range of responsibilities.

1. Library Resources. Library Facilitators researched their chosen area of privilege, selected relevant information resources from the consortial library catalog, and made physical items available for the event. In the months following the event, library facilitators transformed their extensive resource lists into LibGuides, which are now available on the UO Libraries website.
2. Breakout Session Questions. Leaders of the Stacks Crawl Working Group formed a shared set of questions for use during the breakout sessions, but library facilitators were encouraged to modify these or create their own in order to facilitate discussion of their facet of privilege.
3. Breakout Session Rooms. Leaders of the Stacks Crawl Working Group identified the five rooms in the library that would be used for breakout sessions, and assigned a room to each facilitator. Library facilitators were responsible for personally booking these rooms once the rooms had been assigned to them.
4. Experts. Most significantly, library facilitators were charged with identifying and booking panelists from the university community to serve as topic experts for the breakout sessions and/or closing panel.

Our campus and community topic experts/panelists were charged with bringing a wealth of knowledge about their area of privilege to the event, assisting in the facilitation of discussions during breakout sessions, and responding to questions during the panel if they also served as panelists. We provided our scope statement to our panelists, explained the impetus behind the event, and how the logistics of the discussions and panel would operate. With a panel of five experts and no obvious leading area of privilege, it was suggested that we recruit a moderator for the panel discussion. Dr. Sari Pascoe, Assistant Vice President for Campus and Community Engagement, Office of the Vice President for Equity and Inclusion, agreed to take on this crucial role in event.

Intended audience and audience size were critical considerations in the course of planning the event. We represent a university library, and one of our event goals was to highlight the information resources to which we provide access. The university community (students, staff, faculty, etc.), as a major constituent group, was our primary audience.

However, the wider Eugene community also utilizes campus facilities, especially the library, and we wanted to include them in the discussion. The size of our potential audience presented a challenge; such a program could appeal to, and conceivably draw, a large crowd of attendees, but we had no real way of knowing how many people would actually attend. To that end, the space we opted to use for our opening remarks and closing panel lent itself to a flexible number of attendees. In order to know how much refreshment to order from catering, we had to make an educated guess, so we planned for approximately fifty attendees from the university community and Eugene area. We tried to ensure a selection of snacks and beverages that would provide options for multiple palates and dietary restrictions, and our final catering bill came to $300.

By August 2016, the Stacks Crawl Working Group had begun brainstorming on our marketing efforts. During a meeting with the Library's Communications and Marketing Team, we came up with the idea of an activity station where people could create DIY buttons out of old magazines to represent the area of privilege with which they most closely identified or wanted to learn more about. This activity station would be available during the welcome portion of the event, to be used as an ice-breaker. The concept was for people to literally "tag their privilege" by pinning a button on themselves. We liked this idea in particular because we thought it would blend seamlessly into social media promotion. We borrowed a button-making machine from another department, purchased button-making supplies totaling $43.00, and mocked up a few dozen buttons as examples for the event activity. These sample buttons were used in the poster design and in the social media campaign. Throughout the next few months, we remained in touch with the marketing team to attempt to crystallize our marketing vision regarding the layout and placement of posters, and promotion via social media. In all, the marketing department produced and printed our posters, helped develop the idea of the button making station, and shared information about the event via social media. Leaders of the Stacks Crawl Working Group distributed the posters to several UO departments, placed posters in strategic locations throughout campus and beyond, and continued to raise awareness of the event through an email campaign via UO-based listservs.

Our final plan for the event offered an introduction to the concept of privilege using DIY buttons, a breakout session on each area of privilege selected, a chance to interact with the collections related to those areas, and closed with a participatory panel discussion on all areas of privilege. Throughout September and October, the Stacks Crawl Working Group members focused on finalizing resources and confirming panelists, and kept track of individual progress on a logistics spreadsheet. At this point in the process, our goals were to confirm that all of the major planning points of the event were complete, and to track on and resolve any outstanding details. We finalized our catering order, reserved spaces for breakout discussions, and confirmed panelist attendance. As October 2016 came to a close, we scheduled a final check-in with our moderator, expert panelists, and library facilitators to make sure that the intended direction and flow of the event was clear to all participants, and that all understood their responsibilities. Once these were confirmed, the group entered a holding pattern, in which we remained ready to respond to last-minute changes. While there were hiccups in some areas of the work, we felt largely confident that we would indeed hold the event and sincerely hoped that people would show up.

Schematics of Privilege

Despite having involved the Library Communications and Marketing team in the planning process several months in advance of the event, we found ourselves scrambling in the final few weeks of preparation. This had less to do with any failing on the part of our promotional team, and more to do with recent reductions in staffing and a lack of clarity regarding roles and expectations.

The morning of the event dawned unseasonably pleasant, and though we worried this would negatively impact attendance, we had 45 participants. The day before the event, the co-facilitator for the Straight Privilege breakout session, Dr. CJ Pascoe, Associate Professor of Sociology, notified us that she would be unable to attend. This compounded our anxiety. In a bit of a dither, the facilitator of that session, Rachel Lilley, emailed the other two co-organizers, and the dean, who was scheduled to provide opening remarks and introduce all the facilitators. Rachel, however, forgot one key distinction: two Dr. Pascoes (no relation) had been invited to the event, one a co-facilitator, the other the moderator of the panel discussion at the end of the event. Needless to say, what began as a relatively minor inconvenience nearly ballooned into outright panic, with several frantic emails from the dean received before the matter was clarified. With that glitch behind us, we refocused on last-minute preparations.

Light refreshments—sweet and savory snacks, coffee, tea, cider, and water—were provided for attendees during the welcome and introductions, and were available for attendees to revisit when they reconvened for the concluding panel discussion. The button-making station was highlighted and explained at the beginning of the event, and attendees were given time to visit the station. While at the station they were invited to either choose a pre-made button, or create one themselves.

Our dean provided a brief introduction of the library facilitators and topic experts/panelists, and attendees were then invited to join the facilitator of the discussion of the privilege with which they most identified and/or wanted to learn more about. Groups were given five minutes to make their way to one of five assigned rooms in the library, the idea being to introduce attendees not only to new sources, but new spaces within the library. During their breakout sessions, library facilitators and topic experts highlighted resources—both physical and digital—available for further exploration and research, providing printed copies of a list of additional references. Library facilitators also moderated the discussion using a set of questions written to facilitate engagement and advance the discussion. Groups were given twenty minutes for this portion of the event, and a break of approximately ten minutes was scheduled between the end of the breakout sessions and the panel to allow attendees to return to the main meeting area and get settled. Overall, library facilitators reported that their discussions were fruitful and engaged; none of the attendees were combative or defensive, but rather came to their groups with thoughtful questions and comments (e.g. about the definition of privilege, how it has manifested in their lives, and methods they've used to address it).

A more comprehensive introduction of the panelists was provided just before the concluding panel session by the panel moderator. The panelists, most of whom had also served as breakout session topic experts, discussed their backgrounds and expertise, and both defined and spoke to the harm done by their respective areas of privilege/the privilege they "represented." Attendees were given the opportunity to ask questions of the panelists. Questions asked of the panelists, and comments made by attendees, were similar to those presented in the smaller groups. Attendees wanted to know how to address and mitigate specific privileges in the real world, and panelists discussed ways in which interactions could be approached. At the conclusion of the question and answer period, attendees were again given the opportunity to visit the "Tag Your Privilege" button-making station and engage in one-on-one conversations with the panelists and/or members of their breakout session.

We Didn't Bomb

After months of anxiety over preparations, we were rewarded with a reasonably well-attended, well-run event. We anticipated and planned catering for fifty people, and forty-five attended, hitting close to our measured expectations. Attendees were engaged, participated in multiple components, and nearly everyone stayed for the entire two-hour event. Our panelists were pleased and are more than willing to do something similar with UO Libraries in the future.

While it was tempting to end the project on its highest note, we decided to jump right into the Plus Delta analysis while our memories were still fresh. In the hopes that our experience will inspire similar events at other libraries, we offer a summation of what worked for us, what didn't, and what we'd do differently if we knew then what we know now.

1. Audience. First and foremost, have an audience in mind. Ours was "everyone in the UO community" because we wanted to be inclusive, but in retrospect this may have been too broad. If you can narrow the scope, you can better tailor your marketing efforts to the audience.
2. Treats. University catering provided coffee, dessert, and non-dessert samplings for the afternoon affair. A welcoming atmosphere is conducive to collaboration among strangers, especially when the topics may be emotionally intense for some. Also, you can advertise the treats. This particular event was our own invention, and not a standardized, mainstream, easily-communicated idea that lent itself to advertisement. Everybody understands treats.
3. Breakout Sessions. We liked having breakout discussion sessions to introduce attendees to the subject matter and get people talking. This portion of the event could be scalable, as an ongoing lunchtime discussion, for example. Some library facilitators were happy to have topic area experts to call upon during these sessions, and some facilitators felt comfortable leading the discussions on their own. Our library facilitators prepared questions, which some relied upon, and some kept in their pockets. Were we to do this again, we'd book less time for introductions and more time for discussion. We wish we'd had more time for the breakout sessions in their entirety, but this was already a two-hour event. As the event was comprised of several stages, the breakout sessions were limited to twenty minutes so that the groups would have time to make their way to the discussion rooms and back to the main room in time for the next stage. Traveling to different spaces around the library was part of the idea behind the "crawl" feature of

the event and therefore, in our minds, necessary to the core purpose. We liked having separate rooms for the mini-discussions, for their many benefits: they facilitated an intimate discussion, participants were not distracted by other groups, venturing to the separate rooms brought people farther into the library where they could see more of our facility, and rooms were stocked with pre-selected resource material germane to the topic. We were prepared for latecomers by staffing the main event gathering room with a facilitator who directed participants to the appropriate room. This ended up being a wise use of resources, as some panelists surprised us with an early arrival. The library facilitator was available to welcome them and offer refreshments while they waited. Again, have treats.

4. Facilitator. Our dean encouraged us to invite an experienced facilitator to lead the group panel discussion, and we found that to be a worthwhile recommendation. Thankfully, our participatory audience stayed on track, but we felt assured our facilitator would keep the discussion from straying too far off topic or becoming unnecessarily combative. She also kept things moving, which was important, given how much time was allotted for the panel.

5. LibGuides. Library facilitators pooled their resource lists to create LibGuides after the event as part of the library's Diversity and Inclusion website upgrade project. In our case, we were unable to make these in advance of the event, but if you can, they are a desirable outcome useful to the community.

6. Button-maker. The button-making station was a welcome diversion for both the participants and planners. We selected images from popular magazines, created prototypes, and labeled the experience a team-building exercise. At the event itself the buttons served as an ice-breaker, participatory activity, and keepsake. Pre-made buttons provided visuals for the poster, discussed in point seven.

7. Promotion. Communications and marketing staff were integral to the success of our event, and we recommend engaging them early and often. Advertise. Those. Treats. Our communications and marketing team suggested collaborating with professors to increase the student audience at the event by requiring attendance for class. This idea came too late in the project for us to implement, but it is something we would explore were we to put on a similar event. Our marketing team was able to create a poster, which we distributed around campus and spaces beyond, like the public library. The poster was also used to promote the event on the UO Libraries website, as well as across social media platforms.

In essence, we were gratified by our choice to invest so much of our time and resources into planning this event because it was well-received and ran relatively smoothly—or at least appeared that way. We completely subscribed to the old axiom "an ounce of prevention is worth a pound of cure" and it was worth it. At the same time, have fun. People are supposed to enjoy this. You can have fun with serious topics.

Conclusion

We learned a great deal in the course of putting on this event. None of us had ever done something like this before, and we were thrilled and a little bit frightened to try it. As the planning progressed, the shape of our event began to look less like the original stacks crawl we initially envisioned, but an intellectual successor that remained true to our original stated objectives, i.e., to provide a space to talk about privilege and to draw the connection to the library's resources on this topic. Our advice is that everyone is learning, so don't let the fear of mistakes get in the way of doing it at all. Give yourself permission to put on a diversity event in your library. Librarians don't have to be experts in everything, one just needs to know how to gather quality resources, which is what it took to pull off this event. We held *Check(Out) Your Privilege: Library Stacks Crawl and Facilitated Diversity Discussion* a week before the November 2016 election. Our biggest takeaway is that at a certain point you have to let go of perfection and fear because unpredictable things happen. Begin anyway.

WORKS CITED

McKenzie, Mia. 2014. "4 Ways to Push Back Against Your Privilege," *Black Girl Dangerous Press* (blog), February 3. www.bgdblog.org/2014/02/4-ways-push-back-privilege.

United States Census Bureau. n.d. "Quick Facts Eugene, City, Oregon." Accessed September 12, 2017. https://www.census.gov/quickfacts/fact/table/eugenecityoregon,portlandcityoregon/PST045216.

University of Oregon. n.d. "Office of the Registrar Enrollment Reports." Accessed September 12, 2017. https://registrar.uoregon.edu/statistics/enrollment-reports.

Moving Beyond Just Talk

Diversity Programming at an Academic Library

MARTIN L. GARNAR

Introduction

When researching the topic of diversity in academic libraries, the majority of scholarship is focused on diversity within the profession, diversity of collections, and services to diverse populations through outreach and instruction. There are a few examples of diversity programming that push beyond the usual offerings. The Indiana University–Purdue University Indianapolis Library's Diversity Council developed an International Newsroom and hosted a dialogue event inspired by the Human Library (Hanna, Cooper, and Crumrin 2011). The Multicultural Issues Committee of the University of Virginia's library has sponsored speakers and other diversity-related programs for over fifteen years (Ball and Deeds 2006). Though these are not isolated examples, as Gilbert's survey of national liberal arts college libraries reported that 36.4 percent of respondents sponsor some sort of programming series that goes beyond library-focused workshops (2016), they are the exception rather than the rule.

Meanwhile, for the topic of programming and events in libraries, most sources are focused on the activities happening in public libraries. In light of these two trends, it should not be surprising that research on programming related to diversity in academic libraries can be hard to find. This essay will explore one academic library's creation and development of a programming series focused on equity, diversity, and inclusion; discuss how the library quickly became a central partner in high-profile programming events across campus as a result of the success of the series; and engage with the question of how to create a neutral space for dialogue while still promoting social justice.

Background

The University of Colorado Springs (UCCS) is a comprehensive public institution with 45 bachelor's, 22 master's, and five doctoral degree programs offered through six colleges. Founded in 1965, it is one of four campuses in the University of Colorado system and serves over 12,000 students, 29 percent of whom identify as ethnic minorities and 28 percent of whom are first-generation college students (University of Colorado–

Colorado Springs 2017). The Kraemer Family Library is the main library facility for UCCS and enjoys a prime location in the central campus, connected to the university center and serving as a main thoroughfare for a campus geographically restricted by a six-lane road to the south and the rocky Austin Bluffs to the north.

Nicknamed the "Evangelical Vatican," the city of Colorado Springs is the 40th largest city in the country and has a national reputation for being a conservative city, ranking as the fourth most conservative city in a 2014 study (Tausanovitch and Warshaw). Despite (or perhaps because of) this reputation, the UCCS campus has the usual array of diversity-related resources for a state institution, including the Multicultural Office for Student Access, Inclusiveness and Community (*MOSAIC*), the LGBT Resource Center, the Matrix Center for the Advancement of Social Equity and Inclusion, and the Office of the Associate Vice Chancellor (AVC) for Inclusion and Academic Engagement.

Origins of the Programming Series

The year 2015 saw a wave of protests on college campuses across the U.S. related to racial issues, with concerns about discrimination and injustice being raised at schools like Yale University, Ithaca College, the University of Missouri, and Claremont McKenna College (Hartocollis and Bidgood). In response to these events on other campuses, the UCCS chancellor announced a community conversation to which participants were invited "to bring your ideas about how we ensure a campus environment that is truly inclusive and one where issues of importance are brought forward in a timely manner" (Shockley-Zalabak 2015). Campus leaders were encouraged to attend, and as library dean, I wanted to be part of the conversation and see if there were opportunities for the library to be part of any action plans going forward. I was still relatively new to campus, having been in my role for less than three months, so I did not know what to expect at this meeting.

One of the concerns expressed at the meeting was a lack of a space (primarily conceptual, though physical space constraints do plague the campus) for conversations about issues related to equity, diversity, and inclusion, as the likely hosts of such events would either be seen as agents of the administration (e.g., the chancellor's office) or as the usual suspects (the AVC for Inclusion or MOSAIC). If it were the former, participation might be limited by the perception that only officially sanctioned topics could be discussed, while the latter's initiative might be dismissed as preaching to the choir. The chancellor suggested that the library would be an ideal host for such discussions, both conceptually and physically. I readily agreed and took note of those who said they'd be interested in pursuing this. As the initial campus meeting took place on the Friday before Thanksgiving, I waited until after the holiday to reach out to the interested parties, including the AVC for Inclusion and representatives from MOSAIC, the Matrix Center, the LGBT Resource Center, the Faculty Multicultural Affairs Committee (FMAC), and the faculty PRIDE Committee (focused on LGBT concerns). Facing intense end-of-semester schedules, we agreed to meet early in the spring semester, finally finding a date for our initial planning meeting in February. At that meeting, we proposed creating an ongoing dialogue series focused on equity, diversity, and inclusion and agreed to invite the larger campus community to a planning meeting in March. In addition to targeted invitations to people suggested by the AVC for Inclusion, I posted the meeting invitation to the campus email lists for faculty and staff, and was pleased to get over 50 responses from people interested in either attending the meeting or being added to a mailing list for information about the series. To include student voices in the conversation, we asked those with connections to student groups to share the meeting invitation with student leaders.

The initial meeting for the tentatively named "Diversity Dialogues" series had an ambitious agenda, including establishing the name and format of the series, planning the first event, generating ideas for future events, and determining methods for engaging the campus community in what was hoped to be an ongoing conversation. Playing to the library's strengths, which had hosted book discussions in the past, we agreed that the first event would be a facilitated discussion of *Between the World and Me* by Ta-Nehisi Coates. The AVC for Inclusion's office paid for fifteen copies of the book to be distributed by lottery, with volunteers from the planning group serving as facilitators and the director of the writing program supplying discussion questions, having previously taught the book in her class.

As for future events, we developed an extensive list of potential topics and activities, including:

- Responding to current events/concerns on campus
- Flint, MI water crisis
- Election process and issues, including immigration, race, Black Lives Matter
- Digital storytelling: having a StoryCorps-style space in the library to record personal stories related to identity; doing an Instagram campaign on My Mashable Identity; doing a Humans of UCCS series of photos and longer interviews
- Workshop on "Scripting Conflict" for resolving and addressing situations as they happen in the classroom, on campus, etc.
- Struggling with religion; how to incorporate religion with the new experiences at college
- What is inclusive language?
- Police and community relations; responding to confrontations
- Multiracial identities
- Exploring topics for all protected classes as defined by the university's nondiscrimination clause (race, color, national origin, sex, pregnancy, age, disability, creed, religion, sexual orientation, gender identity, gender expression, veteran status, political affiliation or political philosophy)
- Social class
- Turning points in life
- Faculty and staff diversity as it compares to the student body
- Discussion events that encourage people to pair up and travel somewhere on campus as they discuss a topic

For all of the ideas, we stressed being mindful of intersectionality when discussing specific topics. I promised to create a submission form hosted by the library to solicit other ideas from the community, especially since we did not have many students at the initial planning meeting.

After considering a number of options, the group chose to adopt "Just Talk" (suggested by the director of MOSAIC) as the name of the series, playing on the justice aspect of these events as well as the need for people to just talk with each other. The name allows the addition of subtitles for each event without diluting the branding of the series. We talked at some length about whether we'd be adding to event fatigue by scheduling additional programs, since there were already a range of campus events related to equity, diversity, and inclusion offered by a number of offices and departments. Ultimately, the overall consensus was that the Just Talk series would be filling a different niche by providing an ongoing and regular opportunity to come together and discuss these issues. However, we did see the possibility of adding on discussion aspects to existing events. For example, when there's a scheduled movie, speaker, or theatrical event that would otherwise fit in the Just Talk framework, we could organize a "Just Talk After" discussion following the event to complement the program. Though the library doesn't have to be the only location for Just Talk events, the consistency of having a majority of programs there was determined to be desirable. The meeting concluded with assignments to develop ground rules for event discussions, manage the logistics, and develop graphics following the university's brand guidelines to be used in ongoing publicity.

In April 2015, five months after the initial idea was suggested by the chancellor, the Just Talk series launched with the book discussion of *Between the World and Me*. The program began with a review of the Just Talk ground rules, which were adapted from a set of guidelines developed by Paul Gorski as an EdChange project (2015). Despite the fact that we distributed only fifteen books, almost forty people attended the event, and the discussion questions were framed in such a way that all could participate in the conversation. The event received a glowing report in the university's newsletter, which had also promoted the series before its launch. The following month, the series switched from a late afternoon time intended to coordinate with class schedules to a lunchtime slot to better accommodate staff, as most faculty and students were off for the summer.

The Library as Programming Partner

Three events into the Just Talk series, a number of violent incidents shook the globe, including the shootings at the Pulse nightclub in Orlando and terrorist attacks in Nice, Istanbul, and Baghdad, among others (Dorell 2016). The campus leadership felt that it was important to create a space to process feelings and discuss concerns about these tragic incidents, so the AVC for Inclusion was charged with developing a year-long programming series that would eventually be called Moving Forward Through Violent Times. I was asked to be on the planning committee so that this new series could be coordinated with the Just Talk series. I was a little surprised that the Just Talk series would be given such credence so soon after it started, but was pleased to be at the table. We planned for a kick-off event in the fall to be hosted in the library and identified a number of other events already in the works that would fit into the Moving Forward theme so that we wouldn't be competing for an audience.

Meanwhile, concerns about free speech for students on the UCCS campus were publicized on the College Fix, a conservative-leaning website (Hardiman 2016). To underscore its commitment to free speech for all members of the UCCS community, the campus planned another series of programs around academic freedom to be moderated by three people with experience in facilitating dialogue on difficult issues: the chair of the political science department, the director of the university's Center for Religious Diversity and Public Life, and (wait for it) me. I learned this when I was invited to the chancellor's office for a meeting to brainstorm ideas for the campus response and helped shape the series, which ultimately focused on trigger warnings in the classroom, freedom of speech on campus, and the different roles played by the university as pertaining to speakers, including the difference between host and sponsor.

As these two new series got underway, the Just Talk series continued with its own mix of original programming and cosponsored events, including a book club on the play *Disgraced* by Ayad Akhtar, a film on an intergenerational social media training program, two election-related discussions (one pre-, one post-), and the first Just Talk After program in conjunction with an event from the Moving Forward series (an interactive theatrical experience), among others. Though we originally intended for planning meetings to be held every month or two, we soon found that the series was programming itself, as groups across campus were interested in being part of the series and would contact the library to propose ideas. Still, planning meetings were held at the start of each semester to stay in touch with the original group of interested parties and to make sure that we were filling in any gaps in the schedule to guarantee that we were having at least one Just Talk event each month.

Sustaining the Series

As with any programming series, there have been successes and failures. The intergenerational film screening had an audience of just five people, though we still managed to have a lively discussion after the film (and no one had to eat dinner after feasting on the snacks ordered for 30). At the other end of the spectrum, we had almost 50 people show up for our queer poetry open mic night (planned in collaboration with the student LGBT organizations Spectrum and Transmission), including a number of community members. The poetry event was so successful that we launched a separate Just Talk Poetry series in partnership with the student Free Expression (FREEX) club.

As Just Talk was approaching its first anniversary, there were multiple programs each month, with the majority of events being planned by outside groups who wanted to be part of the series. This bodes well for the future of the series, as it takes the pressure off the library to find topics or identify speakers for every event. However, the library is still responsible for managing the logistics of almost every program, since the vast majority take place within the library, thus requiring coordination with the university's event services and catering departments as well as developing and distributing marketing materials for each event. Though I don't mind getting out of the office every now and then, it's probably not the best use of the dean's time to be hanging posters around campus. Thankfully, the library was able to add a new administrative assistant position that includes event coordination and marketing as part of its duties, so I am hopeful that this aspect of program support will become more manageable.

One concern is that the series may become too popular, which may dilute the original intentions of focusing on issues related to equity, diversity, and inclusion through open and honest dialogue. Some topics have been proposed that would stretch the connection to diversity issues, while others would lack the discussion aspect that's crucial to being part of Just Talk. Likewise, there's a danger of being stretched too thin. Even with additional staff support for the series, the number of requests coming in for the second year of programming have made it challenging to keep up, especially if it's not always clear how the request fits into the guidelines of the series. I found myself invited to a planning meeting for a campus event that, on its face, had a strong connection to diversity, but there was no opportunity for dialogue in a meaningful setting related to the event. While I was glad that the planners thought of Just Talk and wanted to include us, I ultimately had to decline to participate on behalf of the library because it just didn't make sense.

The End of Neutrality

At the heart of the Just Talk series is the assumption that it is beneficial to bring together people with different perspectives on a difficult topic so that we can learn from each other and find a way forward. This premise works only if all potential attendees believe that the library will be welcoming to them and their ideas, and takes advantage of the historical view of libraries as neutral spaces, where ideas from across the political and social spectrum are presented without judgment or restriction.

Regarding diversity, the library is likewise seen as an appropriate venue because it does not take sides. In an article on the Culture Showcase series presented by the Ohio University libraries, the authors state that an academic library is uniquely suited to serving as a setting for interaction with members of diverse communities because it is a neutral space (Theodore-Shusta and Dawson-Andoh 2014). However, contrast this with Katy Mathuews's opening statement in her article on social justice in libraries: "The academic library is the common thread among all campus constituents. Open to students, faculty, staff, and community members, the academic library offers services and resources that are accessible to all" (2016). Mathuews does not mention neutrality, instead assuming from the start that libraries are already committed to promoting diversity and social justice. The distinction between neutrality and commonality is important, as it recognizes that libraries have long sided with the marginalized through their promotion of literacy and equitable access to information for all. Likewise, Morales, Knowles, and Bourg argue that "libraries can and should play a key role in promoting social justice; and that a commitment to diversifying our profession, our collections, and our services is critical to social justice work in and for librarianship" (2014).

By definition, the promotion of social justice cannot be a neutral act, as the very idea that social justice is necessary is based upon an acknowledgment that there are injustices that must be addressed. As libraries seek to engage their communities in turbulent times, such as in the wake of racist demonstrations in Charlottesville, VA in August 2017 (Astor, Caron and Victor), they cannot invoke the romanticized ideal of a neutral library. In the case of the Just Talk series, my philosophy is that we will create a space in which a range of opinions can and should be expressed without prejudice to content, but the choice of topic is intentionally not neutral, as I believe we must engage with the topics of equity, diversity, and inclusion if we are to address the systemic problems facing our society.

Conclusion

Eighteen months into the series, Just Talk has become an important player in the programming efforts on the UCCS campus. Currently I am drafting a grant proposal with partners from campus and the community to launch a dialogue series on political polarization using the Just Talk format, and we believe that we can create a model that can be used across the country. Whether or not that grant is funded, the library will continue to position itself as a central partner for dialogue on equity, diversity, and inclusion on campus and in the greater community, and we will continue to promote the power and the promise of coming together to just talk.

Works Cited

Astor, Maggie, Christina Caron, and Daniel Victor. 2017. "A Guide to the Charlottesville Aftermath." *New York Times*, August 13. https://www.nytimes.com/2017/08/13/us/charlottesville-virginia-overview.html?mcubz=0.

Ball, Matt, and Leland Deeds. 2006. "Multicultural Programming Celebrates Fifteen Years at the University of Virginia Library." *Virginia Libraries* 52, no. 2: 41–44.

Dorell, Oren. 2016. "2016 Already Marred by Nearly Daily Terror Attacks." *USA Today*, June 29. https://www.usatoday.com/story/news/world/2016/06/29/major-terrorist-attacks-year/86492692/.

Gilbert, Julie. 2016. "Heroes and Holidays: The Status of Diversity Initiatives at Liberal Arts College Libraries." *College & Research Libraries* 77 (4): 520–535. doi:10.5860/crl.77.4.520.

Gorski, Paul C. 2015. "Guide for Setting Ground Rules." Accessed August 20, 2017. http://www.edchange.org/multicultural/activities/groundrules.html.

Hanna, Kathleen A., Mindy M. Cooper, and Robin A. Crumrin. 2011. *Diversity Programming and Outreach for Academic Libraries*. Oxford: Chandos Publishing.

Hardiman, Kate. 2016. "Professors Tell Students: Drop Class if You Dispute Man-Made Climate Change." *College Fix*, August 31. https://www.thecollegefix.com/post/28825/.

Hartocollis, Anemona, and Jess Bidgood. 2015. "Racial Discrimination Protests Ignite at Colleges Across the U.S." *New York Times*, November 11. https://www.nytimes.com/2015/11/12/us/racial-discrimination-protests-ignite-at-colleges-across-the-us.html.

Mathuews, Katy. 2016. "Moving Beyond Diversity to Social Justice: A Call to Action for Academic Libraries." *Progressive Librarian* (44): 6–27.

Morales, Myrna, Em Claire Knowles, and Chris Bourg. 2014. "Diversity, Social Justice, and the Future of Libraries." *Portal: Libraries and the Academy* 14 (3): 439–451.

Shockley-Zalabak, Pamela. 2015. "Campus Environment Community Conversation." *Communique*, November 12. http://communique.uccs.edu/?p=21321.

Tausanovitch, Chris, and Christopher Warshaw. 2014. "Representation in Municipal Government." *American Political Science Review* 108, no. 3: 605–41.

Theodore-Shusta, Eileen, and Araba Dawson-Andoh. 2014. "Engaging the Campus Community in Conversations on Diversity." *College & Research Libraries News* 75, no. 6: 328–331.

University of Colorado—Colorado Springs. 2017. "About UCCS." Accessed August 6. https://www.uccs.edu/about.html.

Getting Serious
in the Public Library
with "Current Conversations"

Jamie L. Huber, Whitney R. Gerwitz,
Heather M. Wefel *and* Melanie Foster

St. Charles City–County Library District recently implemented a multi-branch series coined "Current Conversations" that addresses serious topics to be discussed within the community. The goal of this series is to invite local experts to the library to present information and facilitate discussion about important issues that are nuanced and potentially controversial. This program series aligns with the Library District's core values of "Freedom to Know," which supports intellectual freedom and openly exchanging ideas that represent a variety of viewpoints, and "Lifelong Learning," which focuses on creating programs that allow patrons to continue their intellectual growth and learning throughout their lives. This essay describes how the series was set up and marketed, and includes some lessons learned from the organizers.

The St. Charles City–County Library serves St. Charles County, Missouri, which has a population of almost 400,000 with more than 90 percent being primarily Caucasian and the median income being over $70,000 with a less than 7 percent poverty rate (U.S. Census Bureau 2016). The Library District, which is about thirty miles west of St. Louis, has twelve branches spread throughout the county with three large regional branches specializing in Government Documents/Consumer Health, Local History/Genealogy, and Business/Nonprofit Services. According to the 2016 Circulation and Services report from the Missouri State Library, it also has the third highest circulation rate for all the libraries in Missouri (Missouri State Library 2016).

Background

As the Government Information coordinator, Whitney Gerwitz receives a variety of questions according to the time of year from "Do you have the Voter's Guide for the next election?" to "How do I find what is in Title 20 of the Code of Federal Regulations from 1998?" After the 2016 election, there were many concerns and questions: Will I lose my health insurance? Will my husband be deported? What will happen to my retirement fund? How does the Supreme Court nomination work? In Missouri, the question of acceptable identification was a concern as the state voted on an amendment to require photo ID when voting. There were so many unknowns and questions that could not yet be answered, so what could librarians do to help answer people's concerns and bring civil discourse to the public?

Since Climate Change and the Environmental Protection Agency were such hot topics during the election, Gerwitz had already planned a Climate Change program. This program sparked an idea between her and her colleague, Heather Wefel. Since libraries serve as a neutral ground for people to come and discuss difficult topics outside of social media, the internet, or their group of friends, what if the library added some more controversial and informational topics for each month? While researching the possibility, Gerwitz and Wefel discovered that other libraries were doing similar types of programming, but on a more limited basis. The original plan for "Current Conversations" was to attempt at least four or five programs every month, but as the planning took place, it became too complicated and time-consuming for one branch to manage alone.

Gerwitz and Wefel reached out to other branches that might be interested by presenting the series idea at a district meeting. Colleagues seemed interested but hesitant, as a lot of the responsibility would fall on the librarians to make sure the programs were not politically one-sided and that both sides of the topic were presented. Out of eleven other branches, two other staff members stepped up to participate in the series—Melanie Foster and Jamie Huber.

Foster facilitated a similar ongoing current events discussion in her branch, called "Let's Talk About It!" The program was born out of a tendency for some patrons to want to discuss sensitive political, social, or religious issues with staff at the reference desk and a book club that strayed from discussing the novel to discussing headlines. "Let's Talk About It!" was a monthly program where anyone can come in and talk about what's going on in the news, locally or globally. It was a place where people can feel safe to openly talk about issues that matter to them without being judged.

Between meetings, Foster kept track of issues that occurred in the news so she would remember them for the next meeting. Much of this was done on her own time, when either watching news shows or listening to the radio. At the meeting, these news headlines were written on a whiteboard simply as conversation-starters, and patrons were encouraged to add anything they would like to discuss. Patrons often brought in newspapers or electronic devices with notes. Due to the intersections between "Let's Talk About It!" and "Current Conversations," Foster was quite willing to get involved with "Current Conversations."

Huber had previously worked as a university women's center coordinator, and was excited to get involved with the "Current Conversations" series due to a passion for creating dialogue around, and critical thinking about, current events and issues of social justice. While the library provides an ample atmosphere for programming on current events and complex political and social issues, she had not yet had the opportunity to work on these types of programs in the library setting.

Planning the Programs

While the structure of monthly themes was set-up to frame the series, there was a substantial amount of flexibility in the monthly topics. The organizers wanted to focus on "hot" topics, but also topics that resonated with patrons in the community. The monthly topics are as followed in the Table 1.

Table 1. Monthly Topics of "Current Conversations"

MARCH	APRIL	MAY	JUNE	JULY
Women's Issues	The Environment	Social Justice	Mental Health	Foreign Relations
AUGUST	SEPTEMBER	OCTOBER	NOVEMBER	DECEMBER
Economics	Government & Grassroots	Technology	Religion	Gender & Sexuality

Between local universities, speakers' bureaus, and non-profit organizations, searching for presenters was fairly easy. Relationships with community organizations and area faculty were helpful because they created networking opportunities to find professional individuals from legitimate organizations who were willing to give a presentation and facilitate a discussion at no cost. Professors from local universities were often willing to speak on their subject expertise and also connected the library with other speakers. Different organizations were researched within the area and there were a few occasions when organizations were used more than once, such as the International Institute of St. Louis, since some have a range of specialization. Some presenters offered the organizers the opportunity to attend their other workshops in order to experience what library patrons would experience. This was very beneficial and led to networking with other individuals and organizations in attendance at these events. Furthermore, attending these programs gave a better understanding of what should be expected from these types of programs, and helped the organizers better understand the need for these programs. Establishing these connections also created more familiarity with resources to be used in the future.

In replicating this program, it is important to note that while many non-profit organizations and local faculty were willing to give free presentations because they are passionate about their mission or research and want to educate others, other organizations or speaker's bureaus may charge fees. It is important to not only vet organizations and speakers, but to also be upfront and transparent about expectations for the programs, including potential speaker's fees.

Marketing

The library was very supportive in helping market the "Current Conversations" series. The library's marketing department gave the series a webslide on the library website where interested patrons could click on the webslide and be redirected to the library's online program registration system. Registration is not required for most adult programs but it is encouraged.

"Current Conversations" was also given valuable ad space in the library's bi-monthly print magazine, "The Kaleidoscope," produced to advertise the classes and events occurring at the library. This magazine is a valuable resource for patrons, which is evident by registration spiking for most programs within days of the release of a new Kaleidoscope.

Like most public libraries, the St. Charles City-County Library runs an annual summer reading program for kids and adults. The Collaborative Summer Library Program (CSLP) theme for 2017 was "Build a Better World," which correlated nicely with the message of "Current Conversations." The reading log for the summer reading program consisted of a game board that patrons "play" in order to complete the program. It allowed patrons to track reading hours as well as activities such as going for a hike or giving back to the community. The library's marketing department used the flip-side of these logs to promote featured programs during the summer and highlighted the monthly themes of "Current Conversations" on the game boards given to thousands of adults in the community.

Even with the promotional assistance given by the library, marketing the series outside the library system was still beneficial. Meetup is an online social networking platform that allows members to browse for groups to join based on their interests or hobbies and members RSVP to events they wished to attend. All "Current Conversations" events were advertised in two Meetup groups—one for people interested in public libraries and the other for local advocacy, which combined makes up over five hundred people.

Table 2. Marketing Venues and Registration for "Current Conversations"

Library Flyer	The Kaleidoscope	Library Website	From a Friend	Other	Library Staff	Meetup.com	TOTAL
26	30	20	8	3	6	17	110

The Table 2 indicates how library patrons registered for all of the "Current Conversations" programs that took place. It does not indicate the people who attended without registering (as it is not required) or people who registered but didn't attend. The table shows that traditional marketing through the Kaleidoscope and through posted signs throughout the library had the most impact. The field labeled "Other" could be marketing on Summer Reading game boards, personal Facebook/Instagram accounts, or a public online calendar with the St. Louis Post Dispatch.

Programs

A wide variety of programs occurred as part of the "Current Conversations" series, but a few example programs are described below to give an idea of the programming that was offered.

March: Women's Issues

HUMAN TRAFFICKING

Huber's first "Current Conversations" program focused on human trafficking, which was gaining a great deal of local, national, and international attention. Local chapters of the American Association of University Women and the newly formed St. Charles Outreach Coalition against Human Trafficking are working to raise awareness about these issues in St. Charles County. For this program, the Anti-Trafficking Coordinator for the International Institute of St. Louis gave a presentation and facilitated a discussion.

The presentation provided facts and statistics about different types of human trafficking, and shared common signs of trafficking. The presenter also shared videos in which survivors of trafficking shared their stories, and then led attendees in an engaging activity in which they were presented with a card depicting a graphic novel-style visual scenario and then utilized a storytelling approach to determine what was going on in the scenario. This activity helped the attendees understand the different types of trafficking, as well as how traffickers control their victims. Patrons who attended the program left stating that they learned a lot, and on subsequent visits to the library have shared how they have remained vigilant for signs of trafficking in their own communities.

April: Environment

Climate Change

The program on Climate Change was scheduled before the series was formed and one could say it was the catalyst that helped start this series. The presenter, a professor of Atmospheric Sciences at St. Louis University, was found through a speakers' networking site called Climate Voices where one may find a local speaker on climate change. He used interactive polling through the audience's smartphones and hands-on activities that demonstrated the global effects of climate change. One activity consisted of everyone standing in a circle and he started by throwing a bean bag to one person. That person then threw the bean bag to another individual within the circle. Everyone had to remember who threw the bean bag to them and to whom they threw the bean bag. Once that was established, it started again with one bean bag, then two bean bags, then three, and the number increased to where the bean bags were completely out of everyone's control. It was a great demonstration on how climate change has progressed and opened up a lot of people's eyes. After the class, one attendee commented that he was shocked that not more people showed up because this was such a serious topic that needed to be discussed and proceeded to say he was going to share this information with everyone.

May: Social Justice

Prison Reform

A representative from the Criminal Justice Reform Initiative at Lindenwood University presented on prison reform and brought prison cheesecake she "baked" from ingredients that prisoners can only purchase from the prison commissary. The audience was very engaged by the presentation and felt it gave them a realistic view of small luxuries that are missed when a person is in prison. The presenter focused on portraying prisoners as human beings and emphasized that whatever happens within the prison system affects the success or failure of an individual when integrated back into society. After the event, Gerwitz felt that this session accomplished the goal of allowing people to learn from those who are at the very heart of an issue in order to get a different perspective.

Global Gender Justice

At Huber's branch, she focused on global gender justice. A local gender studies faculty member served as the presenter and facilitator, and began by providing background information about international women's issues, including information about United Nations campaigns and initiatives. Following the background information, she utilized curriculum based on the *Half the Sky: Turning Oppression into Opportunity for Women Worldwide* documentary, which included brief clips from the film and interactive activities. These activities were based around the ideas of critically exploring UN policies, examining poverty—including the feminization of poverty—on a global scale, and discussing small ways to make a difference for what might seem like insurmountable problems. Attendees engaged in a lively discussion and suggested ideas for future programs, including a program about gender identity.

SHARING OUR STORIES ON RACE

One of Foster's programs for the social justice component of "Current Conversations" included the program, 'Sharing Our Stories on Race.' To her knowledge, there had never been a program at the library purely devoted to discussing race or diversity. While St. Charles County is becoming more diverse, it is still a majority Caucasian county and a program that focused on race could be a sensitive topic. To get an idea of how to present a program like this in the library, staff attended a program in St. Louis called "Listen. Learn. Talk." put on by the Diversity Awareness Project, an organization that helps promote diversity and open dialog in the St. Louis Metropolitan area. The program explored the difference between debate and dialogue and also how to best communicate with others who are different than oneself.

Staff also attended a second program entitled, "Listen. Talk. Learn More," which was a continuation of the first session. It explored what comes after the initial dialogue and went deeper into some of the common stereotypes people often make about others of different races or backgrounds. This session also focused more on being aware in daily interactions with others and the intersectionality of race, class, gender and other identities.

Attending both programs provided a good grasp of how to host a program like this in the library, including how to organize a facilitated discussion. It also allowed the development of partnerships and networking with organizations that might be interested in helping to facilitate similar programs at the library. It became apparent that having a professional facilitator is highly recommended to help navigate controversial or sensitive discussions. A facilitator also ensures that the environment is neutral, the group stays on topic and that everyone has a chance to be heard. Since having a professional facilitator to get the audience to talk about race issues and diversity was instrumental to the success of this program, organizers reached out to the National Conference for Community and Justice of Metropolitan St. Louis (NCCJ-STL), which led to a presenter from Intrinsic Change, an organization that provides Motivational Interviewing (MI) services to businesses and other community organizations.

The presenter from Intrinsic Change was not only a licensed social worker, but also a trained facilitator in subjects dealing with diversity. Foster talked with him about the "Current Conversations" series and the goals of the program. He suggested the title 'Sharing Our Stories on Race' as it imparts a more casual setting for a potentially uncomfortable discussion. There were only 6 patrons at the program, but the small size provided an intimacy which invited them to be more open in sharing their stories. The patrons who attended said that they truly enjoyed the program and would like to see more programs like this at the library.

Attendance

Despite a healthy internal marketing campaign, the attendance for "Current Conversations" was disappointing. From March to June, there were nineteen programs scheduled and seven of those programs were cancelled due to lack of minimum registration (5). The twelve completed programs had a mean attendance of 8.5 and a median of 5 while the smallest attendance was four and the largest was thirty.

St. Charles City–County Library often hits capacity for children's programs (100+) but adult programs are a harder sell. Craft programs, book clubs and trivia nights do well but educational programs typically have lower participation. It was a gamble planning this series when it came to prospective attendance. The 2016 presidential election generated a lot of renewed interest in political and social issues on all sides of party lines. Advocacy and activism were spiking all across the nation, so there was hope this would translate into high attendance numbers. Unfortunately, we never got close to capacity at any of the events. It could be hypothesized that interest in advocacy and activism cooled as the year progressed.

The theme for June was Mental Health and it was the worst month for attendance. If cooling of civic engagement was not a factor, it was a struggle answering why this month had such poor attendance. Indeed, five of the seven programs in June were canceled due to low registration. Perhaps it is something about the topic itself that stymied attendance. Undoubtedly, the stigma against mental illness is still very strong but so is the stigma against openly discussing racism, immigration and gender/sexual identity.

Achieving healthy attendance figures was very important yet there was not an exclusive concern with just impacting the people that physically attended the programs. On program evaluations, attendees were asked if they discussed the topic with anyone since the program, and all respondents affirmed they had discussed the topic with multiple people.

- "Yes, family and friends who are new to the area too."
- "I shared with my co-workers about what I learned—- 10 ladies and my boss."
- "My daughter, husband, friends."

This was not the only good news. Results from the program evaluation indicated attendees had a positive experience.

- 100 percent felt the program they attended was presented in a positive and neutral manner.
- 100 percent felt comfortable asking questions.
- 10 out of 13 respondents reported an increase in their level of knowledge after the program.

Challenges and Lessons Learned

As indicated, individuals who have attended programs that are part of "Current Conversations" have provided positive feedback. The programs, however, have not been without challenges, with attendance being a major challenge. In part, this was due to getting the word out, and highlights the previously discussed importance of marketing. The program organizers have found that directly contacting specific organizations with interests aligned to the programs can increase attendance, as can making connections with faculty who are willing to offer students extra credit for attending a program. However, for best results, this has to be done in a personal, organized manner, and with enough time for a group or professor to incorporate the idea into their plans.

Also, while many community members are interested in serious issues, those who have limited free time might very well choose an evening activity that is more focused on fun and relaxation. The fact that programs include discussing serious issues and engaging in discussion around them can intimidate individuals and deter them from attending an event, even if they are interested in the topic. Trying to balance program descriptions and titles with both the gravity the subject deserves and an enticing hook to draw in attendees is an important, but often overlooked, component.

Another important aspect learned was that topics were more intriguing if applicable to a local issue. For example, the most successful program was during the month on environmental issues regarding a local site known as the Weldon Spring Site, which was formerly a munitions and uranium refinement plant during World War II and the Cold War. People were intrigued because it was, figuratively speaking, in their backyard. While planning future programs, staff asked presenters to focus more on regional effects of the specific topic to make it more personal for attendees.

Despite some challenges, the organizers feel that overall this has been a successful series, and plan to continue efforts with bringing this type of programming to the St. Charles City-County Library District. Staff may have been overly ambitious when planning the programs for 2017, however, they hope to continue their efforts into the next year but possibly on a smaller scale in order to help keep interest in social issues alive. Instead of four or five programs a month, it may be more successful to have two per month so as not to overwhelm potential attendees. Hopefully, our learning experiences can also inform others who are interested in implementing similar programs.

WORKS CITED

Missouri State Library. 2016. "Circulation and Services." Accessed August 4. http://www.sos.mo.gov/CMS Images/LibraryDevelopment/FY16CircServices.pdf.

U.S. Census Bureau. 2016. *Quick Facts*. Retrieved from https://www.census.gov/quickfacts/table/PST045215/ 29183.

PART VII

Expanding Teaching

Teaching Social Justice with Special Collections and Archives

Critical Information Literacy and Primary Source Analysis

JULIE M. PORTERFIELD

Introduction

Any dialogue on the role of diversity and social justice in libraries is likely to include the concept of critical librarianship, meaning a practice of librarianship that is "episte-mological, self-reflective, and activist in nature (Garcia 2015)." Critical librarianship borrows from the work of critical theorists. However, the idea of activism is also inherent to the history and practice of librarianship. Libraries have long been partners with the cause of democracy and freedom by making information freely available. As the current social and political climate urges librarians to consider how they might play a more active role in efforts toward diversity and social justice, the activist role of librarians seems more important than ever. There are numerous ways to implement a critical approach to librarianship, including teaching and learning information literacy through a critical lens. In fact, critical information literacy offers an opportunity for librarians and other information professionals to move beyond simply providing information resources to empowering their patrons to use those resources in meaningful and civically engaged ways. Archives, special collections libraries, and other institutions that maintain archival, rare books, and manuscript collections, can play an important role in these activities by utilizing their collections to teach critical information literacy.

Using critical teaching techniques, archivists and librarians can build learners' information literacy skills in several ways. The primary sources found within these repositories provide first-hand accounts and experiences that can be analyzed to form critical conclusions about the authority of the source and the context in which it was created. This kind of classroom consciousness-raising builds confidence in learners to advocate for their own needs, as well as empathy for the experiences of others for whom they might also advocate. In addition to the resources found within these repositories, understanding the process of collecting and maintaining these types of collections can be a tool for thinking critically about gaps and silences found in archival records, and how collective memory is shaped.

As libraries and archives are aiming to diversify their collections, create inclusive environments for patrons, and implement the social activism of critical librarianship, critical information literacy using archival material and rare books provides an opportunity to achieve all of these goals. It is a means by which archivists, librarians, and allies can move beyond profession-wide calls for diversity to meaningful social justice activism. It is a way to empower learners, whether they are undergraduates, graduates, K–12, or community members, to use the evidence found in collections to form their own critical conclusions, and take action for change.

Archives and Social Justice

In the past fifty years, archival repositories have made progress in transitioning from passively collecting the records that make their way to repositories by chance to actively seeking and collecting primary sources that document experiences that are underrepresented in archival collections. With concentrated efforts to collect underrepresented voices in the archival record, collections, though still not fully representative, are more diverse than they have been historically. As a result, these repositories are uniquely situated to teach information literacy skills related to primary sources and archival repositories in a way that promotes social change. Though these institutions have begun their diversity efforts within the realm of their collecting practices, for this work to be truly impactful, the collections must also be used in a critical way. Teaching and learning through a critical lens is one way to achieve this next level of diversity.

Archives and special collections libraries have a long-standing relationship with social justice, albeit an inconsistent one. Repositories for archival records and rare books are bound up in their power to legitimize an experience by collecting proof of it. However, the reflexive is also true. The power to give credence to an experience is also the power to invalidate it by failing to provide a record of it. "Archives have always been about power, whether it is the power of the state, the church, the corporation, the family, the public, or the individual. Archives have the power to privilege and to marginalize. They can be a tool of hegemony; they can be a tool of resistance. They both reflect and constitute power relations (Schwartz and Cook 2002)." How archival professionals have grappled with this responsibility has varied over time, but the conversation has almost always revolved around matters of appraisal. Appraisal is the process of assessing material for its research value, and selecting what to collect and what not to collect. Though this focus has impacted diversity in collections, it neglects the critical element of use.

Early archivists practiced a form of collecting known as custodial appraisal. In custodial appraisal, archivists are merely the custodians of the records that make their way to archival repositories. Their role is not to assign value. This type of selection is predicated on the assumption that archivists are only the caretakers of archival records, not the arbiters of what has lasting scholarly value. In other words, the creators of the documents in question already deemed them valuable by creating them for a bureaucratic or state purpose; therefore, they must have lasting value (Tschan 2002). Custodial appraisal was also partially a result of the audience for archival repositories. At the time of its inception, the users of archival records were primarily professional historians. Thus, a change in the approach of historians would ultimately cause archivists to reconsider their appraisal methods. Archives were not exempt from the rhetoric of social change taking place in the 1960s and early 1970s, and neither were historians. This time period saw the advent of the new social history, which aimed to incorporate segments of society, who had previously been omitted, into the historical narrative. It did not take long for this historiographic change to impact repositories. In an effort to better service their patrons, repositories slowly began to collect records relating to African American history, women's history and feminism, labor history, etc. Although several decades later collections found in libraries and archives still do not represent every experience, they include a more diverse set of experiences than they ever have previously.

The mere existence of diverse collections in archival repositories is nearly as passive as not collecting them at all. True activism in the archives means taking one's expertise from the closed stacks to the classroom. Depending on the institution, this may include non-course-related outreach to community groups, or it might encompass course-related instruction with post-secondary or K–12 students. No matter the audience, it means helping learners understand the necessity of archival repositories in democracy, as well as teaching the situated, specialized information literacy skills it takes to utilize them to become informed and active citizens. Or, in short, archival and primary source literacies.

Critical Information Literacy and Archives

When compared to the long history of archival appraisal outlined above, teaching and learning activities that include archives and special collections are a relatively young area of expertise. With an historical focus on professional historians as expert users, it was assumed that patrons already possessed the specialized information literacy skills that are necessary to successfully navigate research at an archival repository. However, with time, users of archival resources have transformed to include scholars in disciplines outside of history, community members researching family histories, K–12 students completing projects and assignments, and many other users at various levels of experience in the realm of archival research. As a result, institutions that maintain rare and archival collections have begun to consider the role they can play in aiding their patrons to cultivate information literacy skills.

Information literacy as it relates to archives and special collections can generally be broken up into two types of literacies: primary source literacy and archival literacy (Prom and Hinchliffe et al. 2016, 9–13). Primary source literacy concerns itself with the skills a learner needs to analyze and utilize primary sources, i.e., archival material and rare books. For instance, examining the historical context of a primary source impacts a learner's ability to interpret the author's authority, and make a judgment regarding whether or not the information found in the source is accurate and supports their information needs. Alternatively, archival literacy refers to the proficiencies that a learner needs to navigate research in the specialized environment of archival repositories. Whether it is a large state archives, a university archives, or a small historical society collection found in a public library, archives possess unique features, and understanding these features can help users more effectively access and utilize archival resources. For example, understanding that archival collections are named for their creators, not necessarily their subject matter, can change the way a learner approaches searching for them online. Both of these sets of skills can be taught formally in a structured classroom, or informally, such as at a reference desk. No matter the setting, primary source and archival literacies form the information literacy skills that are necessary to utilize the resources found in archival collections.

Information literacy is commonly defined as having the skills necessary to locate, evaluate, and use information. However, in the spirit of critical librarianship, "critical information literacy is a deliberate movement to extend information literacy further than the acquisition of the research skills of finding and evaluating information. Instead, it is the 'reframing of conventional notions of text, knowledge, and authority' in order to ask more reflective questions about information" (Simmons 2005). Its roots are found in critical educational theories that were developed by educators, who were concerned with how education might inform and impact social change. Librarians interested in critical librarianship adopted some of these teaching techniques to information literacy, and critical information literacy was born. Succinctly, critical information literacy focuses on teaching consumers of information to think critically about the social context of information, and how information might be used to promote social change. Despite the fact that diversity efforts in archives have traditionally been focused on collecting, rather than use, the long-standing relationship between archives and social justice makes primary source and archival literacies natural fits for implementing critical information literacy as critical librarianship.

There are several elements of primary source and archival literacies that provide the opportunity to harness the social justice power found in archives, manuscripts, and rare books. At its core, archival literacy is understanding archives. It is knowing what is unique about the way that institutions across a spectrum of shapes and sizes, which all maintain archival material, operate and provide service. It is discerning the ways that these unique features can be advantageous to a user's research; and, as a result, it also means recognizing the ways that they might be a disadvantage for a user. In other words, archival literacy illuminates inequalities. These inequalities can include the cataloging, arrangement, and description work of librarians and archivists. For example, the vernacular that a community group uses to describe themselves, or their activities, might not be the terminology an information professional uses to describe the contents of a collection. This is a barrier to search and discovery that privileges one group over another, and does not service the culture that the collection documents. Critical archival literacy provides space for users to be open and vocal about the biases that they uncover in discovering and accessing a collection. Understanding archives also includes understanding the role of archives in democracy and collective memory. It is knowing that, despite diverse collecting efforts, there are still gaps and silences in the historical record that archives keep. This might seem like an overwhelming thing to teach, but it is very relatable. For a user, it's a simple question: is my experience represented here? What about the experiences of others who are different than me? Critical archival literacy allows for opportunities to identify what is missing, and to consider the consequences of not being included.

In many ways, the elements of critical primary source literacy are similar to those of critical archival literacy. The main difference is that critical primary source literacy can focus on a specific primary source, or group of sources, rather than considering all archival repositories as a whole. Of course, a user who is proficient in primary sources would be able to transfer skills, such as document analysis, from one source to another.

However, many of the critical questions remain the same. A primary source literate user considers each element of a source, and determines what is represented, and not represented, and who is advantaged and disadvantaged. The process of drawing these conclusions can be call primary source analysis. Users analyze primary sources in a variety of settings from undergraduate research papers to genealogy research. In any case, primary source analysis is a focused and scalable activity. As a result, it can be less overwhelming, and an ideal way to leverage the advantages of archival material in critical librarianship.

Critical Primary Source Analysis and Social Justice

Like many critical approaches to teaching, critical information literacy aims to eliminate hierarchy where possible, and empower learners to participate in determining their own learning objectives. Thus, a critical approach to teaching primary source analysis guides, but does not prescribe. Most importantly, it encourages users to be critically reflective as they examine a source, and promotes an activist response to the inequities that they uncover. An adaptable and scalable way to achieve this is to provide a guide, or series of open-ended questions for a user to consider, while remaining available to answer questions and triage roadblocks. In a group setting, peers can also provide this support, and the group may reach some of their critical conclusions together. However, this kind of primary source analysis guide can also be useful in reference settings, where the patron might be a first-time archives user. Since the end goal is for users to apply their analysis to social justice activism, the guide provided should lend itself to these kinds of conclusions. Fortunately, librarians and archivists can draw on the historical relationship between archives and social justice and the composition of archival records to build a foundational guide for users to begin their analysis.

Every archival record, no matter its format has three parts. Whether it is a letter, a financial ledger, a first edition of a published work, or any other type of document, it contains content, context, and structure (Pearce-Moses 2005). Since content, context, and structure is ubiquitous, it is a great way to frame a primary source analysis guide. Of course, this means beginning by explaining each part to a user, and giving examples of what they might find. Nevertheless, asking users to identify the content, context, and structure of a primary source can lead them to the kind of socially-conscious conclusions and activities that critical librarianship and critical information literacy aim to achieve.

Content can be described as what a source says, or what image it portrays. It is important to note that it can be facts, or opinions, but it is the explicit message that is being communicated. Content supports diversity and social justice by allowing users to appreciate the experience of the source's creator, which might be similar or different from their own. Other forms of critical teaching and learning have traditionally used consciousness-raising, an activity in which learners share their experiences, and identify common and dissimilar experiences with the goal of inspiring empathy and social activism. In the case of content, the experience of the source's creator is a substitute for the experiences of classroom peers. As a result, it can still serve as a guide for critical primary source analysis in settings, such as reference, when only one user may be present. In outreach and classroom settings, librarians are also able to select material with the content that is particularly suitable for critical analysis, because its biases are obvious.

For example, an anti-women's suffrage pamphlet from the turn of the century, or a work published by a white supremacist group.

Context is the circumstances under which a source was created. It can be as broad as the larger historical context at the time of creation, or as narrow as the biographical background of the creator. Of the three elements, context allows users to be the most critical in their inquiry, but it is also the least explicit. While analyzing context, it is often useful for users to consult catalog entries, finding aids, and other secondary sources to provide more background information. Librarians wanting to implement a critical primary source analysis activity might consider preparing secondary sources to consult for context in advance, when primary sources are pre-selected, and reliable go-to secondary sources for when users select their own material. Context demonstrates issues of diversity and social justice in a less obvious way than content, but can be critical to a user's understanding of a source. For instance, knowing that a diary was written by a woman or person of color during a time period in which they were denied access to education illuminates the source as rarer, and representative of a perspective that is underrepresented in the written record.

Structure is simply the format and makeup of the source. It can be a book, a letter, a pamphlet, or any medium. It can be bound in vellum, or written on scratch paper. There is a wide array of possibilities, and the structure of a source can tell a user, who is critically analyzing it, important things about the social context of its creation. For example, in the case of a rare book with a particularly ornate binding, a user might conclude that it was likely inaccessible to working class individuals.

The final element of a guide for critical primary source analysis is asking users to combine their content, context, and structure findings into some final conclusions. Specifically, what inequities have they uncovered, and how exposure to the experiences found in the source has impacted their views. In an outreach or class group, this might include questions and discussion with peers. In a one-on-one reference setting, it might simply be asking a user what they learned from a source, or how it impacted their research. Ideally, librarians, archivists, and other information professionals, who endeavor to implement critical teaching and learning techniques, like critical primary source analysis, would be able to tie users' research to their activism and community involvement. However, this will not always be the case. There is no guarantee that a user will take action on the things that they've learned from a primary source. Nevertheless, considering how archives reflect social inequality, even if it's only during their encounter with a library professional, still addresses how institutions with archival material can extend their social justice work beyond collecting to use.

Conclusion

For librarians looking for new and impactful ways to implement elements of critical librarianship into their practice, critical information literacy using archives can be a way to renew and extend a personal or institutional commitment to diversity and social justice. Activities, such as primary source analysis, not only require considerations of diversity and inclusion from library professionals, but go further to empower users to draw their own social justice conclusions. Furthermore, teaching and learning critical information literacy with archives is useful across a variety of institutional settings. Even libraries that do not maintain their own archival material can take advantage of digitized collections, and primary source sets, such as those supplied by the Digital Public Library of America (DPLA). Although archival material may not be the first resource that many information professionals think of when implementing critical librarianship, archives have always played an important role shaping collective memory and documenting culture. The next step in critical librarianship is enabling users to utilize archival material in informed and civically engaged ways.

WORKS CITED

Garcia, Kenny. 2015. *Keeping Up with … Critical Librarianship.* ACRL. http://www.ala.org/acrl/publications/keeping_up_with/critlib.

Pearce-Moses, Richard. 2005. *A Glossary of Archival and Records Terminology.* Chicago: Society of American Archivists.

Prom, Christopher J., and Lisa Hinchliffe, eds. 2016. *Teaching with Primary Sources.* Chicago: Society of American Archivists.

Schwartz, Joan, and Terry Cook. 2002. "Archives, Records, and Power: The Making of Modern Memory." *Archival Science* 2 (6): 1–19.

Simmons, Michelle Holschuh. 2005. "Librarians as Disciplinary Discourse Mediators: Using Genre Theory to Move Toward Critical Information Literacy." *Portal: Libraries and the Academy* 5 (3): 297–311.

Tschan, Reto. 2002. "A Comparison of Jenkinson and Schellenberg on Appraisal." *The American Archivist* 65 (2):176–195.

Research Skills in International Issues and Social Justice Programs

Talking Points and Literature Review

Paul Jerome McLaughlin, Jr.

Introduction

University students can benefit their careers, their communities, and their schools by learning about and taking part in social justice courses and programs. Introducing students to human rights and social justice research topics and teaching them to examine interactions between cultures, economic systems, and individuals has been found to aid them in their studies and in their personal lives (Madden et al. 2017). Training in how to see human rights and social justice issues in a broad context is needed for students preparing to go into professions such as family counseling, children's services, health care support, and many other social services positions (Johns 2017).

As part of their professional responsibilities to prepare students to think and conduct research in a critical manner and to support social justice efforts, librarians must teach students to be cognizant of detrimental political and social situations that could be overlooked due to their inconspicuous natures (Roberts and Noble 2016). Human rights and social justice research training requires that researchers link the information available, the legal principles involved, and the social impacts of legal rules and schemes in an understandable manner (Jaeger et al., "The Virtuous Circle," 2015). Putting human rights research into context can be a difficult task not only due to its complexity but also due to the need to put information into a format relatable to every day experiences. Students must be able to approach a human rights or social justice issue without making determinations whether there is a right or wrong in the situation they are presented, break down the underlying causes of the issue, and be able to craft solutions that not only benefit their communities but also global society (Akbar 2015). To solve human rights and social justice problems, students must take into consideration the issue's economic and cultural causes so they can construct solutions that end the financial and social motivations for these problems (Thompson 2016). Learning how to approach human rights and social justice issues using a broad perspective can help prepare students to adapt their mind-sets as the United States becomes more diverse and international due to globalization.

Libraries can have a pivotal role in teaching students the value of social justice initiatives and their impacts on communities by allowing students access information on human rights and social justice initiatives and teaching them how to conduct human rights research. Libraries can help students learn about research methods and social justice by conducting programs that focus on researching human rights and social justice issues (Jaeger et al., "Libraries, Human rights, and Social Justice," 2015). As part of their programs, libraries can reach out to local and international organizations that defend human rights and combat social problems to exchange information and expertise, making connections for themselves and their students. The connections made with students and organizations in their community can help libraries meet their goals in being hubs for civil service groups and educational centers for civil and human rights while bolstering their positions in the community (Jaeger and Sarin 2016).

Reasons for Using International Human Rights Issues to Introduce Students to Human Rights and Social Justice Research

The rules that govern individuals' lives can be seen as not only the laws created by the courts and other governing bodies of a nation, but also as the organizations and systems that allow them to live their lives (Cotterrell 2017). Researching human rights topics allows students to gain insights into the conflicts between ideologies about what is legal, what is moral, and what is sacred among groups (Criddle 2014). Learning about international human rights and social justice issues helps students understand the ramifications that societal norms can have in a way that researching an issue from a single country's perspective cannot.

Choosing human rights topics and social rights issues such as child marriage, child labor, or gender equality on an international scale not only allows students to learn how such topics are dealt with in their home country, but also how different cultures address these issues and craft solutions that fit their economic, legal, and social frameworks (Forsythe 2017). Through library programs, students can be shown that research on human rights and social justice issues can be done using a variety of free and reliable online sources and through academic databases.

Using International Human Rights Research to Encourage Understanding of Economic and Social Causes of Human Rights and Social Justice Issues on a Local Level

Those seeking to implement societal changes must conduct research to understand the cultural issues and history regarding them so that reforms can be implemented with as little resistance as possible. This helps activists avoid having the problem they are trying to eradicate shift in form or create new problems as citizens adapt (Shelton 2015).

To understand the context of a human rights or social justice issue on a local or international scale, students must study the international agreements that impose a duty on a nation. They must also understand the legislative and non-legislative steps that a nation takes to address that issue which exposes the student to international agreements that cover the human rights issue they are interested in (Goodhart 2015).

Often with human rights and social justice issues, such as child marriage, changing the laws regarding such issues is not enough to end harmful practices (Maswikwa et al. 2015). Human rights and social justice problems have economic and social causes that must be understood before a student can gain insights into why an issue does not prove much of a problem to address in one country while remaining a serious challenge to control in another (Koenig 2017). To make meaningful strides against social injustice, the issue being studied must be understood from the economic and social levels and then worked against using a mix of local and national laws, education efforts, and societal changes. While introducing students to international human rights and social justice initiatives, instructors should emphasize that a deeper understanding of the problems they are examining and for which they are seeking solutions must be formed. Students should be aware that human rights and social justice concerns could be viewed in a different manner in societies that are not their own which could lead into insights they were not expecting (Sabbagh and Schmitt 2016).

The Positive Effects of Libraries Teaching International Human Rights to Students

Positive Outcomes for Students

Without being introduced to the content of human rights and social justice work and the types of information that need to be gathered for social justice programs to succeed, students may have limited views of what social justice is, the kinds of issues it involves, and careers in social justice initiatives (Torres-Harding et al. 2014). By being introduced to researching human rights and social justice issues, students gain the opportunity to study academic articles, international and local statistical information, and governmental publications that are available to them. They also learn to utilize those resources to create the informational base they will need to understand a social justice issue. Teaching students about human rights and social justice matters can help them break away from thought patterns that are often ingrained into students: that the societal norms have no inherent issues and cannot or should not be changed (Kumashiro 2015). Students who are introduced to international human rights and social justice research learn about social justice groups around the world. They can see the impacts such groups have by participating in programs that help gather data and create research collections aimed at improving human rights and social conditions.

Learning how to conduct human rights and social justice research can have a strong impact on students who are interested in social work (Sue et al. 2016). Students who seek careers in social work have multifaceted professions that require them to use their skills to aid individual citizens, act as pillars of their communities, and remain within the ethical and legal bounds of their professions (Morgan 2016). Due to the increase of immigration around the world, social workers must be able to find cultural information and laws pertaining to immigration and human rights to assist those new to the legal and social care systems they are entering (Congress and Chang-Muy 2016). Local laws often change to match the standards of international law regarding issues such as children's rights and health care decision-making; that requires that social workers keep current with trends in international law that could impact their work (Braye and Preston-Shoot 2016). Learning about international human rights law also introduces students to human rights and social worker organizations and sources of information they otherwise may not have been exposed to if their studies focused on domestic sources.

Positive Impacts for Libraries

The American Library Association has stated that libraries can be a key resource in fighting inequity of all kinds and should be involved in social justice activities (Morales et. al. 2014). Reaching out to appropriate groups in order to create human rights and social justice programs allows libraries to better connect to their community and to promote themselves as being vital for community growth and wellbeing. To make the most productive connections, libraries must study their communities, learn what information or services are needed, and then contact potential patrons and organizational partners interested in attending or conducting human rights programs (Jaeger et. al., "The Virtuous Circle Revisited," 2015). By reaching out to their patrons and local human rights groups to learn what informational needs are not being met, libraries can tailor their programs to best fit their communities, provide information to those who need it most, and partner with groups that have specialized knowledge for patrons.

Creating a Program on International Human Rights Research

Choosing a Topic to Include in a Presentation

Library programs focused on human rights and social justice research do not need to create specialized resources due to the amount of free online information (de la Peña 2014). Following Volokh's method for choosing a topic, librarians should ask students to do preliminary research on a subject that is current, that has not been resolved, and that has enough information on it so that a possible solution to the problem can be formulated (2016). One such topic could compare child marriage practices in the United States to other countries' and the impacts that the lack of having a federal law that establishes a uniform minimum age for a child to be married among the states has on young children who enter or are forced into marriage. Instructors can frame the session by showing students how they can use free sources on the Internet to research child marriage, corresponding laws, and construct a possible solution to the problem using legal and social reforms.

Teaching Students to Use Internet Searches for Reliable Information

Online resources often present the most efficient and effective way to introduce students to international research by allowing access to international human rights documents and also due to students' familiarity with searching the Internet for information (Gazzini 2016). Using Internet, including social media, is an accepted professional research strategy (Browne-Barbour 2016). Teaching students to be proficient in Internet searches prepares them for searching for information matters in a multidisciplinary manner which allows for a deeper understanding of the topic they are researching (Ndulo 2014). To compose effective online search strategies, students should be taught to focus on the fundamental aspects of their topic and use them as their search key terms. To find the key terms, students should be taught to think of the main concepts of a topic much like they would in a book's index, input those terms into the search engine of their choice, and then combine the terms with the search engine's Boolean operators to find precise results (Woods 2016).

Introducing Students to Free International Sources, Guides and Statistics

Students tend to use technology and digital sources to find the authoritative materials, but their success can be low due to lack of training in conducting online searches and determining sources' reliability (Henderson et. al. 2015). Students should be shown that international human rights information is available through a variety of free authoritative websites, such as the Law Library of Congress'(law.gov) and GlobalLex (nyulaw-global.org) which is maintained by New York University's School of Law (Svengalis 2016). Both the Law Library of Congress' website and GlobalLex can be searched by topical categories or by the name of the country examined and give information about the governmental systems for each jurisdiction. Introducing students to international organization websites such as Amnesty International (www.amnestyusa.org) and the United Nations Office of the High Commission (www.ohchr.org) provides them with sources for international law and a variety of reliable human rights statistics (Goodhart 2016). Students should be made aware that being able to find statistical information on human rights and social equity data is often a key part in ensuring that human rights issues are understood so that effective solutions can be created (Schnakenberg and Fariss 2014).

Teaching How to Research Possible Solutions for a Human Rights Issue

Human rights issues are difficult to address on the individual and societal levels. To plan a possible solution to human rights concerns, students must understand the problem they are researching from an economic and sociological standpoint so that they could construct solutions that address the causes of the practices driving the human rights violations (Sajeda et. al. 2016). Using sites such as Amnesty International and the United Nations, students can research and better understand the motivations for human rights violations and find programs that have been effective in reducing them. Students can be taught to research human rights issues that have similar contributing factors, such as child marriage and female genital mutilation, so that they can find methods and programs that have been successful in reducing violations and then adapt them to create solutions for other cases (Ellsberg et al. 2015).

Conclusion

Presenting research sessions on human rights law has a variety of benefits for libraries and their patrons. For students, whether they are focused on going into the legal field or social service careers, learning the processes and methods of conducting research on human rights topics and their possible solutions will prepare them for their professions. For libraries, developing and conducting human rights research sessions affords them an opportunity to reach out to their communities and provide programs that require little capital investment. It allows libraries to have a meaningful impact on their communities while creating new partnerships and elevating their visibility.

WORKS CITED

Akbar, Amna A. 2015. "Law's Exposure: The Movement and the Legal Academy." *Journal of Legal Education* 65(2): 366–372.

Braye, Suzy, and Michael Preston-Shoot. 2016. *Practicing Social Work Law*. London: Palgrave Macmillan.

Browne-Barbour, Vanessa S. 2016. "Why Can't We Be Friends: Ethical Concerns in the Use of Social Media." *South Texas Law Review* 57(4): 551–557.

Congress, Elaine, and Fernando Chang-Muy, eds. 2016. *Social Workers with Immigrants and Refugees*. New York: Springer Publishing Company.

Cotterrell, Roger. 2017. *Living Law: Studies in Legal and Social Theory*. New York: Routledge.

de la Peña McCook, Kathleen. 2014. "Librarians as Wikipedians: From Library History to Librarianship and Human Rights." *Progressive Librarian* (42): 61–81.

Ellsberg, Mary, Diana J. Arango, Matthew Morton, Floriza Gennari, Sveinung Kiplesund, Manuel Contreras, and Charlotte Watts. 2015. "Prevention of Violence Against Women and Girls: What Does the Evidence Say?" *The Lancet* 385(9977): 1555–1566.

Forsythe, David P. 2017. *Human Rights in International Relations*. New York: Cambridge University Press.

Gazzini, Tarcisio. 2016. "A Fresh Look at Teaching International Law—A Few Pedagogical Considerations in the Age of Communications." *Leiden Journal of International Law* 29(4): 971–978.

Goodhart, Michael. 2016. *Human Rights: Politics and Practice*. Oxford: Oxford University Press.

Henderson, Michael, Neil Selwyn, Glenn Finger, and Rachel Aston. 2015. "Students' Everyday Engagement with Digital Technology in University: Exploring Patterns of Use and 'Usefulness.'" *Journal of Higher Education Policy and Management*, 37(3), 308–319.

Jaeger, Paul T., Katie Shilton, and Jes Koepfler. 2016. "The Rise of Social Justice as a Guiding Principle in Library and Information Science Research." *Library Quarterly* 86(1): 1–9.

Jaeger, Paul T., Natalie Greene Taylor, and Ursula Gorham. 2015. *Libraries, Human Rights, and Social Justice: Enabling Access and Promoting Inclusion*. London: Rowman & Littlefield.

Jaeger, Paul T., Nicole A. Cooke, Cecilia Feltis, Michelle Hamiel, Fiona Jardine, and Katie Shilton. 2015. "The Virtuous Circle Revisited: Injecting Diversity, Inclusion, Rights, Justice, and Equity into LIS from Education to Advocacy." *The Library Quarterly* 85(2): 150–171.

Johns, Robert. 2017. *Using the Law in Social Work*. London: Learning Matters.

Koenig, Matthias, ed. 2017. *Democracy and Human Rights in Multicultural Societies*. New York.

Kumashiro, Kevin K. 2015. *Against Common Sense: Teaching and Learning Toward Social Justice*. New York: Routledge.

Madden, Paul E., Catherine Wong, Anne C. Vera Cruz, Chad Olle, and Mike Barnett. 2017. "Social Justice Driven STEM Learning (STEMJ): A Curricular Framework for Teaching STEM in a Social Justice Driven, Urban, College Access Program." *Catalyst: A Social Justice Forum* 7(1): 25–37.

Maswikwa, Richter B., Nandi J. Kaufman, and A. Nandi. 2015. "Minimum Marriage Age Laws and the Prevalence of Child Marriage and Adolescent Birth: Evidence from Sub-Saharan Africa." *International Perspectives on Sexual & Reproductive Health* 41(2): 58–68.

Morales, Myrna, Em Claire Knowles, and Chris Bourg. 2014. "Diversity, Social Justice, and the Future of Libraries." *Libraries and the Academy* 14(3): 439–451.

Morgan, R. 2016. "Developing Skills of Leadership Through Service Learning: Alice's Adventures in Wonderland and Path to Effective Leadership." *Tennessee Law Review* 83(3): 915–930.

Ndulo, M. 2014. "Legal Education in an Era of Globalisation and the Challenge of Development." *Journal of Comparative Law in Africa* 1(1): 1–24.

Roberts, Sarah T., and Safiya Umoja Noble. 2016. "Empowered to Name, Inspired to Act: Social Responsibility and Diversity as Calls to Action in the LIS Context." *Library Trends* 64(3): 512–532.

Sabbagh, Clara, and Manfred Schmitt, eds. 2016. *Handbook of Social Justice Theory and Research*. New York: Springer.

Sajeda, Amin, Johana Ahmed, Jyotirmoy Saha, Irfan Hossain, and Eashita Haque. 2016. *Delaying Child Marriage Through Community Based Skills-Development Programs for Girls, Bangladesh Association for Life Skills Income and Knowledge for Adolescents Report.* New York: Population Council.

Schnakenberg, Keith E., and Christopher. J. Fariss. 2014. "Dynamic Patterns of Human Rights Practices." *Political Science Research and Methods* 2(1): 1–31.

Shelton, Dinah. 2015. *Remedies in International Human Rights Law.* Oxford: Oxford University Press.

Sue, Derald Wing, Mikal N. Rasheed, and Janice Matthews Rasheed. 2015. *Multicultural Social Work Practice: A Competency-Based Approach to Diversity and Social Justice.* Hoboken: John Wiley & Sons.

Svengalis, Kendall F. 2016. *Legal Information Buyer's Guide & Reference Manual.* Guildford: New England LawPress.

Thompson, Neil. 2016. *Anti-Discriminatory Practice: Equality, Diversity and Social Justice.* London: Palgrave Macmillan.

Torres-Harding, Susan R., Cheronda Steele, Erica Schulz, Farah Taha, and Chantal Pico. 2014. "Student Perceptions of Social Justice and Social Justice Activities." *Education, Citizenship and Social Justice* 9(1): 55–66.

Volokh, Eugene. 2016. *Academic Legal Writing Law Review Articles, Student Notes, Seminar Papers, and Getting on Law Review.* Saint Paul: Foundation Press.

Woods, Roberta. 2016. "Analytical Search Strategies: A Tip Sheet with Examples for Teachers and Students." *Perspectives: Teaching Legal Research and Writing* 24(1 & 2): 59.

Advocating for Diversity Through Embedded Librarianship

Faith L. Bradham

Embedded Librarianship as Advocacy

One of the greatest joys of librarianship is serving everyone in a library's community. However, many librarians have little experience with a large number of the groups that their libraries serve. Librarianship is mostly made up of white, able-bodied women (Davis and Hall 2007). Nearly 80 percent of librarians are non–Hispanic white, and nearly 84 percent are women (Bureau of Labor Statistics 2016; Davis and Hall 2007; Department for Professional Workers 2016). This is a serious lack of diversity within a group that serves the deepest needs of America's many and varied communities. Although nearly every librarian I've encountered cares passionately about serving the needs of each population in their community, many have little frame of reference for the needs of groups such as undocumented immigrants, people of color, people with disabilities, etc. This lack of preparedness for the diverse needs of library users shows itself differently depending on the library. Academic librarians might encounter more opportunities to work with different ethnic groups, international groups, and student success groups; public librarians might overwhelmingly experience the needs of poverty and homelessness, and school librarians might work with children dealing with mental illness or who have difficult home lives. When talking to fellow librarians, I have observed that many feel as if they are floundering to serve the needs of their diverse populations.

One way that librarians can feel more connected to the groups their libraries serve is through embedment. Embedment emphasizes discovering the needs of library users by becoming an integral part of those users' community. Embedded librarianship "moves librarians out of the traditional library setting... and into a new framework for providing library services. It shifts the emphasis from reactively answering research requests in a vacuum to developing a unique understanding of what customers need and delivering proactive results" (Riccio 2012, p. 1). As a result, I believe that embedment is necessary for librarians to work meaningfully with diverse populations. The needs of diverse library users may vary depending on the type of library being used, but the need for librarians to interact purposefully and meaningfully with these users remains the same across librarianship. Embedment creates a unique environment of trust that allows librarians to know the needs of the group they are embedded in. They can then advocate for that group in very tangible ways.

I came to this conclusion after embedding into an all-black student success program at my college called the Umoja Community. This essay describes how this embedment changed my practice of librarianship to be more receptive of and responsive to the needs of the black community at my college and in my city. It also details best practices for this type of embedment. Although I present a case study of embedment within an academic context, I offer advice and methods that can be applied to any type of library.

Bakersfield College and the Grace Van Dyke Bird Library

I am a Reference Librarian at Bakersfield College in Bakersfield, California. Bakersfield is located in California's Central Valley, midway between Los Angeles and Fresno. Bakersfield College (BC) is one of three schools in the Kern Community College District, and is the only community college serving Bakersfield, a city of half a million people. In Fall 2017, BC had an unduplicated headcount of over 30,000 students (California Community Colleges 2017). BC graduates the highest percentage of students in Kern County (Data USA 2015). Of BC's students, 66 percent are Hispanic or Latino, 21 percent are white, and 4 percent are African American (California Community Colleges 2017). This means that, although BC's Hispanic population is very high, its African American population is well under the national average of 13.3 percent (United States Census Bureau 2016).

BC's Grace Van Dyke Bird Library is the center of student research at BC. There are 5 full-time tenure-track faculty librarians: 4 Reference Librarians and 1 Technical Services Librarian. Each of us conducts dozens of one-time library orientations per semester in addition to teaching research skills workshops, spending 2–3 hours per day on the reference desk, maintaining relationships with teaching faculty, and serving on various campus committees. My personal philosophy of librarianship points strongly toward serving underprivileged and underrepresented groups, and many of my strengths lie in outreach and student engagement. This philosophy drives me to engage in targeted library intervention.

The Umoja Community

The Umoja Community is a California Community College student success program that uses curriculum and pedagogy responsive to the legacy of the African and African American diasporas (Umoja Community 2016). There are over 50 Umoja programs at community colleges across California, as well as 2 Umoja programs at public universities in California. Umoja works with each campus to integrate the core goals and principles of Umoja into each college mission's goals and strategic plan. As such, Umoja varies from program to program while keeping a unified mission and message across the state.

The Umoja program at Bakersfield College is called Umoja African American Success Through Excellence & Persistence (ASTEP). It consists of 1.5 years of enrollment in a learning community where students take two English courses, two student development courses, a math course, a leadership course, and Library B1: Introduction to Library Research. Library B1 is a one-credit, transfer-level course. By adding the library to the learning community, students learn the fundamentals of college-level research while they are taking their transfer-level English course. Embedding the library into the program also means that the Umoja ASTEP students have a dedicated librarian during their entire time in the program.

Embedding the BC Library into the Umoja Community

I joined the Umoja faculty team in the summer of 2016, after the faculty lead for the Umoja ASTEP program approached the library about incorporating a library element into the program. Due to my drive to work with underserved students, I happily volunteered to work with this community. Umoja ASTEP was the first Umoja program in the state to embed the library into its program. As a result, there was some difficulty in figuring out how to keep me in my role as a librarian for all BC students while leaving me enough time to devote to my duties as Umoja librarian. Although my official instructional role with Umoja extends only to the one-unit Library B1 course, my responsibilities as a member of the Umoja ASTEP community at BC reach far beyond this. I participate in the Umoja Summer Bridge that occurs before students begin the Umoja program, in each Umoja student celebration, act as the Umoja liaison librarian, and teach the Umoja ASTEP students basic library skills in the semester before they take my Library B1 course. In addition, I accompany the Umoja ASTEP program to the Umoja Conference each fall, and attend the Umoja Summer Learning Institute, an intensive faculty training session, each summer.

Now in my second year with the program, I have found a good balance between my regular work functions and my function as Umoja librarian. Yet, time is an important consideration when embedding. Embedded librarianship, by definition, requires librarians to leave the library and invest time into the group they are working with. This can feel daunting. However, embedment has unreplicable results. Because of the sheer amount of time I spend with Umoja, I have been able to form closer relationships with the faculty and with past and present Umoja students than I have with any other faculty or students at BC.

Umoja's Impact on My Librarianship

Working within the Umoja community has been incredibly engaging and fulfilling. It has also caused my practice of librarianship to change. There are three main takeaways from my work with Umoja:

1. Traditional information literacy curricula are not inclusive of diversity.
2. Learning cultural norms is essential for embedded work.
3. Gaining trust as an outsider can be difficult.

Traditional Information Literacy Curricula Are Not Inclusive of Diversity

While teaching my first semester of Library B1 to the Umoja ASTEP students, I found myself betrayed by the information literacy curriculum my library uses. It is common knowledge that the traditional academic canon is highly white and male, and thus highly exclusionary toward non-male genders and people of color. However, in my blind white privilege, I hadn't quite realized just how insidious this exclusivity truly was. This became obvious when I began teaching about source authority and evaluation skills. When putting together an assignment for students to look up an author in the database *Gale Biography in Context* and qualify the author based on the biographical information found there, I realized that many prominent African and African American authors and scholars did not have entries in this database. Students who qualified an African American author with this tool would assume that this author was not sufficiently authoritative to use as a source in a college-level research paper. Moreover, several evaluation shortcuts my library teaches proved exclusionary. When using education and academic credentials as primary indicators of authority, my students concluded that Ta Nehisi-Coates was not an authoritative voice to use in their research papers about issues in the African American community. They also came to this conclusion about several leaders of the Black Lives Matter movement. Because these leaders do not work in academia and do not have advanced degrees, my students decided they would not be authoritative voices in a paper on police brutality and racial discrimination.

Ta Nehisi-Coates and leaders of the Black Lives Matter movement are clearly authoritative voices, particularly for papers focusing on the African American community. But traditional library resources for evaluation failed to help my black students realize this. After realizing that these resources were exclusionary, I vetoed teaching these in this class and in all future iterations of my Library B1 course. Instead, I began focusing on the critical thinking skills necessary to evaluate nuanced pieces of information. I believe that instilling these critical thinking skills in students empowers them much more than relying on the crutch of evaluation tools.

Not all libraries have formal information literacy courses or have such a focus on source evaluation as academic libraries. However, it is necessary for all librarians to acknowledge that librarianship is, traditionally, very white and that the tools and resources we provide to library users have a possibility of being exclusionary to people of color. When working with diverse groups, we must carefully evaluate the tools and resources we provide to these groups to ensure that these truly work for the needs of these groups and do not further alienate them from the library.

Learning Cultural Norms

Umoja classrooms are different than other classrooms. At BC, Umoja ASTEP students take classes with each other every day. This has both positive and negative impacts in the classroom. Since the students are close with each other, it is very easy to encourage class discussion and participation in group activities. However, the classroom is much louder and disruptive than an average classroom. Umoja faculty can expect many more interruptions in their lectures than usual. Yet, even beyond these distractions (which are normal for any group of students that spend a lot of time together), I discovered several cultural norms within the Umoja ASTEP community that were different from my own. Students felt very lax about time and punctuality. I had difficulty starting class earlier than 10 minutes after the official start time because the students trickled in late and wanted to spend time chatting with each other and me before settling down to the day's topic. I spent the first semester of my Umoja Library B1 course fuming over this before I investigated.

I realized several things. My students were not trying to disrespect me by wanting to chat before we started class. They simply needed time to center their attention and form bonds with me as their instructor. They had close relationships with their other Umoja faculty, whom they saw more frequently than me, and wanted a similar relationship with me. As a result, I started incorporating different icebreakers into the beginning of class as a way to segue into the day's work. This worked extremely well. It made the students feel as though I cared about them, and helped everyone get in the right mode to begin learning. I also learned that the students only had a 30-minute break between their Umoja English course and my course. They were struggling to find time to eat lunch between classes, and their tardiness was often due to the length of the cafeteria line rather than disrespect for class time.

Once I knew the cultural norms for my Umoja students, I became an immensely better teacher and librarian to them. However, to do this, I had to investigate why my students were acting certain ways rather than simply make assumptions about them. After I did this, I was able to make changes to my class that accommodated both my learning outcomes and my students' cultural expectations. This resulted in a more productive learning environment. The same principle holds true for any library. In public libraries, programs do not always turn out exactly as planned, and it can be extremely easy to fall into frustration rather than do the work of discovering why program attendants acted in certain ways. Investigation is especially important when doing embedded work. If a public librarian is embedded into an advocacy group for homeless library users, s/he will need to investigate the cultural norms of those users in order to effectively serve them. Otherwise, s/he will invariably be frustrated when these users do not act how s/he expects them to. Doing this work saves frustration on both sides, and can lead to a much deeper connection between users and librarian.

Gaining Trust as an Outsider

One of the biggest challenges I continue to face in my embedment with Umoja is gaining the trust of my students. I am white, and was nervous the first day I taught the students in my official capacity as professor. I was worried they would see another white person telling them what to do, and that they would be resistant to me as a member of a black-focused group. All of these would have been very valid responses. I did not address my whiteness to the Umoja students in my first year with Umoja and I regret this. I did succeed in winning the students' trust by showing that I was a safe person to talk to and that I cared about them and about their academic and personal success, but this took a great deal of time and effort.

For example, despite a fairly strict late work policy in my Library B1 course, students consistently turned in work 1–2 weeks late, or failed to turn it in at all. This severely impacted their grades in my course. When I asked individually, some told me they felt overwhelmed by the assignment and decided not to turn it in. I was frustrated that they didn't ask me for help, but the students told me they were afraid I would treat them like they were stupid if they asked for help. As a result, I changed my assignment schedule so that every student was required to make an individual appointment with me before turning in their first class assignment. Since they were forced to come to me for help at the beginning of the semester, this made them feel more comfortable asking for help in the future. In addition, many students used these individual appointments to tell me about personal difficulties that were impacting their performance in class. Having this individual time with students helped form bonds of trust between us.

As a community college librarian in a county with a poverty rate of 22 percent (Data USA 2015), I expect my students to face heavy responsibilities and difficulties. However, the difficulties my Umoja students were dealing with were often even weightier than I expected. I discovered that one student was tired and doing poorly on assignments because she had to walk 6 miles home from work in the wee hours of every weekend night, since her shifts lasted until after the buses stopped running. She was exhausted and scared for her safety. She was very cautious about telling me this information, but once I made the effort to draw her out, listen to her story, and try to find solutions to her issues with her commute as well as her understanding of the course material, she became one of the best students in my class. Knowing this information not only helped me understand this student's performance in my class, but also helped her feel as though I could be trusted, and that I cared about her and her academic success. She knew that I would not dismiss her as a "bad" or "lazy" student, and she continued coming to me for help when needed.

Gaining this trust with this student and my other students was difficult not only because I was an authority figure, but because I was an outsider. The students are well aware of the fact that I am white and they are black, and they hesitate to trust me like they do the black Umoja faculty. In my second year of work with Umoja, I made a point to discuss my whiteness with students. At the Umoja 2017 conference, Tim Wise, a white man, was a keynote speaker. Some students were vocally resistant to a white person being featured as a keynote speaker at a conference for and by African Americans. After hearing the Umoja ASTEP students' thoughts about this, I brought up my own whiteness with them over lunch and asked if they had opinions or questions about me being their Umoja librarian. When the students heard that I would step aside if a black librarian was hired and willing to work with Umoja, and that I had volunteered to work with Umoja because I cared about the well-being of black students at BC, they became much less guarded around me. For the rest of the semester, students made a point of stopping by my office to chat whenever they were in the library. This interaction with the students has high-lighted how incredibly important it is for any librarian doing embedded work in a community to which they are not native to address their status as outsider with the community members. They need to give these members the chance to express their feelings about the librarian's inclusion in the community. Only then can a mutual trust begin to grow.

Implications of Embedment

Embedment into Umoja has not only changed my own practice of librarianship but has broader implications for the way the library at BC serves Umoja ASTEP students and all black students at BC. It has even caused changes for the overall Umoja Community.

Implications for the Grace Van Dyke Bird Library and Bakersfield College

Several changes to the BC library curricula and outreach have occurred due to my work with Umoja. With the realization that the source evaluation tools we teach students are exclusive of diverse perspectives, many of the BC librarians have begun teaching source evaluation with a greater focus on critical thinking skills rather than traditional evaluation tools. This shift is not only inclusive of diverse perspectives, but is more applicable to the current internet age. Students are highly likely to encounter propaganda and fake news while researching, and will need to apply critical thinking skills when evaluating these sources. This has also caused us to create new resources that are more inclusive of all perspectives. We have created a Fake News LibGuide, and are working to create an Umoja-specific LibGuide and other LibGuides for African-American Studies, Chicano Studies, and many more.

Finally, the library has begun creating programming with Umoja in mind. Now that we are aware of the specific needs of Umoja ASTEP students, we have adapted existing programs to be inclusive of these needs. Examples include creating an interactive book display using Umoja principles for Black History Month, and asking an African American scholar to be the library's annual author visit for 2018. Because I am a conduit to the needs of needs of the Umoja ASTEP students, all librarians are now better able to serve Umoja students. In addition, I can advocate for the needs of these students in the various campus committees I am part of. My embedment into Umoja has made both me and the BC library as a whole a much better advocate for the Umoja ASTEP students and, I hope, all African American students at BC.

Implications for Umoja

The state-wide Umoja Community did not have any programs that included a library component before I began working with the Umoja ASTEP program at BC. Now that I have been with Umoja for two years, other programs have picked up on the idea of including the library in their learning communities. At the last training session that I attended, I met three other Umoja librarians. This shows that library embedment can have implications for both parties in the embedment. While the goal of embedded librarianship is to provide better, more targeted library access to the group the library is embedded in, embedment also has the possibility to change the targeted group. Whether we are in an academic, public, school, or an archival or special collection library, the possibility for change remains the same. Embedment not only changes how the library is able to advocate for the group it is embedded into, but allows that group to become more aware of how the library can help them. This creates the possibility for that group to change and to be more receptive of library services. As a result, embedded librarianship is an incredibly powerful tool that can have far-reaching, positive changes for all parties involved in the embedment. Embedding librarians into different diverse groups gives libraries the tools they need to advocate successfully for all of their many and varied constituents.

Works Cited

Bureau of Labor Statistics. 2016. "Current Population Survey: Household Data, Annual Averages, Table 11." Accessed December 6, 2017. https://www.bls.gov/cps/cpsa2016.pdf.
California Community Colleges. 2017. "2017 Student Success Scorecard: Bakersfield College." Accessed December 6, 2017. http://scorecard.cccco.edu/scorecardrates.aspx?CollegeID=521.
Data USA. 2015. "Bakersfield: Kern County, CA." Accessed December 6, 2017. https://datausa.io/profile/geo/kern-county-ca/#education.
Davis, Denise M., and Tracie D. Hall. 2007. "Diversity Counts." *American Library Association.* Last modified January 2007. http://www.ala.org/aboutala/sites/ala.org.aboutala/files/content/diversity/diversitycounts/diversitycounts_rev0.pdf.

Department for Professional Employees, AFL-CIO. 2016. "Library Workers: Facts & Figures." Last modified June 2016. http://dpeaflcio.org/programs-publications/issue-fact-sheets/library-workers-facts-figures/#_ednref23.

Riccio, Holly M. 2012. "Embedded Librarianship: The Library as a Service, Not a Sphere." *American Association of Law Libraries*. Accessed December 11, 2017. https://www.aallnet.org/mm/Publications/products/aall-ilta-white-paper/embedded.pdf.

Umoja Community. 2016. "About Umoja." Accessed December 6, 2017. https://umojacommunity.biz/about-umoja.

United States Census Bureau. 2016. *Quick Facts: United States*. Accessed December 6, 2017. https://www.census.gov/quickfacts/fact/table/US/PST045216.

About the Contributors

Joshua **Becker** is the information literacy and assessment librarian at Southern New Hampshire University in Manchester. He serves as a reviewer for *American Reference Books Annual* (*ARBA*) and *Choice Charleston Advisor* (*ccAdvisor*). His research interests include outreach to diverse populations, embedded librarianship, assessment, and universal design. He obtained his MLIS from the University of Illinois, as well as a MAT in English education from Boston University.

Celeste **Bocchicchio-Chaudhri** is the early literacy librarian at the Children's Library in the Boston Public Library. She obtained her MLIS from Simmons College in 2016. Before becoming a librarian, she earned a BA in anthropology and religious studies from the Indiana University of Pennsylvania, an MA in South Asian studies from the University of Michigan, and spent three years in the graduate program in women's studies at Emory University where she studied critical theory.

Ian **Boucher** began as a video editor with a BA in film studies and communication from the University of Pittsburgh, and earned his Master of Library and Information Science at Kent State University, becoming a librarian to advocate for information literacy. Since 2013, he has worked in a library in Rocky Mount, North Carolina. His research interests include the roles of motivation in information seeking behavior and the roles of film and superhero comic books in cultural discourse.

Faith L. **Bradham** is a community college librarian in Bakersfield, California. She obtained her MLS from Indiana University and has a student-centered philosophy of librarianship that focuses on student outreach and engaging diverse populations with the library. She hails from Houston, Texas, but has made Bakersfield, California, her home for the past two years. She feels passionate about the community college mission and plans to continue serving it.

Jeremy **Brett** is the processing archivist as well as the curator of the science fiction & fantasy research collection at Cushing Memorial Library & Archives, Texas A&M University. He is an organizing member of the Concerned Archivists Alliance, as well as the current chair of the Diversity Committee for the Society of Southwest Archivists. He received a BA in history from George Washington University (1997), and an MA in history and MLS from the University of Maryland, College Park (1999).

Damon **Campbell** specializes in serials and acquisitions work, and received his MLIS from University of Illinois in Urbana-Champaign in 2007. His library career spans 17 years, from student to librarian. He has worked in libraries in several states, and is the acquisitions librarian at the University of Oregon Libraries as well as a member of the Library Diversity Committee.

Anna J. **Clutterbuck-Cook** serves as a reference librarian at the Massachusetts Historical Society. She was a founding member of the LGBTQ Issues Roundtable within New England Archivists (2013) and went on to serve as the organization's inaugural Inclusion and Diversity Coordinator (2015–2017). She is an organizing member of the Concerned Archivists Alliance. She earned her BA in women's studies and history from Hope College (2005) and her MA in history and MLS in archives management from Simmons GSLIS (2011).

Matthew **Conner** has an MLS and a Ph.D. in American literature from the University of Illinois at Urbana-Champaign. He is a reference and instruction librarian at the University of California–Davis and is former president of the Librarians' Association of the University of California (LAUC). He has published articles on instructional pedagogy, library outreach, and a book with the American Library Association (ALA) Press on the future of academic libraries.

Tracy S. **Drake** is an archivist at the Chicago Public Library in the Vivian G. Harsh Research Collection. A native of Chicago, she graduated from Eastern Illinois University with a BS in African American studies, an MA in history from Roosevelt University and an MS in library science from the University of Illinois. Her research and work is centered upon utilizing technology and new media into the archival space.

Su **Epstein** holds a doctorate in sociology from the University of Connecticut and began her career teaching criminology. Leaving academia, she earned her MLIS from Simmons College and subsequently worked in a variety of libraries ranging from newspaper to private school. She is the director at the Saxton B. Little Free Library in Columbia, Connecticut. Her writing has appeared in *Creative Management of Small Public Libraries, Handling Job Stress: Tips by Librarians*, as well as the blog *Public Libraries Online*.

Cindy **Fesemyer**'s professional life is devoted to providing equal access to tools of wellbeing for all. Following fourteen years in nonprofits, she left it all behind for library school. Since graduation from library school in 2012, she has served as the director of the Columbus (Wisconsin) Public Library. She also teaches for the UW–Madison iSchool, is a trustee for the Madison Public Library and teaches community engagement to librarians around the country.

Carrie **Fishner** is the director of the Resnick Library at SUNY Delhi, an adjunct instructor in the school of liberal arts and sciences, and actively involved in the SUNY Librarians Association, currently serving a term as president. In her past, she was a residence hall director for two different universities, as well as working in other student life departments. Her research focuses on the library as a bridge between the aspects of academics and student life on college campuses.

Melanie **Foster** is an adult services librarian at the Kathryn Linnemann Branch of the St. Charles City-County Library, St. Charles, Missouri. She has a master of library and information science from the University of Missouri–Columbia. She established the current events discussion group, "Let's Talk About It!" and is interested in library programs that engage patrons in meaningful dialogue and the honest exchange of ideas.

Laura **Francabandera**, a librarian working for Credo Education and Robert Gordon University Library, received her MLIS from San Jose State University. She passionately advocates for those who are often overlooked and for equity in all facets of the library and speaks about technology, social justice, and accessibility at conferences across the country. She has written a book about accessibility, *Making Library Websites Accessible* (Rowman & Littlefield 2018), as well as facilitated online webinars and in-person workshops.

Erica **Freudenberger** is a frequent collaborator who works with libraries to create community-led change. She is the outreach & engagement consultant at the Southern Adirondack Library System, and formerly led the Red Hook Public Library, a finalist for *Library Journal's* "Best Small Library Award," garnering five-star library ratings from 2013 to 2016. She took part in the *Re-envisioning Public Libraries* pilot with the Aspen Institute, and the American Library Association's Libraries Transforming Communities initiative. She is a 2016 *Library Journal* Mover & Shaker.

Carolyn **Frey** is the associate director of library services at Grace Doherty Library at Centre College, Danville, Kentucky. She has worked with the Posse Program at Centre College as a mentor of a cohort of students from Boston who receive a full scholarship to attend Centre and also as a member of the Grissom Scholarship Committee. The Grissom scholarship provides a fully funded college experience for a group of first-generation college students.

Martin L. **Garnar** joined the University of Colorado–Colorado Springs as dean of the Kraemer Family Library and professor of library science in 2015. He is a graduate of the University of Denver (MLIS '00) and the State University of New York at Binghamton (MA history '95, BA history and geography '93). An active member of the American Library Association, he serves as the chair of the ALA Committee on Diversity.

Whitney R. **Gerwitz** is the consumer health and government document reference paraprofessional at the Middendorf-Kredell Branch of the St. Charles City–County Library District, St. Charles Missouri. She specializes in government information and coordinates the Federal Depository Library Program for the library district. She has a MA in military history from Norwich University and helps connect veterans to resources within the community. She is passionate about creating innovative library programs that allow patrons to explore ideas outside their comfort zone and ask serious questions.

Vera **Gubnitskaia**, an art fellow at Crealdé School, Winter Park, Florida, received library degrees from Moscow Institute of Culture (Russia) and Florida State University. She has worked in public and academic libraries in Russia and the United States and has presented at Florida Library Association and Florida Literacy conferences. Active in publishing, she has contributed essays and coedited multiple professional anthologies. She is a book reviewer for *Journal of International Women's Studies, Small Press Review, Florida Library Youth Program Newsletter.*

Lydia **Harlan** holds a BA in film from Emerson College and an MLIS from San Jose State University. She combines her interest in libraries and popular culture through co-curation of both the popular reading collection and the video game collection. Her library career began at the County of Los Angeles Public Library, as a teen librarian, before becoming a community library manager. She has been with the University of Oregon since 2012, and serves on the Library Diversity Committee.

Andrew **Hart**, research librarian for the Ohio BWC Library, Columbus, Ohio, obtained his BA in criminology from Ohio State, his MSLS from Clarion University, and his MSS from Ohio University. He is a former prison librarian with experience in academic, special collections, and government libraries. He is a Certified Public Librarian (CPL), a member of the American Library Association, and contributed to *Genealogy and the Librarian* (McFarland, 2018). He writes monthly articles for Public Libraries Online.

Elizabeth **Hobart** is a special collections cataloging librarian at Pennsylvania State University, University Park. She obtained her MLS from Indiana University, and has previously held positions at Indiana University's Lilly Library and UNC–Chapel Hill. Her research interests include user-centered descriptive practices, catalog assessment, and implicit bias in Library of Congress Subject Headings.

Jamie L. **Huber** is an adult services paraprofessional at the Corporate Parkway Branch of the St. Charles City–County Library, St. Charles, Missouri, and a gender studies instructor at Lindenwood University. She holds a Ph.D. in communication, a graduate certificate in women's studies from Southern Illinois University and is enrolled in library and information sciences coursework from the University of Missouri. Her work has appeared in *Kaleidoscope, Affilia, Communicating Women's Health* (Routledge, 2015), and *Gender Issues and the Library* (McFarland, 2017).

Zoe **Jarocki** is the undergraduate success librarian at San Diego State University and a member of the Chicana and Chicano Studies Archives Advisory Committee. She is the subject librarian for the Center for Latin American Studies, and the Chicana and Chicano studies and Spanish and Portuguese language and literature departments. She has an MLIS from University of California, Los Angeles.

Sarah C. **Johnson** is a substitute assistant professor at Hunter College Libraries (City University of New York). She is both an instruction librarian and a licensed social worker (LMSW). She is currently working to develop a field placement for master-level social work (MSW) students at her institution with local, public libraries. She serves on the ACRL EBSS Social Work Committee.

Elliott **Kuecker** is the collections management librarian and college archivist at Oxford College of Emory University, where he works and lives in Oxford, Georgia. He researches and writes on labor, sexuality, and LIS studies, and is pursuing a Ph.D. in educational theory and practice (critical studies) from the University of Georgia. He has been published in *Progressive Librarians Guild*, *In the Library with a Lead Pipe*, and *NoMorePotlucks*.

Amanda **Lanthorne** is the university archivist at San Diego State University and a member of the Chicana and Chicano Studies Archives Advisory Committee. She works to preserve, organize, and provide access to archival collections related to university history as well as local and regional history. She is interested in documenting underrepresented groups in an effort to foster inclusivity and empathy. She has an MA in Middle Eastern studies from Columbia University and an MLIS from San Jose State University.

Rachel **Lilley** was born and raised in Roseburg, Oregon. She holds two Bachelor's degrees—history and anthropology—from Oregon State University, and a Master's degree certification in archives and records management from Western Washington University. She works as the public services assistant in Oregon State University's Special Collections and Archives Research Center.

Paul Jerome **McLaughlin**, Jr., is an instruction and reference librarian at Florida Agricultural and Mechanical University College of Law, Orlando, Florida. He obtained his MLIS from the University of Alabama and earned his Juris Doctorate from the Valparaiso University School of Law. He has published articles on the impacts of social media use on law librarians and possible pedagogical approaches to teaching legal research methods.

Carrie **Moran** is the head of user services at the California State University San Marcos Library. Prior to this role she was the user engagement librarian at the University of Central Florida. Her research focuses on creating safe spaces for users in person and online by blending empathy with UX and service design. She is committed to promoting social justice and inclusivity in libraries and higher education.

JJ **Pionke** is the applied health sciences librarian at the Social Sciences, Health, and Education Library at the University of Illinois at Urbana-Champaign. His research focuses on disability and accessibility in libraries.

Leah **Plocharczyk** has an MLS and an MA in sociology. She is assistant director of the John D. MacArthur Campus Library at Florida Atlantic University in Jupiter, Florida, where she oversees all aspects of the library's operation. She is active in mentoring students as well as leadership and library outreach. She has published articles on library collaboration with marine mammal stranding networks and conflict management within libraries. Hosting a book club for the Academy for Community Inclusion students brings her great joy.

Julie M. **Porterfield** serves the Penn State University Libraries as the instruction and outreach archivist and WGSS library liaison, State College, Pennsylvania. Her work focuses on women and feminism in archives, archival outreach to campus and community groups, and teaching archival and primary source literacies with critical pedagogical techniques. Additionally, she is an active member of the Reference, Access, and Outreach Section of the Society of American Archivists, serving as a member of the steering and teaching with primary sources committees.

Jami **Powell** is a library systems specialist at Grace Doherty Library at Centre College, Danville, Kentucky. In addition to administering library technologies, she makes sure to spend plenty of time in public services where she can connect with students and the daily "heartbeat" of the library. She is an active leader and participant in campus groups like Beloved Community, Posse scholars, Nonviolent Communication/Intergroup Dialogue practice group and the Diversity and Community Committee.

Leandra **Preston-Sidler** is an associate lecturer in women's and gender studies at the University of Central Florida, Orlando, Florida. She teaches courses including girls studies, virtual girls, third wave feminisms, theories of masculinities; gender and technology. Her Ph.D. is in texts and technology and her research interests include biotechnologies, girls and digital literacy, and identity in virtual communities. In 2007, she founded Animal Safehouse of Brevard, a foster network for pets of women in domestic violence shelters.

Aimée C. **Quinn** is an assistant professor and the government publications librarian at the James E. Brooks Library, Central Washington University, Ellensburg, Washington. She is responsible for developing federal and state depository services and outreach to Central Washington citizens and helping with e-government services to the campus and broader citizenry. The Social Justice and Human Rights Dialogues (discussed in her essay) are one avenue to that partnership.

Maureen **Rust** is an assistant professor and student engagement and community outreach librarian at the James E. Brooks Library, Central Washington University. She is responsible for developing and promoting library outreach programming for the student, campus, and the greater Ellensburg (Washington) communities. Maureen serves on several campus and community committees, including the steering committee for the campus-wide Social Justice and Human Rights Dialogues at CWU.

Carol **Smallwood** received a MLS from Western Michigan University, MA in history from Eastern Michigan University. She is an active editor of professional anthologies. Recent examples are *Librarians as Community Partners: An Outreach Handbook* and *Bringing the Arts into the Library* (ALA); *Library's Role in Supporting Financial Literacy for Patrons* (Rowman & Littlefield, 2016); *Gender Issues and the Library* (McFarland, 2017); *A Matter of Selection* (Poetic Matrix Press, 2018). Her library experience includes school, public, academic, special, as well as administration and library systems consultant.

Kai Alexis **Smith** is the subject librarian at Cal Poly Pomona in Pomona, California. She liaises to the College of Environmental Design as well as the ethnic and women's studies and foreign languages departments. She has a MSLIS from Pratt Institute in Brooklyn, New York. She is a member of the Hip Hop Librarians Consortium and enjoys when her work and research intersect with art and activism.

Lisa **Tessier** is an assistant professor for the School of Liberal Arts and Sciences at SUNY Delhi. She has co-taught design at SUNY Environmental Science and Forestry (ESF) and art at Capital Community College. She has also worked for two landscape architecture firms in New York and the Center for Community Design Research at SUNY ESF. Her research focuses on creating engaging learning experiences in both online and face-to-face classes, and on the interconnections between art and health.

Tonyia J. **Tidline** has a Ph.D. and masters in library and information science and is concerned with the intersection of librarianship and matters of environmental and social justice. She regularly teaches management, research methods, and foundation classes in library and information studies. Her research interests include sustainability and resilience, and visual literacy.

Melissa **Villa-Nicholas** is faculty at Harrington School of Media and Communications and Graduate School of Library and Information Studies (LIS) at the University of Rhode Island (URI). Her research interests include the history of Latina/os with information technologies and information spaces, Latina/o socio-techno practices, new media studies, and race/class/gender technology studies. She teaches LIS students on inclusion, race and racism, intersectionality, and use and users of information.

Heather **Walker-White** is the library communications coordinator at Southern New Hampshire University, Manchester. She works with a variety of organizations, both on and off campus, creating and sustaining productive partnerships within the university and in the broader community. Her research interests include academic library leadership; outreach and community engagement; and usability and user experience. She received her MLIS from Drexel University, as well as a MS in applied psychology from Sacred Heart University.

Heather M. **Wefel** is an information services librarian at the Middendorf-Kredell Branch of the St. Charles City–County Library, St. Cloud, Missouri. She graduated from Wayne State University with a master of library and information science. In her career, she strives towards introducing social services into public libraries and educating the public on serious matters. She is passionate about intersectional feminism and loves Ruth Bader Ginsburg.

Amber H. **Williams** is a librarian with Spokane County Library District, Spokane County Washington. She recognizes the role the library plays in helping the community reach its aspirations, one of which is a quality education for children. In her eleven years with SCLD, she has introduced programs such as free snack for children in Deer Park, free lunch at the North Spokane and Spokane Valley libraries and a variety of other food related programs.

Index